My dear friend to ask,

@

CASS
Dec. 2012

Also by MARLENA DE BLASI

A Thousand Days in Venice

A Thousand Days in Tuscany

Regional Foods of Northern Italy

A TASTE OF SOUTHERN ITALY

ORIGINALLY PUBLISHED AS

Regional Foods of Southern Italy

Ballantine Books

NEW YORK

A TASTE OF

Southern Italy

Delicious Recipes and a Dash of Culture

Marlena de Blasi

Published in the United States by Ballantine Books,
an imprint of The Random House Publishing Group,
a division of Random House, Inc., New York.

BALLANTINE and colophon are registered
trademarks of Random House, Inc.

Originally published in hardcover under the title
Regional Foods of Southern Italy in slightly different form
in the United States by Viking, a member of
Penguin Putnam Inc., New York, in 1999.

LIBRARY OF CONGRESS CATALOGING-IN-PUBLICATION DATA

De Blasi, Marlena.
A taste of Southern Italy: delicious recipes and a dash of culture / Marlena de Blasi.
p. cm.
Originally published under title: Regional foods of Southern Italy. New York: Viking, c1999.
Includes index.
ISBN 0-345-48723-0
1. Cookery, Italian—Southern style.   I. Title.
TX723.2.S65D435 2006
641.5945'7—dc22   2005053590

Printed in the United States of America on acid-free paper.

www.ballantinebooks.com

2 4 6 8 9 7 5 3 1

FIRST EDITION

Book design by Jaye Zimet

Dear Fernando,

I have loved you from Paris to Carmel-by-the-Sea
and from Mont Blanc to Lampedusa.
I love you when you wear sunglasses to shave,
and your purple beret at the morning market,
when your hair smells of wood smoke.
I love you when you sing.

CONTENTS

PREFACE
A PERSONAL NOTE

Though I've lived in Italy for twelve years now—the first three in Venice, two more in the tiny Tuscan village of *San Casciano dei Bagni* and these last seven in the Umbrian hilltown of *Orvieto*—this book was begun longer ago than that, in a very early era of my American journalist's life. Food and wine were my subject and Italy, with her endless gastronomic glories, was my beat. Journeying far off the predictable routes, I would tuck myself into the hamlets and villages between the cities, down the road from a cheesemaker in Sardinia, in a watermill behind a lemon grove near Amalfi and, during a gelid February in Abruzzo, in an empty eleventh-century monastery, which noble edifice I set ablaze by lighting a fire in a hearth with a chimney suffocated by doves' nests. But these were just the beginnings, precursors to what has become a lifetime of adventures as we—the Venetian I married and I—proceed in an almost unbroken journey up and down and all over the face of this, perhaps, the most splendid country on earth.

When I sat down in the winter of '98 to write this book in the barely restored stable that was our home in Tuscany then, my desk pushed as close to the hearth as I could get it without scorching it—there was no other source of heat save the fireplace— I remember how afraid I'd been, afraid of forgetting something, some phrase, someone's eyes, some sort of light. But it was all safe. I sat there with my memories and page after page of notes scratched in fancy journals and on pretty hotel vellum, on rough white butcher's paper, knowing that this would be a work made with great affection. Italy had, even by then, given me a thousand ways to love her, especially that part of her that begins at Rome.

It has always been true for me that to know a place, I must first know how it eats and drinks. Everything that doesn't happen in bed happens at table. Hence, this is, quite naturally, a cook's book. But as much and more even, it is a storybook, a gathering of small rhapsodies, impressions, initiations, romantic notions from a land where these are plentiful as stones.

The portraits of the people herein are true. They represent the astounding generosity, the simplicity of the southern Italian who, summed up, can be among the most gentle of humans. Spurred as often by the southerners' rejoicing in our curiosity as by our own impulses, Fernando and I pummeled the steeps of goat paths that masqueraded as country roads and snaked over thin mountain passes. We trekked into the farthest-flung villages and promenaded sunwashed avenues of great cities. Persuaded always by kindness, we went as far as the edges of her, to the tiniest, last pieces of Italy that crumble into the Mediterranean and float closer to Africa than to the peninsula itself. Whether we asked for a wine or wild celery, an heirloom formula for *caponata*, a method to caramelize the flesh of a yellow pumpkin, another one for *gelato* with wild rice, to bake bread in a three-hundred-year-old *forno*, to gain passage on a tuna-harpooning vessel, to sleep in a feather bed, they were ours. But still I cannot tell you that the south is all of pleasure. She presents jolts, delusions, her primitiveness causes predicaments. Nonetheless, as you will see, she is clever at insinuating her sentimental self inside your own. At least that's how she was and how she is, still. But who knows for how long?

As I was once afraid of forgetting something, now I fear more the truth that nothing stays the same. As are all chroniclers who are charmed by their subject, I mourn the vanishing pieces of it, its inexorable passages, caused by nature or made by man. *That* was then and so *this* cannot be. All this is to say, hurry.

Somewhere about 40 B.C., Horace wrote, grievingly, about the sour taste of the wild leeks—once sweet as hyacinth bulbs—which grew up from the stony flanks of his Lucanian village—now the region of *Basilicata*. And he liked neither the way in which Marcellus' tomb was being cared for nor the strange tilt of the headdresses that the younger village women had taken to. He'd been gone a year.

Maggio, 2005
Via del Duomo 34
Orvieto

INTRODUCTION

The food of Italy's southern regions comprises a much more varied cuisine than that of the north. Many still think that southern food is all of a piece, a slim repertoire of dishes unfailingly announced by a great whiff of garlic and brought forth deep in a wash of some thickish red sauce. Not true. Southern food has a range of style and savor that sweeps from piquant to delicate, embracing restraint and sensitivity as often as it demonstrates aggressiveness. It is created by cooks with the courage to let a food be, to let it taste like its own good self. Southerners revere the purity of flavors and textures of a food. They are content to tear a few leaves of wild mint over a roasted fish, to grill fat prawns in lemon leaves, to roast suckling lamb in a terra-cotta pot with a great heft of sweet butter. It is a cuisine that aspires to dignity even in the midst of insufficiency. It is called *la cucina povera*—cooking of the poor—and it is so in the sense that it was and is and shall be always a cuisine that, from necessity, asks its own short litany of components, stuffs primordial to each piece of each province of each region of the south.

Southerners coaxed up what they might from patches, more often than not, all of stones and sand, collected weeds and herbs from seashores and mountainsides and ancient woods. With rough-ground grains they baked coarse, thick-crusted breads and rolled out their own rustic versions of pasta. When they had flesh to eat, it was from the hunt or fished up from rivers and the sea. Following herds of sheep and goats gave them milk and cheese. Courtyard animals were often a luxury in the south. A man from Calabria told me once that his father thought himself a rich man when there was surfeit enough from his table to fatten a pig. But who can call a food poor such as swordfish cured under sea salt and set down on the table with a puckery lemon marmalade, or wild hare cooked with honey and chestnuts or poached quail set to cool in a sack of wild herbs?

More often than do northerners, southern Italians still eat as did their forebears. Those who can now afford to eat from the universal Italian table still mostly choose the comfort of their ancestral dishes, they being nourished by the thread of sameness the old foods provide. A southerner's way of cooking and eating is part of his patrimony as much as are the ruins of a Greek temple. Southern food is the wellspring of nearly three thousand years of the impresses of tribes and conquerors from the Etruscans through to the last reign of the Bourbon kings, each of them having inlaid some ornament of its own cuisine into the southern culture. Southern food is African and Byzantine, Spanish, French, and Greek. On the moors of Sardegna, it remains the food of Stone Age hunters.

When one cooks from a specific region, a sincere curiosity about its history, its persona is at least as important as a recipe. As one studies the ways of a people with their food, one sometimes finds paths into their psyche, how they think and dream, what comforts or excites them, their expansiveness, the breadth of their hearts, even. So much sociology can be read from cuisine. But not always. In Italy, the northerner is as foreign to the southerner as though he were of another breed. Some say the schism has all to do with the northern industrial "prosperity" willed by ambition and commitment versus the southern resolve that only destiny prevails. Others say it is simply the heredity of ancient invasions, that southern cunning is Saracen while northern postures recall Austrian severity. I am still trying to understand it. What I do see, though, is that the northern spirit is closed, tight, and operates often from fear, while the southern guise is open, ready to receive and beyond fear. I see, too, that their dissonance has nothing to do with butter and olive oil.

In this work I do no wearisome gymnastics to measure out the dishes, giving you two soups, three versions of pasta, a roast, a fish, and five sweets from each place. If I liked six dishes that featured chile pepper, it is those six dishes that I present to you. I offer what I found, the good things that were offered to me as traditional and characteristic, things that I sought, things that were surprises, all without trying to write some classic tome. The recipes are rarely those that are employed in Italy, they being meant for components and attitudes and culture that belongs there. When one cooks the food from another place, lacking its earth and its air, its sun and water and the hand of its own ancestor, one can expect to bring only a parody to the table. Most often food is meant to be gathered and caressed into its own goodness near to the place where it and the cook were born. Believing this, I did not go about waving press credentials, begging cooks and chefs and grandmothers to unbind gastronomical secrets that I might carefully copy them down and offer them to you as gospel. Almost never did I speak to anyone of writing a book about his food. It just wasn't necessary. The southerner is, by his nature, open-handed, generous, responsive. Hence, what follows in these pages is a very personal collection of dishes inspired by the typical cooking of the south. They are foods I learned about by watching others cook them, by cooking together with southern cooks, sometimes by living and working, for a while, with southern families and always by tasting and feasting and still more feasting. Hence, when I title a recipe—for example, *Pesce Spada sulla Brace alla Pantesca*—I am telling you that it is Roasted Swordfish "in the style of Pantelleria," that is, inspired by the cooking of Pantelleria. I worked with traditional ideas adapting them into recipes that will give one the clearest opportunity to succeed at creating dishes that speak to and reflect the authentic and genuine foods of the southern regions of Italy. I do not make whimsical substitution or offer personal expression, as does the New York chef who presents *caponata* built with fennel rather than eggplant. But you would neither cook with mutton fat nor eat the intestines of a goat and so, though these are very much a part of the southern legacy, I do not ask it of you.

This is not a book about technique. Italians, in general, are not technicians and southerners are even less so. You will find no implication, no promise here that, with perseverance, you will cook like an Italian. You will never cook like an Italian, any more than you will look like one, nor think like one, nor make love like one, nor have his fears, his dramas. Nor can he do these things as you do them nor feel the things you feel. These are as intimate as our thumbprints and can neither be lent nor acquired.

Finally, lest it seem strange that this book on Italian food speaks not a word about Parmigiano Reggiano, let me tell you why this most splendid of all the earth's cheeses which, along with *aceto balsamico tradizionale, culatello di Zibello, olio extravergine di* Laudemia, *pasta di semola di grano duro di* Giuseppe Cocco, is always safe in my *dispensa,* is not here present. It is because the argument of this work is the food of eight regions of Italy's south. The indigenous cheese of these regions of pasturelands is one made from ewe's milk. Parmigiano Reggiano—the real one—is made from cow's milk in the northern region of Emilia. Though it and its counterfeit versions are available nearly everywhere in Italy, the everyday cooking of the south is done with the salty piquancy of its own pecorino.

LAZIO

As we cross over the sweet, southern Tuscan flanks into the region of Lazio, we must trim our expectations. Light thins, impressions narrow, and the silvered rhapsody of Tuscany smudges into the blacks and greens and browns of the humble countryside of the Alto Lazio. Pastures and sheepfolds separate sandy-eyed villages sleeping through time. Some of them, rich with untrumpeted pasts unhunted by travelers, are hemmed by Etruscan *necropoli*, tombs excavated, preserved, beckoning small, whispered ingress into an elegant and precocious culture. The city of Tarquinia, the villages of Sorano, Sovana, Pitigliano, Sutri, Vetralla, Nepi, Civita Castellana, and Tuscania hold up smoked looking glasses into the essentially impenetrable story of Etruria.

And then there is Rome.

An ecstasy of secrets wrapped in lies and dreams is Rome. The ages ache in our throats as we float on her memories. Raised up from pagan huts huddled on wooded hills,

Rome is the sublime issue of grinding wills and destinies dyed in blood, and into her earth are planted the most splendid conceits of power and beauty. Know them, touch them all, and still you shall not know Rome. One can recount her story, trample over her breast—never touching her heart—feel the shifts of her mood shivering one's skin. Still you shall not know her. Look up at her. See a splendid ruin of the Republic containing a medieval church that, in its turn, was re-dressed for the Renaissance, then persuaded into the Baroque—one springing, tumbling forth from another—in an unfading rhythm of resurrection from spoils. If you search her well, she will give up to you some shard of her mystery. But never mistake her smile for transparency.

It is enough, I suppose, that we are of her, of her crooked, confounding descendance of demons and heroes and saints. Perhaps, then, it is first our own shams and treacheries we must loosen, all the better to illuminate her. It helps to approach Rome as an innocent.

Even Romans will tell you they know only the places of her in which they live, where they walk, where they buy bread and take coffee and go to Mass. Pieces of her enchant them as they do us. Yet she is not a crumbled and ornamented old dame to be held gingerly, unclose, as if she were only her unembraceable stones. Rome is new and young and becoming, she is of kindness and possibility. Guileless midst the improbable drape of her ruins, she is gold-dusted and bewitching, engaging life, daring it, ravishing every bittersweet crumb of it.

A morning in March offers a walk to the Teatro di Marcello and a nearby temple dedicated in 431 B.C. to Apollo. Pediments, pilasters, remnants of the Empire are the precious litter strewn about the wooded patches of weeds and grasses. And there among them is one taking the sun. Her headrest is a fragment of marble column, supine, lustrous in the grass. Unself-consciously pivoting her amplitude under the cupolas of black pine and oleander, she bathes her face in unshaded heat. A string bag filled with nodding, long-stemmed artichokes, and lavender roses waits beside her on the smoothed stump of another stone. In a single one of her moments, she has gathered up to her the sunlight, artichokes, roses, and some quiet, undesigned reckoning with her past. She is, after all, a Roman and would have nothing less.

Go at nine of a morning to a bar in Piazza Sant' Eustachio to drink Rome's best coffee, and standing there with you, upholstered in cashmere and Scottish tweed, lips powdered in sugar from his custard-filled croissant, will be a prince. Too, you will find the neighborhood's respected carpenter, a seller of rare books, a restorer of antiquated furniture, two chefs in crisp whites, a wine merchant, and, as dramatic tint for the proscenium, there will be a revolving brigade of red-and-blue-varnished *carabinieri*. The prince, the carpenter, the wine merchant, and the *barista*, the barman, all live in a nearby palazzo and have been neighbors for years. They and the others collect in the bar at more than several junctures of the day and evening, reviving or soothing themselves with the hour's appropriate cups, engaging in the life-giving ritual of empty discourse. And one can establish one's presence among them after, say, three consecutive mornings.

Thus assured, then, that one is a pilgrim rather than a passerby, the prince might inquire where and how well one dined last evening, or if one has yet seen the Fontana di Giacomo. The carpenter, having recently had a hand in a small project at the Palazzo Spada, upstages the prince by wagering that surely one has never even heard of Borromini's great *trucco*—trick—tucked inside the palazzo's museum. One or another of them or some multiple faction of the bar's cast will offer ceremonious escort into the field, teaching as artlessly as did the sunbather, informing, assuaging, if only for those moments, one's longing to know Rome.

About the Cuisine

Roman food is bawdy, vivid, radiant; it invites communion. Resonating the Roman appetite, it is, at its voluptuous and medieval heart, *la cucina povera*. The Empire's gusto for luxury and extravagance was long-ago faded in the pungent steams of a cauldronful of oxtails softening in a great bath of tomatoes and wine. To build the cuisine of Rome one must have, nearby, a thatch of mint—wild or peppery and an untimid hand with it— artichokes—those globe-shaped and adolescent ones too young to have suffered the growth of an evil choke and those tinier yet, tight-hearted and purple-lipped—the blunted fear of, if not an earnest yearning for, the viscera and the tail of an ox, the willingness and the grace to dance round a pot of bubbling oil, an absorbing passion and reverence for vegetables and fruits, and, finally, an indifference to sweets. A pitcher full of roses, overblown, their beauty bruised, their perfume fat and full, is also welcome.

Coda alla Vaccinara

OXTAILS BRAISED IN TOMATOES AND WHITE WINE
IN THE MANNER OF THE ROMAN BUTCHERS

Serves 4

Roman ox butchers, known as i vaccinari, *have been attributed authorship for this most characteristic dish* of la cucina povera romana. *Honored as savvy, inventive cooks, the butchers were and are wont to pot up the most particularly toothsome nuggets plundered from the great beasts. The tail of an ox, though it surrenders inconsiderable flesh, is of the tenderest texture and most delicate savor to be gleaned from the whole bulk of him.*

 1 oxtail (about 2½ to 3 pounds), whacked into 2- to 3-inch
   pieces
 3 ounces salt pork
 1 large bunch of flat-leaf parsley
 4 fat cloves garlic, peeled and crushed
 1 large yellow onion, peeled and minced
 2 small carrots, sliced
 Hearts and leaves of 2 large bunches of celery, the hearts sliced,
   and the leaves chopped
 1 small, dried red chile pepper, crushed, or ⅓ to ½ teaspoon
   dried chile flakes
 2 cups dry white wine
 ½ cup tomato puree
 1 cup water
 1½ teaspoons fine sea salt
 Freshly cracked pepper

Rinse the oxtail and place it in a large soup pot, covering it with cold water. Over a lively flame, bring to a full boil. Immediately drain the oxtail, setting it aside and discarding the water.

With a mezzaluna or very sharp knife, mince the salt pork with the leaves of the parsley and the garlic to a fine paste. In a large terra-cotta or enameled cast-iron casserole, over a medium flame, warm the aromatic paste. In it, brown the pieces of oxtail, turning them about in the fat, sealing them well.

Add the onion, carrots, celery leaves, and the crushed chile, sautéing them a bit in the hot fat before adding ½ cup of the white wine and permitting it to evaporate. Add another ½ cup and, again, let it evaporate. Add the remaining wine, the tomato puree, water, sea salt, and generous grindings of fresh pepper, bringing the mixture to a quiet simmer.

Cover the pot tightly and very gently braise the oxtail for 4 hours, stirring every ½ hour or so. Add the celery hearts and continue to braise, the pot covered, for ½ hour.

Permit the oxtail to luxuriate in its bath for at least 1 hour or as long as overnight in a cool place or in the refrigerator. Slowly reheat the oxtail and present it in shallow bowls with oven-toasted bread and cold white wine.

Mezzancolli al Cognac

PRAWNS BRAISED IN WHITE WINE AND COGNAC

Serves 4 to 6

A patently rustic treatment of the prawns that presses us to a dramatic sort of dance in front of the flame as we toss the fat, handsome things about in the hot oil, their briny perfumes dissolving up in great vapors around our heads. A bottle of fine Cognac perched on the kitchen shelf seems an occurrence as common in Rome as is the one filled with the simple white wine from the hills just outside its gates. Here, the bottle is used to a fine end, scenting the seething, sputtering flesh of the prawns inside their bronzed, vermilion shells.

> 1½ pounds large prawns or medium langoustines, unshelled
> ½ cup extra-virgin olive oil
> Fine sea salt
> 1 cup dry white wine
> 1 cup Cognac
> Juice of 1 large lemon
> Freshly ground pepper

Rinse the prawns and dry them on absorbent paper towels.

Heat the oil in a very large terra-cotta or enameled cast-iron casserole and, over a lively flame, sauté the prawns, tossing them about in the oil until their shells turn angry red and are beautifully browned, 5 or 6 minutes. Salt them generously, adding the wine and the Cognac, letting the prawns drink in all the bubbling liquids for 2 to 3 minutes, depending on the size of the prawns.

Remove from the flame and give the prawns a benediction of lemon juice and generous grindings of pepper before presenting them, in their casserole, with jugs of cold white wine.

Trippa alla Romana

TRIPE IN THE STYLE OF ROME

Serves 4 to 6

For nearly a century, the mattatoio, the slaughterhouse, of Rome was fixed, south of the city's center and flanked by Porta San Paolo and the Piramide di Caio Cestio, in the quarter of Testaccio—a hillock formed by the dross of terra-cotta amphorae that held olive oil and other comestibles imported into the city. Of an eloquent, uncompromised Roman character, the quarter grew up simple little houses in whose kitchens were cooked the humble remains of the butchers' art, transforming the offal into i piatti fortissimi—the strongest plates—to serve to the workingmen for lunch. Il mattatoio has long since been relocated, but the Testaccio still practices the most orthodox Roman gastronomic traditions, building dishes such as nervetti in insalata, a salad of poached calves' feet, coda alla vaccinara, (see page 4), pajata, the grilled or braised intestines of a calf or an ox, and trippa. As prosaic as are the formulas for these dishes, the manner in which they are presented is also prescripted.

First, if the proprietor in any one of the neighborhood's tabernae—Romans swing easily in and out of Latin, as in this usage for taverns—doesn't approve one's general look or demeanor, he will point, steely, to a little sign marked COMPLETO, reserved, that is fastened, permanently, handily for such occasions, to a rope of salame suspended from the rafters. If he does deem to seat one, neither he nor his colleagues will be charmed if one speaks Italian. It is only the dialect of Rome that is shouted in the Testaccio. It seems best to communicate, through eye-rolling and hand-flailing, that one wishes all decisions to be made by the house, that one is armed with magnificent appetite, and that one shall remain serene and unrepining at whatever part of whatever animal may be set before one. Our place of choice to be fed like a Roman is called Da Felice, an unsigned post in Via Mastro Giorgio. We go always of a Saturday so we can always eat tripe.

Soaked in water and vinegar, urging the nastiness from its pores, the tripe is poached before it is sautéed in a battuto (the fundamental vegetable, herb, and fat flavoring for a sauce) of pancetta, olive oil, and garlic, then braised overnight on the quietest flame in tomato, white wine, and wild mint. A Saturday ritual in the Testaccio, as well as in every genuine osteria and trattoria in Rome, la trippa is served in deep bowls, under a dusting of pecorino, with chunks of rough bread and a jug of Frascati. Food of the poor is this tripe, flotsam conjured into a flavorful, cockle-warming stew, one that a sage Roman wouldn't trade for a big, bloody beefsteak, not even one flounced in truffles.

> 2 pounds honeycomb veal or oxtail tripe
> 3 ounces pancetta
> 4 fat cloves garlic, peeled and crushed
> 5 tablespoons extra-virgin olive oil
> 1 large yellow onion, peeled and thinly sliced
> 1 14-ounce can plum tomatoes, with their liquids

2 teaspoons fine sea salt

½ teaspoon ground cloves

1 bay leaf

3 cups dry white wine, plus more if necessary

1 small, dried red chile pepper, crushed, or ⅓ to ½ teaspoon
dried chile flakes

1½ cups torn fresh mint leaves

Just-grated pecorino to taste

The tripe should first be rinsed, bleached in vinegar, rinsed again, and poached, all of which your butcher or specialty grocer may be able to do in advance for you. Rinse the tripe and, with kitchen shears, cut it into 1-inch-wide strips, then cut the strips into 4-inch lengths. Cover the tripe with cold water and, over a moderate flame, bring it to a gentle simmer and poach for several minutes. Drain the tripe, rinse it under cold water, and set aside.

With a mezzaluna or sharp knife, mince the pancetta with the garlic, making a fine paste. Over a medium flame in a large terra-cotta or enameled cast-iron casserole, warm the pancetta/garlic paste in 2 tablespoons of the olive oil and soften the onion in the fat for 3 or 4 minutes, taking care not to let it color. Add the tomatoes, the sea salt mixed with the cloves, the bay leaf, the wine, and the prepared tripe, bringing the combination to a quiet simmer.

Cover the casserole tightly and cook for 2½ hours, undisturbed. Remove the lid, stir, and add a few spoonfuls more of the wine if the liquid seems scant. Replace the cover and continue to cook the tripe, over the gentlest flame, for another ½ hour. Test a piece of the tripe for tenderness. It is cooked properly when its texture is tender, though still pleasantly chewy—al dente, as you would cook pasta. Continue the slow cooking until this stage is reached.

Remove the tripe from the flame and permit it to rest for at least 1 hour, or as long as overnight.

Just before serving the tripe, warm 3 tablespoons of the olive oil in a tiny saucepan and flavor it with the crushed chile. Set the scented oil aside. Slowly reheat the tripe, not permitting its liquids to reach the boil and stir in the chile oil and 1 cup of the mint. Let the tripe rest for a minute or two. Mix the just-grated pecorino with ½ cup of the mint.

Ladle the tripe into warmed deep bowls, dusting each of them generously with the pecorino/mint mixture.

La Vignarola

THE WINEMAKER'S WIFE'S STEW

Serves 6

Not so many springtimes ago, I knew it was a Roman birthday for which I yearned, convinced that the salve of the place would soften the edges of a long sadness. Arriving crumpled and unslept on that morning, I slid my two dusty bags under the purple flounce of the bed in my genteelly shabby room at the Adriano and bolted off to the Campo de' Fiori. I needed lilacs. I explained to the flower merchant in the market my desire to bring più allegria—*more cheerfulness—to my little hotel room, that I was preparing for a sort of birthday party. He amplified the girth of the sweet-smelling sheaves I'd chosen and dispatched his helper to carry the towering bouquets through the twisting streets back to the Adriano. His field of vision completely contained inside thickets of blossoms, the porter left me to play front guard, to scream commands and admonitions back at him, staging a droll farce that could happen only in Rome.*

Safe inside the hotel with the lilacs, I purloined a large metal wastebasket from the reception hall, tied up its middle in a length of green silk, and installed the great, weeping blooms at the foot of my bed. I raced back to the market to fill two baskets with tiny, blushed velvet peaches still on their branches and hung them from wall sconces and draped them over mirrors and bedposts and on the roof of the dour, mustard-colored armoire. I collected breads from the forno *(bakery) in Via della Scrofa, not so much to eat but for the comfort of their forms and their scents. I unwrapped the Georgian candlesticks I always carry with me from their cradle in my old taffeta skirt, threw open the shutters to beams of a rosy moon, and the birthday room was ready.*

I'd collected a beautiful supper at Volpetti: a brace of quail, each reposing on a cushion of roasted bread—depository for their rosemary juices—olives crushed into a paste with capers and Cognac, a stew of baby artichokes, new peas, and fava beans scented with wild mint and called, mysteriously, la vignarola—the winemaker's wife—and a small, white, quivering cylinder of sweet robiola (fresh handmade cow's milk cheese). I laid the feast on the dressing table, serving myself only bits of it at first. But little explosions of goodness insinuated themselves, and the quiet supper urged me into the goodness of the moment. Hungers found, strategies resewn. Happy birthday.

During the time I lived at the Adriano, I went each morning to the market in Campo de' Fiori, stopping to chat with my flower man, he introducing me to the lady with the slenderest, most delicate asparagus, which I devoured raw, like some earth-scented bonbon, and the one with the baby blood-red strawberries collected in the forests of Lake Nemi up in the Alban Hills. A ration of these beauties I vanquished each afternoon between sips of icy Frascati from my changing caffè *posts along the* campo. *With those weeks as initiation, I might have stayed the rest of my life in the lap of that neighborhood, that village within Rome so contained and complete unto itself, and surely would never have known a single lonely day. More than she is a city, Rome is a string of small provinces, fastened one to the other by old fates.*

4 tablespoons plus ⅓ cup extra-virgin olive oil

4 ounces pancetta, minced

1 large yellow onion, peeled and minced

2 pounds spring peas, shelled

2 cups dry white wine

2 pounds fresh fava beans

Fine sea salt

6 to 12 baby artichokes, with several inches of their stems intact

Freshly cracked pepper

Zest of 1 lemon, finely shredded

2 fat cloves garlic, peeled, crushed, and finely minced

1 cup torn fresh mint leaves

In a large sauté pan over a medium flame, warm 1 tablespoon of the olive oil and brown the pancetta for several minutes. Soften the onion until transparent in the fat, taking care not to color it. Add the peas and the wine, bringing the combination to a simmer. Cover the pot, its lid askew, and gently simmer the peas for 20 minutes or less, until barely tender. Remove the fava beans from their pods and cook in boiling sea-salted water for 12 to 15 minutes or until they are nearly tender, rather like the al dente stage in cooking pasta. Set aside.

Blanch the artichokes in boiling salted water for 3 minutes. If they are of the purple-lipped variety and no larger than a small plum, leave them whole, barely trimming their tender petals and scraping at their stems a bit. If they are somewhat larger, give the stems a scrape or two and slice them in half, lengthwise, removing any signs of a more than embryonic choke.

In another sauté pan, over a lively flame, warm ⅓ cup of olive oil and sauté the artichokes, salting them generously, adding freshly cracked pepper and tossing them about for several minutes or until they are nearly tender. Transfer the artichokes and their accumulated juices to the sauté pan with the peas and pancetta, sautéing the mixture for 2 or 3 minutes just to finish cooking the artichokes.

In a small saucepan, warm 3 tablespoons of olive oil with the lemon zest and the garlic, taking care not to color the garlic. Set the scented oil aside.

Add the blanched favas and the mint leaves to the sauté pan, gently heating the components together and taking care not to let them reach a simmer.

Remove from the heat, stir in the lemon/garlic-scented oil, and serve *la vignarola* as an antipasto or a first course, warm or at room temperature, with oven-toasted bread and cold white wine.

Baccalà in Guazzetto

SALT COD BRAISED WITH TOMATOES, RAISINS, AND PINE NUTS

Serves 6 to 8

Baccalà *is of ancient Roman favor. The methodology of its preservation was one cultivated during their campaigns in the north, where they learned to embalm a catch of the great, fat cod under unpounded crystals of sea salt, reviving it for meals both festive and humble. Stoccafisso differs from* baccalà *in its fundamental cure, as it, having no encounter with salt, is simply hung out to dry in the winds moaning up from the North Sea. In either case, once plumped in its renaissance bath of cold water, the cod flesh is tender and, when cooked gently, its flesh takes on an almost creamy texture. The yield of a correctly reconstituted and properly cooked fish, well conserved in either way, is quite the same. This is an unexpectedly delicate dish, the raisins foiling any saltiness that might linger in the fish, while the Cognac softens the acidity of the tomatoes.*

> 2 pounds *baccalà* or *stoccafisso*
> Flour for coating fish
> ½ cup extra-virgin olive oil
> 4 fat cloves garlic, peeled and crushed
> 1 teaspoon fine sea salt, plus more as needed
> Freshly cracked pepper
> ⅓ cup dry white wine
> 2 14-ounce cans plum tomatoes, with their liquids
> ½ cup golden raisins, plumped in 6 tablespoons warmed Cognac
> ⅔ cup pine nuts, lightly toasted

To prepare the *baccalà*, pound it heartily with a wooden mallet, then lay it to rest in very cold water for 48 hours. Change the bathwater several times each day. Drain and rinse. Poach the fish in barely simmering water for 3 minutes. Drain, remove the skin and bones, and cut into 3- to 4-inch pieces. Dry the prepared *baccalà* on absorbent paper towels and roll the pieces about in a bit of flour, coating them well but not too thick.

In a large, shallow terra-cotta or enameled cast-iron pan over a lively flame, warm the olive oil and scent it with 2 of the crushed cloves of garlic, tossing them about until they take on some color. With a slotted spoon, remove the 2 cloves of garlic and discard them. Brown the flour-dusted *baccalà*, putting only those pieces into the pan that will fit without touching, permitting them to color and crust on one side before gently turning them, crusting the other side. Sprinkle lightly with sea salt and freshly cracked pepper as you proceed. As the *baccalà* is sautéed, remove it to absorbent paper towels. When all of the *baccalà* is golden, soften the remaining 2 cloves of garlic in the remaining oil, taking care not to let them take on color.

Rinse the pan with the wine, stirring, scraping at the residue, and permitting the wine to reduce for a minute or two. Add the tomatoes, 1 teaspoon of sea salt, and the plumped raisins with their Cognac juices, bringing the mixture to a simmer and reducing the sauce for 15 minutes.

Carefully position the fish in the sauce, spooning the juices over them. Cover the pot and, over a gentle flame, bring the liquids just to a simmer, braising the fish gently for 5 minutes.

Now the dish can be presented, or it can wait, without harm, covered for several hours. Never reheat the dish, but offer it at room temperature. Just before serving, strew the *baccalà* with the toasted pine nuts.

Carciofi alla Giudia

ARTICHOKES IN THE MANNER OF JEWISH ROME

Serves 4

It was nearly eleven on Saturday and Fernando was standing under the open roof in the rain, tender, silvered glissades of it plashing quietly, as it has for two thousand years, onto the black and white marble of the temple floor. He, not minding, stood directly in the puddle, its depths caressing the tops of his shoes, looking up at the sky like a child in wonder, the water settling in fine mists on his cheeks and eyelids. He turned fifty that morning in the Pantheon. His spiritual birthday thus celebrated, he pronounced that his carnal festival was to be solemnized in not less than six of his preferred ostarie/trattorie/ristoranti. Fernando wanted to eat artichokes.

More, he wanted an artichoke crawl—a critical journey up and down the vicoli (narrow streets), an earnest search for great, golden-green, crisped Roman roses—as many of them as he might vanquish in a day and its evening in a half dozen genuine houses—we were in search of the one perfect carciofo alla giudia. Ten years ago, I might have propelled him into the arms of the trattoria da Giggetto, when I was still convinced of the authenticity of its cooking. Sidled up as it is to the edge of the Portico d'Ottavia, perhaps it was only the taberna's majestic old neighbor that wooed me. Fernando had his own ideas.

At midday, we made quick aperitivi e antipasti visits to Arancio d'Oro in Via Monte d'Oro and La Campana in Vicolo della Campana, taking only one or two artichokes and a glass of white wine. We would settle in at Agata e Romeo in Via Carlo Alberto for a proper lunch that would start with another of the little beauties. The evening's gallop would open at Tram Tram in Via dei Reti before a stint at Il Dito e la Luna in Via dei Sabelli, where we would crunch on more fried thistles. Our palates veneered in stainless steel, our bellies convulsing, plumped, we brushed sea salt and crisp freckles from our lips and our chests and stepped at last inside the dimmed sanctum of Piperno in Via Monte dei Cenci. Murmuring something to our waiter about not having much appetite, he assured us that he would carry to us only those plates that could titillate a dead man. He started us with a salad of puntarelle—*a thick-bladed wild grass collected in the Alban hills—glossed in sauce of anchovies. Then came the misty comfort of* stracciatella, *chicken broth scribbled with a paste of egg and pecorino. Expert by now, able to whiff their very presence from twenty meters, we knew then the artichokes were only moments away. He set them down, clucking over their beauty, assuring us their salty vaporousness would coax our hunger. He was right. We continued with* la coda alla vaccinara—*oxtail stew—*abbacchio—*roast suckling lamb—a few crumbles of a hard, piquant* pecorino pepato—*peppered pecorino—a soft brown pear, and sealed it all with a great fluff of roasted chestnut mousse that we ate with small silver spoons.*

> 6 to 8 cups peanut oil
> 4 to 8 globe artichokes, with several inches of their stems intact
> Juice of 1 lemon
> Fine sea salt
> Freshly cracked pepper

Select carefully the vessel in which you will fry the artichokes, as half their bulk must be immersed in the hot oil to cook them properly. In a large pot or deep fryer, warm the oil over a medium flame to ensure it heats evenly, without cold spots. Peel the artichoke stems to reveal their tender cores, tear away the hard petals, and trim the tips of the softer petals. Immerse the artichokes in very cold water, acidulated with the lemon juice, for ½ hour.

Remove the artichokes from their acidy bath, drying them carefully on absorbent paper towels.

Hold each artichoke by its stem or its stem end and forcefully slam it down onto a wooden board or marble slab to flatten it, spreading out its petals. Tuck generous pinches of sea salt and pepper between its petals.

When the oil is very hot—but not at the maximum temperature of your deep fryer—place as many of the artichokes as will fit in the pan, stems up, leaving ample space for each of them to float about freely. Fry the artichokes for 6 to 7 minutes, turning often with tongs. Raise the heat to its maximum level and fry the artichokes for an additional 6 minutes, or until they've blossomed into great, bronzed, green roses.

Remove the artichokes from the oil to rest a moment on absorbent paper towels and then mist them—using a plant mister—with iced, sea-salted water, the spritz ensuring the fried thistles' delectable crunch.

Serve them as fast as you can, but only to people who are excited to eat them.

Carciofi alla Romana

ARTICHOKES IN THE STYLE OF ROME

Serves 4

These are Rome's other artichokes. Softened rather than crisped in their oil bath, they are of an extravagant goodness.

8 globe artichokes, with several inches of their stems intact
Juice of 1 lemon
8 ounces *pancetta affumicata* or bacon
6 fat cloves of garlic, peeled and crushed
1 cup fresh mint leaves, plus a few torn leaves for garnish
¾ cup extra-virgin olive oil
1½ cups dry white wine
2 teaspoons fine sea salt
Freshly cracked pepper

Peel the artichoke stems to reveal their tender cores, tear away the hard petals, and trim the tips of the softer petals. Remove their chokes before immersing the artichokes in very cold water, acidulated with the lemon juice, for ½ hour. Remove the artichokes from their acidy bath and dry them carefully on absorbent paper towels.

With a mezzaluna or a sharp knife, mince the *pancetta affumicata* with the garlic and the mint, making a fine paste. Tuck the paste deeply between all the petals of the artichokes.

In a large terra-cotta or enameled cast-iron casserole over a medium flame, heat the olive oil and immerse the artichokes, stems up. Gently cook the artichokes for 3 or 4 minutes, then add the wine, the sea salt, and generous grindings of pepper.

Cover the casserole and braise the artichokes over a gentle flame for 30 minutes or until the thistles are tender and yield easily to the point of a sharp knife.

Remove the casserole from the flame and permit the artichokes to rest for ½ hour.

Serve the artichokes, glossed with their own juices, at room temperature or cold, strewn with a few torn leaves of mint. A single artichoke might do as an antipasto, but a pair of them are necessary for a first or second course.

Una Terrina di Vitello alla Romana

A TERRINE OF VEAL IN THE MANNER OF ROME

Serves 8 to 10

In several of the finest of Rome's gastronomie (prepared food shops) and rosticcerie, one finds a reading of this coarse sort of country pâté, prepared by the Romans with the prowess of French charcutiers. Sometimes, its middle will hide the Cognac-steeped livers of game, while others are studded with hazelnuts or truffles or wild mushrooms. This one, though, has become one of our "house" terrines. Some evenings, we like to make a supper of it and a good bread and wine. We have been known, more than once, to use it to build little panini, sandwiches, which we wrap in yellow napkins and hide inside my purse with a small silver flask of red wine to take with us over the mountain to Chianciano when we go to see a film. It tastes so good in the dark.

2 pounds veal, cut from the leg, ground

1 pound breast of chicken, ground

6 ounces prosciutto, ground

½ pound fresh Italian-style sausage

2 medium white-skinned potatoes, peeled, boiled in
    sea-salted water, and mashed with 1 tablespoon
    extra-virgin olive oil

2 cups just-grated pecorino

6 large eggs, beaten

1 tablespoon fine sea salt

Freshly cracked pepper

4 fat cloves garlic, peeled, crushed, and minced

1 cup flat parsley leaves, chopped with ½ cup fresh oregano
    leaves

⅔ cup white raisins, plumped in warm white wine

1 cup pistachios, shelled and lightly roasted

⅓ cup Cognac

Preheat the oven to 375 degrees.

    In a large bowl, combine all the ingredients, mixing them vigorously until well combined. Pat the mixture into a terrine constructed of terra-cotta, enameled cast iron, or ceramic, compacting it nicely.

    Place the terrine in a larger pan with several inches of hot water, covering it with its own lid or one fashioned from aluminum foil and bake the terrine for 1 hour and

15 minutes. Lift its lid and if the juices of the meat are running clear rather than pink, the terrine is cooked.

Remove the terrine from the oven. Remove its lid and place several thicknesses of foil over its surface. Weight the terrine with some heavy object, permitting it to cool thoroughly. Remove the weight and the foil, re-covering the terrine tightly with plastic wrap—and its own lid—refrigerating it for a day or two. Slice the terrine at table or turn it out onto a board, cutting it into thin slices.

Abbacchio Pasquale

THE ROAST SUCKLING LAMB OF EASTER

Serves 4

Abbacchio, *a long-ago Roman term for a newborn lamb, is the prescripted dish of Easter. And older than history is the innocent, rousing scent of it roasting with branches of wild rosemary, curling out from the kitchen doors of the* trattorie *in the Trastevere on Sundays in the spring, beckoning one to table together.*

> 2 legs suckling lamb (each about 2 pounds)
> 4 fat cloves garlic, peeled and crushed
> 2 tablespoons fresh rosemary leaves
> 10 to 12 large leaves fresh sage
> 4 teaspoons fine sea salt
> ¼ cup plus ⅓ cup extra-virgin olive oil
> Juice of 1 lemon
> 1½ pounds tiny, new, white- or red-skinned potatoes
> Freshly cracked pepper
> 2 tablespoons fennel seeds
> 1¾ cups dry white wine
> 3 ounces anchovies, preserved in salt

Preheat the oven to 450 degrees.

Wipe the lamb with absorbent paper towels, and with a small, sharp knife make ½-inch slits, ½-inch deep, over the flesh. With a mezzaluna or a sharp knife, mince the garlic, rosemary, sage, and 2 teaspoons salt together, making a paste. Rub the paste over the incisions, urging it inside them and using any remaining paste as a general rub for the lamb.

Mix ¼ cup of the olive oil with the lemon juice and massage the scented oil over all the surfaces of the lamb. Set the lamb aside.

Wash and dry the potatoes, cutting in two or three pieces any that are larger than a prune, and place them in a bowl. Add 2 teaspoons salt, generous grindings of pepper, the fennel seeds, and ⅓ cup of the oil, rolling the potatoes about in the oil and coating them well. Turn the potatoes out into a roasting pan just large enough to contain them comfortably.

Place a rack, its legs resting inside the roasting pan, over the potatoes and on it position the legs of lamb. The lamb must be sitting directly over the potatoes so its juices will fall directly on them. Pour ½ cup of the wine over the lamb (letting it fall wherever it will over the potatoes) and roast the whole for 15 minutes.

Rinse the anchovies, dry on paper towels, and remove their heads and bones. Crush lightly with a fork and set aside.

Lower the oven's heat to 375 degrees and continue roasting for another 20 to 25 minutes, basting it two or three times with more wine or until a thermometer inserted into the thickest part of the meat registers 130 degrees. At this point, the flesh will be pink and full of rosy juices, some of which will have already drizzled down onto the potatoes. One could roast the lamb a bit longer—until the thermometer reads 135 degrees, risking those gorgeous juices. Remove the whole roasting contraption from the oven and lay the lamb to rest on a carving tray.

Remove the potatoes to a warmed bowl. Pour off most of the fat remaining in the roasting pan and place the pan over a lively flame, stirring, scraping at its residue, and adding the remaining wine and the anchovies. Reduce to make a simple pan sauce. Carve the lamb at table, presenting it with the roasted potatoes and the pan juices.

Find a simple Frascati if you can and chill it down to its toes. Otherwise, any of the whites from the Castelli Romani—the hills of Rome—will do nicely, as would an Est!, Est!!, Est!!! from Montefiascone.

Uno Stufatino di Vitello

A LITTLE BRAISE OF VEAL

Serves 4

Here is a simple presentation of the components of Rome's saltimbocca *embroidered with spring peas and tomatoes.*

> 4 ounces prosciutto
>
> 2 ounces pancetta
>
> 5 fat cloves garlic, peeled and crushed
>
> 9 large leaves sage
>
> 1 tablespoon extra-virgin olive oil
>
> 2 pounds veal, cut from the leg in 3-inch chunks
>
> 2 teaspoons fine sea salt
>
> 2 cups dry white wine
>
> 7 ounces canned plum tomatoes, with some juices
>
> 1 pound spring peas, shelled
>
> Zest of 1 lemon

With a mezzaluna or a sharp knife, mince the prosciutto, pancetta, 3 cloves of garlic, and 6 leaves of sage together to make a paste.

In a terra-cotta or enameled cast-iron casserole over a medium flame, warm the olive oil and heat the fragrant paste, sautéing it for a minute or two.

Dry the veal on absorbent paper towels and, a few pieces at a time, seal the veal in the hot fat, coloring it well on all sides. Remove the veal to a platter and proceed until all of it has been treated. Toss the veal with the sea salt.

Add half the wine to the still-warm casserole, stirring and scraping at the residue and permitting it to reduce for a minute or two. Add the tomatoes, the remaining wine, and the veal and bring the mixture to a quiet simmer.

Cover the casserole, its lid barely askew, and braise the veal for 40 minutes. Add the peas and continue the gentlest braise for another 20 minutes, or until the meat is melting into its sauce. Permit the *stufatino* to rest for at least ½ hour or as long as several hours. Just before serving the veal, mince 2 cloves of the garlic, 3 sage leaves, and the lemon zest nearly down to a powder with a mezzaluna or a very sharp knife.

Slowly reheat the *stufatino*—or, on a warm evening, present it at room temperature—ladling it into shallow bowls, dusting it with the garlic/sage/lemon mixture, and offering it with cold white wine and warm, just-toasted bread.

Gnocchi di Castagne con Porcini Trifolati

CHESTNUT FLOUR DUMPLINGS WITH A SAUCE OF WILD MUSHROOMS

Serves 4

Twenty kilometers from our home sits the bustling Latian village of Acquapendente. There we find our trustworthy pork butcher, our *panificio di famiglia* (family bakery), and the only shop between Rome and Florence where Erich can find the music of Astor Piazzola. Hence, Acquapendente is a sort of vortex for us.

It is on early Friday mornings when it beckons us most plaintively, the day the market—the mercato—comes to town. It is a good-enough market at any time of the year, but steeled in late January fogs is how we like it best. From our home in San Casciano dei Bagni, higher up by four hundred feet and, in winter, sitting nearly always in crystal air, we descend the narrow, sloping road past the sheepfolds, past the ostrich farm, away from the new, gold sun, fresh from its rise, and into the thick, purply mists of the rough little place. Wrapped in our woolens we stroll the abundant tables of green-black Savoy cabbages and violet broccoli, baskets of potatoes and turnips unwashed of their Latian earth. Here and there are lit small, consoling charcoal fires in funny little tripod burners over which the farmers thaw their ungloved hands. Just outside the fray are the humbler posts, those that beg no rent, that are had for their predawn staking.

The farmers, sober in the unpacified cold, unwrap their often meager stuffs—a basket of chestnuts, one of cauliflower, and once, a man, standing beside his little pile of pumpkins, held a brace of pheasant, still dripping their blood on the frozen ground, his booty from a predawn hunt—offering them at far lower prices than those asked by their more prosperous colleagues inside the village. It was there, too, at the Friday mercato in Acquapendente that a woman from Bolsena, who was selling just-ground chestnut flour, sat on the edge of her table and wrote out this most wonderful recipe.

The smokiness of the chestnut flour enlarges upon the forest scents of the mushrooms, the whole combining into a sensual sort of rusticity. If chestnut flour is not to be found at your specialty store, substitute whole wheat or buckwheat flour and mix 3 ounces of canned, unsweetened chestnut puree with the mascarpone.

The Gnocchi

12 ounces whole-milk ricotta

3 ounces mascarpone or natural cream cheese, softened

½ cup just-grated pecorino

3 large eggs

4 tablespoons chestnut flour, plus additional as needed

1½ teaspoons fine sea salt

Generous grindings of cracked pepper

1 teaspoon freshly scraped nutmeg

Force the ricotta through a fine sieve into a large bowl. Add the mascarpone, the pecorino, and the eggs, beating with an electric mixer only until mixture is smooth.

Combine the flour, salt, pepper, and nutmeg and stir them into the ricotta mixture, combining all into a thick paste. Cover the bowl tightly with plastic wrap and permit it to rest in the refrigerator at least 4 hours, or as long as overnight.

Roll portions of the rested, chilled dough into ropes about ¾ inch in diameter and 10 inches in length. Cut the ropes into 1-inch lengths and place them on a tray lined with a clean kitchen towel sprinkled with chestnut flour. Roll the gnocchi about in the flour. Repeat the process until all the gnocchi are coated. Cover the gnocchi with another clean kitchen towel and permit them to dry while you make the sauce.

The Sauce

⅓ cup extra-virgin olive oil
3 fat cloves garlic, peeled, crushed, and finely minced
1½ pounds fresh, wild mushrooms (porcini, chanterelles, cèpes,
    portobelli, etc.), wiped free of grit, trimmed, and thickly sliced
1½ teaspoons fine sea salt
Freshly cracked pepper
2 cups dry white wine
½ cup flat-leaf parsley

In a large sauté pan over a medium flame, heat the olive oil and cook the garlic until it is transparent, taking care not to color it. Add the mushrooms, sprinkling with sea salt and generous grindings of pepper. Toss the mushrooms about in the fat, until they give up their juices. Add the wine and bring to a quiet simmer.

Cover the pan with a skewed lid and, over a gentle flame, permit the mushrooms to absorb their juices and the wine until they are plumped and soft, about ½ hour. Mince the parsley leaves and stir into the mushrooms.

Cover the pan and let the mushrooms rest for a few minutes while you cook the gnocchi.

In a large pot, bring abundant, sea-salted water to a boil and drop in the gnocchi.

As the gnocchi begin to rise to the surface, remove them with a slotted spoon and place in a warmed, shallow bowl. When all the gnocchi have been cooked, pour over the barely reheated mushrooms and all their juices and portion onto plates or shallow bowls.

Pasta alla Gricia

PASTA WITH PANCETTA AND PECORINO

Serves 4

From the somber mountain village of Amatrice in the Abruzzo—one of the areas from which have emigrated, to other regions of Italy and throughout the world, many cooks and chefs—was born the famous pasta all' Amatriciana, *prepared faithfully by the pilgrim cooks wherever they go. One evening in Rome, an Abruzzese cook asked if he might offer a different pasta to us, the one most nostalgic for him. What he presented was, indeed,* pasta all' Amatriciana, *simply made without tomatoes. In dialect, its name contracts into* gricia.

> 6 ounces salt pork, minced
> 1 large yellow onion, peeled and finely minced
> 1 small, dried red chile pepper, crushed, or ⅓ to ½ teaspoon
>   dried chile flakes
> Coarse sea salt
> 12 ounces bucatini or other dried string pasta
> 2 cups just-grated pecorino
> Freshly cracked pepper

Place the pasta cooking pot filled with abundant water over a lively flame while you prepare the sauce.

In a sauté pan over a medium flame, heat the salt pork, permitting it to color and crisp and give up its perfumed fat. With a slotted spoon, remove the crisped salt pork and leave it to rest on absorbent paper towels.

In the remaining fat, sauté the onion until translucent, taking care not to let it color, and add the crushed chile, stirring it about with the onion. Remove the pan from the flame.

The water should be boiling and ready to receive the pasta now. Add the sea salt to the boiling water with the pasta, cook it to al dente, and drain. Reserve ½ cup or so of its cooking water. The pasta should still be somewhat wet. Place it in a warmed, shallow bowl.

Pour the onion over the pasta along with 1 cup of the pecorino and several tablespoons of the pasta cooking water. Grind pepper very generously over all and toss the pasta, coating each strand. Strew the pasta with the crisped salt pork and grind over more pepper.

Present the pasta, passing the remaining pecorino and the pepper grinder.

Pasta ai Pomodori Verdi

PASTA WITH GREEN TOMATOES

Serves 4

The cooling green tint of the sauce, its reserved, sensual sort of piquancy, make this a pasta good for high-summer lunch or supper after insalata di cantalupo *(see page 22).*

> 1½ pounds firm-fleshed green tomatoes, coarsely chopped
> 1 small purple onion, peeled and coarsely chopped
> 1 cup torn fresh basil leaves
> 2 teaspoons fine sea salt
> ¾ cup extra-virgin olive oil
> 4 fat cloves garlic, peeled, crushed, and finely minced
> 1 small, dried red chile pepper, crushed, or ⅓ to ½ teaspoon
>   dried chile flakes
> 1 cup freshly made fine bread crumbs
> 12 ounces bucatini or other dried string pasta
> Coarse sea salt
> ½ cup capers preserved under salt, rinsed and dried
> Just-grated pecorino

In the bowl of a food processor fitted with a steel blade, pulse the tomatoes with the onion to a coarse puree. Turn the mixture out into a bowl, stirring in the basil and the salt. In a small saucepan, heat ½ cup of the oil and soften the garlic in it, taking care not to let it color. Remove from the flame, add the chile, and permit the chile to steep for a minute or two before pouring the warm oil into the tomato puree. Stir the sauce well and set aside.

Brown the bread crumbs in ¼ cup of the oil. Cook the pasta to al dente in abundant, boiling, sea-salted water. Drain the pasta but leave it somewhat wet.

Return the pasta to its cooking pot and toss the pasta with the sauce, coating each strand. Add the capers and toss once again.

Turn the pasta out into a shallow bowl. Sprinkle with the browned bread crumbs and the pecorino.

Insalata di Cantalupo

A SALAD OF FRESH FIGS, MELON, AND MINT

Serves 2

Should there be, one day in your life, both a handful of still-warm-from-the-tree ripe figs and the juice-dripping flesh of a melon, go quickly to find leaves of mint, some good green olive oil, and the juice of a lemon to make this little salad. Use only flawless components and arrange them for someone wonderful with whom to rhapsodize over it. You might, then, need heady, appropriate conversation. You could choose to speak of Platina—one Bartolomeo Sacchi—the Vatican librarian and author, in 1475, of Platine de Honestate Voluptate. *The work's argument concerns the history of Roman cuisine and was the first officially published cookbook since those written during the Republic. Or you might want to chatter a bit about Cantalupo in Sabina—the Singing Wolf of the Sabines—once a papal garden property outside the Roman walls where a strain of tiny, orange-fleshed melons were cultivated, they, no doubt, being the precursors to those we call cantaloupe. Perhaps you might choose not to speak at all, thus distracting nothing from the sweet little figs.*

> 4 to 6 plump, ripe green or purple figs
> 1 small, very ripe cantaloupe or other orange-fleshed melon
> 1 generous handful of fresh mint leaves
> 2 tablespoons finest extra-virgin olive oil
> 2 tablespoons just-squeezed lemon juice

Halve the figs vertically, not peeling them, and lay them, in some pattern that pleases you, on two large plates. Halve the melon horizontally, removing its rind and seeds, carving each half into ¼-inch slices and laying these on the plates. Tear the mint leaves and strew the fruit with them. Drop the oil in tears over the figs and the lemon juice over the melon. Serve the salads with iced *moscato* or any fine, ambered sweet wine.

Un Natale Romano

A ROMAN CHRISTMAS

The Roman Christmas seems a festival inviolate. It remains treasured, recalling, permitting, if only for a day or two, families, friends, to stay inside the sympathy of tradition. *La vigilia,* the eve of Christmas, is kept with the ritual presentation of a fish and seafood supper that dictates serving *capitoni arrostiti su rami d' alloro*, eels roasted over branches of bay—some version of which has been eaten since the days of the Republic, when Romans bought eel at the *pescheria* in Portico d'Ottavia.

Until a decade or so ago, as the bells rang two on the morning of *la vigilia*, the mayor of Rome opened the gates of Il Cottio, the wholesale fish market in Via Ostiense, to a bawdy constituency who awaited his hurtling of live eels out to them—a Christmas gift of food and of force, pagan symbol of the Roman's own potency and immortality. Though this folkloric event is no more, one spies countless Romans on the morning of Christmas Eve, straining with great, sloshing buckets, transporting their slithery prizes.

He prefers female water snakes. Some are nearly a meter in length and of a weight that often exceeds four kilos. If he is a traditionalist, he takes the snake live. At home, most often at the hands of his wife, the beast is beheaded, cleaved into great, still-slithering chunks, speared onto thick branches of bay, then bathed in a potion of red wine, olive oil, and garlic. The eel is roasted over a wood fire and given a benediction of red wine vinegar just as it is taken, crusted, fire-blackened, to the table. And *i capitoni* are just one offering.

Each family stays fixed to its own unstinting litany of dishes for the eve of, the day of, and the day after Christmas. Our Roman friends, an extended family of twenty-two plus their children, collect in the ancestral home several days before the festival, ostensibly to shop and cook and bake together. Several levels of posturing and harrumphing first ensue. There seems always some attempt at trimming the traditional menu. But whose dishes should be cut? And why? Have they not been appreciated all these years? Doors slam, screams are muffled in half a dozen lace-trimmed handkerchiefs, sibilant oaths are heard, until someone proposes that they simply do things as they have done them always, as they shall do them always. Then begins the gala in earnest.

We have been honored guests at their Christmases, dancing our parts in the breathless, herculean pageant of preparation. Precisely penned lists are posted stating allotments of time in front of the burners, at the wood-fired ovens, at the fireplace. Those who pull midnight or five-in-the-morning slots search to illuminate the wisdom of working at those hours, sometimes nimbly bartering them for more temperate times. And, somehow, as the church bells of San Roberto ring nine, all contingencies—ruffled, starched, curled, swathed, scented—gather near the seventeenth-century fireplace to raise their glasses in thanksgiving and then to sit together at the great wooden bishop's table with its ritual eighteen candles alight.

Here follow the dishes that, unfailingly, comprise the grand Christmas Eve supper and the lunch that follows on the day of Christmas. Recipes are given for the dishes most characteristic of the feasts. An asterisk indicates that the recipe follows the menu.

Cena della Vigilia
CHRISTMAS EVE SUPPER

Spuma di Tonno
A MOUSSE OF TUNA

Gamberoni Arrostiti
PRAWNS THREADED ON OLIVE BRANCHES AND WOOD-ROASTED

Puppidi Fritti
(AN ANCIENT OVAL BASKET LAID IN WHITE LINEN AND CRADLING AN IMMENSE
TANGLE OF CRISP, TINY FISH, FRIED GOLDEN. THIS DISH IS MADE ALWAYS BY A
PUGLIESE COUSIN WITH LOCAL FISH, HE INSISTING ON GIVING THE DISH ITS
PUGLIESE-DIALECT NAME.)

I Capitoni
EEL ROASTED ON BRANCHES OF BAY

Taglierini con Lumachine
SLENDER STRINGS OF HAND-ROLLED PASTA WITH TINY SEA SNAILS
SEARED IN GARLIC AND ANISE-PERFUMED OIL

Pasta con le Acciughe
PASTA WITH SALT ANCHOVIES, CAPERS, GARLIC, AND CHILE

Pasta con i Ricci
PASTA WITH SEA URCHINS

Frittelle di Baccalà*
FRITTERS OF SALT COD

Branzino Arrostito con Rami d' Alloro, Limone, e Capperi*
SEA BASS ROASTED WITH BAY BRANCHES, LEMON, AND CAPERS

Salmone Arrostito
SALMON BATHED IN BLOOD-ORANGE JUICE AND ROASTED OVER
OLIVE WOOD BRANCHES

Broccoletti con Uvette e Briciole
ROMAN BROCCOLI WITH RAISINS AND TOASTED BREAD CRUMBS

Cicoria Saltata con Aglio e Peperoncino
BITTER GREENS SAUTÉED WITH GARLIC AND CHILE

Pangiallo Antico Natalizio
THE ANCIENT SAFFRONED FRUIT BREAD OF CHRISTMAS

Frittelle di Baccalà

FRITTERS OF SALT COD

Serves 6 to 8

1½ cups all-purpose flour

12 ounces beer

2 pounds *baccalà* or *stoccafisso* (prepared according to instructions
    on page 10)

1⅓ cups heavy cream

2 large egg whites

4 to 6 cups peanut oil

2 lemons

Place the flour in a medium bowl and stir in enough beer to form a batter the consistency of heavy cream. Cover the batter and set aside.

Place the prepared *baccalà* in a large bowl and, with two forks, finely shred the fish. Stir in the cream, blending the elements until thick.

In another bowl, beat the egg whites until they form stiff but not dry peaks. Gently fold the egg whites into the creamed *baccalà*.

In a large, deep sauté pan or a deep fryer, heat the peanut oil over a medium flame. With your hands, form ovals of the *baccalà* mixture, about 3 inches or 2 inches, then quickly dip them in the beer batter. Fry the fritters in the very hot oil. Cook the fritters until deeply golden before turning them, then cook the other side, and remove them with a slotted spoon to absorbent paper towels. Present the fritters as fast as you can, with wedges of lemon and cold white wine.

Branzino Arrostito con Rami d' Alloro, Limone, e Capperi

SEA BASS ROASTED WITH BAY BRANCHES, LEMON, AND CAPERS

Serves 6

1 3½- to 4-pound sea bass, cleaned, scaled, and filleted
2 large branches of fresh bay leaves or several large branches of
    rosemary
1 large lemon, very thinly sliced
⅓ cup capers, preserved under salt, rinsed and dried
Fine sea salt
¼ cup extra-virgin olive oil
¼ cup dry white wine

Preheat the oven to 450 degrees.

Dry the fish well with absorbent paper towels and split it in two. Place 1 bay branch or 2 rosemary branches on one side of the fish, then the slices of lemon, one overlapping the other. Strew the lemon slices with the capers and anoint the whole with sea salt and a few drops of the oil. Re-form the fish, massaging it with more of the oil and laying it in a shallow terra-cotta or enameled cast-iron casserole. Cover the fish with the remaining branch of bay or the remaining branches of rosemary.

Roast the fish for 10 minutes, then adjust the heat to 375 degrees and continue to roast for another 10 minutes or until a skewer inserted into the bass emerges extremely hot.

Remove the bass from the oven, pour over the white wine, permitting it to steam and hiss up into vapors while you carry the fish to table.

Serve the bass with no other accompaniments save its own good juices, a bit of oven-toasted bread, and very cold white wine.

Pranzo di Natale
CHRISTMAS DAY LUNCH

Brodo di Cappone
CAPON BROTH

La Nociata
PASTA WITH WALNUTS, SUGAR, AND CINNAMON

Il Tacchino Ripieno
TURKEY MARINATED IN COGNAC, STUFFED WITH CHESTNUTS
AND TRUFFLES, AND SPIT-ROASTED OVER A WOOD FIRE

Cardi Gratinati
GRATINÉED CARDOONS

Cipolline in Agrodolce
SMALL ROASTED ONIONS IN A SWEET AND SOUR SAUCE

Piselli con Pancetta e Salsicce
PEAS WITH PANCETTA AND SAUSAGE

Melograni, Rami di Sedano, Noci Arrostite
POMEGRANATES, CELERY STALKS, AND ROASTED WALNUTS

La Crostata di Prugne Secche Speziate*
A SPICED PRUNE TART

La Crostata di Prugne Secche Speziate

A SPICED PRUNE TART

Serves 8

First, know that you are about to bake the earth's most delectable prune tart. If you wish to make it with fresh plums, you must sugar them, according to their own sweetness and your own need to taste sugar rather than fresh fruit. The same adjustment is necessary should you use fresh apricots or nectarines or peaches. Then simply proceed with the recipe.

> 1 tart crust recipe (page 216)
> 14 ounces plump pitted prunes
> ½ cup dark rum
> 1¼ cups mascarpone
> 1 large egg, slightly beaten
> ¼ cup heavy cream
> ½ teaspoon just-grated nutmeg
> 1-inch stick cinnamon, grated
> ¼ teaspoon ground cloves
> ¼ teaspoon just-cracked pepper
> ⅓ cup very bitter orange marmalade
> 1 tablespoon dark brown sugar

Preheat the oven to 400 degrees. You will need a 10- to 12-inch tart pan with a removable bottom, buttered, and lined with the tart crust pastry. Cover the pastry-lined tart tin with plastic wrap and place it in the freezer while you make the filling.

Place the prunes in a small saucepan with the rum, heating the two over a low flame until the rum nearly boils. Remove from heat. Cover the pot and permit the prunes to steep.

Place the mascarpone, the egg, the cream, and the remaining ingredients in a bowl, beating them together with a wooden spoon. Drain the prunes, reserving any remaining drops of the rum.

Remove the pastry from the freezer, unwrap it, and position the drained prunes in it. Gently spoon or pour the spiced mascarpone over the prunes and bake the tart for 20 minutes, then adjust the temperature to 350 degrees and continue to bake for 15 to 20 minutes more or until the crust is deep gold and the prunes all hidden beneath the bronzed skin of the cream. Brush the hot tart with the few drops of reserved rum and cool it on a rack for 20 minutes.

Present it still warm or, better still, at room temperature with tiny glasses of iced moscato.

Antica Pizza Dolce Romana di Fabriziana

THE ANCIENT SWEET BREAD OF ROME IN THE MANNER OF FABRIZIANA

or

Il Pane della Ninna Nanna

LULLABY BREAD

For 2 beautiful breads

Neither very sweet nor pizzalike in the flat, savory pie sort of way, this is a gold-fleshed, orange-perfumed cake-like bread that, if baked with care, will be tall and elegant, its crumb coarse yet light and full of the consoling scents of yeast and butter.

Fabriziana is one of the several "middle" names of the Roman countess with whom I learned to bake the confection in the cavernous old kitchen of her villa that looks to the gardens of the Borghese. Ours were clandestine appointments, with our yeast and our candied orange peels and the tattered recipe book of her mother's cook. You see, Fabriziana had never cooked or baked in her life, had never made anything from a pile of flour and a few crumbles of yeast. Forbidden in the kitchen as a girl, her adulthood has been always too fraught with obligations to permit interludes in front of the flames. But in the years we have been friends, she has always demonstrated more than a kind interest in my cooking, sitting once in a while, rapt as a fox, on an old wrought-iron chair in my kitchen as I dance about. And one day when I told her I was searching for a formula for an ancient, orange-perfumed Roman bread, she knew precisely where to find the recipe. Trailing off in some Proustian dream, she said she hadn't thought of the bread in too many years, it having been her favorite sweet at Christmas and Easter. Once she even requested that it—rather than some grand, creamy *torta*—be her birthday cake. She told of poaching slices of it from a silver tray during parties and receptions, stuffing them deep into the pockets of her silk dresses to eat later in bed, after her sister was safely asleep, so she might share them only with her puppy.

So it was that we decided to make the bread together. Wishing to avoid the chiding of her family and, most of all, her cook, we chose to do the deed on mornings when the house would be safe from them. It was wonderful to see Fabriziana at play. Flour and butter were forced under her long, mother-of-pearled nails, and her blond-streaked coif, mounted to resist tempests, soon fell into girlish ringlets over her noble brow. With a few mornings' worth of trial, we baked Fabriziana's lullaby bread, the bread of her memories. And once, on a birthday of mine, the countess came fairly racing through my doorway proffering a curiously wrapped parcel that gave up the telltale perfumes of our bread. The countess had learned to bake indeed.

The Starter

1 tablespoon active dry yeast or 1½ small cakes of fresh yeast
½ cup warm water
½ cup all-purpose flour

The Dough

4 cups all-purpose flour
1½ teaspoons fine sea salt
3 tablespoons sugar
6 large eggs, lightly beaten
2-inch stick cinnamon, grated
Finely grated zest of 2 large oranges
2 tablespoons aniseeds
⅓ cup plus 2 tablespoons Cointreau
10 tablespoons sweet butter, slightly softened, plus additional
    for molds
1 cup candied orange peel, finely chopped
Juice of 1 large orange
2 cups confectioners' sugar

To make the starter, place the yeast in a small bowl, add the water, stirring, permitting the yeast to soften and activate for 15 minutes. Stir in the flour, forming a smooth batter. Cover the bowl with plastic wrap, until the contents double.

In a large bowl, using an electric mixer or a wooden spoon, beat the flour, salt, sugar, and eggs. Add the rested, risen starter and beat the batter hard for 5 minutes with the mixer or for 7 minutes by hand.

In a small bowl, combine the cinnamon, orange zest, aniseeds, and ⅓ cup of Cointreau and incorporate them into the batter. Cover with plastic wrap and permit its mass to double—about 1½ hours—at which point the batter will have transformed itself into a rather stringy and elastic but still very soft dough. Beat in the softened butter with your hands, breaking down the fiber of the dough and urging it to smoothness. Last, beat in the candied peel.

Butter the surfaces of two molds—Kugelhopf tins, Bundt cake tins, high-sided charlotte molds, or soufflé dishes, or, perhaps best of all, those very deep aluminum tins with removable bottoms often used to bake angel food cakes—and pour or spoon in the dough evenly between the two. Cover the molds with clean kitchen towels and permit the *pizze* to rise for an hour or so or until they have reached the tops of the molds. Preheat oven to 400 degrees.

Bake the breads for 7 minutes, adjusting the temperature to 350 degrees and continuing the bake for 50 to 60 minutes or until the breads have taken on a dark, gold skin and are risen well above the rims of their molds. Permit the *pizze* to cool slightly, then turn them out of their molds, setting them upright to cool thoroughly on wire racks.

Meanwhile, make a simple glaze by beating 2 tablespoons of the Cointreau and the orange juice into the confectioners' sugar. Cover the glaze and beat it again after about thirty minutes. When the breads are fully cooled, spoon the glaze over the domes of the bread, permitting it to drip, as it will, down their sides. Let the glaze dry and repeat the process once or twice more, using it up.

Gelato di Fragole di Nemi

GELATO OF WOOD STRAWBERRIES WITH BASIL, HONEY, AND PEPPER

Makes about 1½ quarts

Caligola, *Caligula—the diminutive in the dialect of the Empire for* shoe—*was the name given to Caio Cesare, despot of the Empire in* A.D. 37. *And it was under the murky waters of the small volcanic lake of Nemi, south of Rome, that were excavated, earlier in this century, two of the emperor's small sailing ships—toy boats, really—from which his madness commanded droll, demonic games played in the shadows of the lake forest, the once-sacred woods of Diana's mythical hunts.*

Now the pine and oak forests about the little lake of Nemi seem serene enough, whispering up nothing of the old horrors of the place. There, in May, begin to push up from the velvety black earth the most gorgeous and tiny wild strawberries. We like to go there then, for the festivals that celebrate them, to eat them, cool and fresh from their woodsy patches. And on a Sunday last June, as the season for them was ending, we lunched in the town of Nemi, hoping to find one last dose of the berries for dessert.

Sitting out on a shaded terrace that looked to the main square, we watched the promenading of the few citizens not yet seated at table. A little ruckus came up behind us from two boys jousting with silvered plastic swords. One of them was a robust sort of chap, thickset, his patrician black-eyed face in profile to us. His adversary was a waif of a boy, a miniature of the other with the same legacy of splendid form and feature. The small one was losing the battle. I tried not to feel every blow I saw him take, the bigger one thrusting the blunted end of the toy sword into his spare middle over and over again. The little one was crying, then, but hardly in surrender. His pain was evident, his fear, too, I thought, yet he stayed to fight. Then, throwing his weapon to the side, the victor began to use his hands to pummel him. The diners around were unmindful. I begged Fernando to do something, to stop them. He told me sternly with his eyes that we must do nothing.

I got up and walked, nonchalantly, over to them. "Buon giorno, ragazzi. Come stiamo? Come vanno le cose?" "Hi, boys. How are you? How are things going?" I asked inanely, as though they had been shooting marbles. Gentlemen to the core, the bigger one said, "Buon giorno, signora. Noi stiamo bene, e lei?" "Good day, my lady. We are well, and you?" "What is your name?" I asked, playing for time so the little one might catch his breath. "Io sono Alessio e lui si chiama Giovannino." "I am Alessio and he is called Giovannino," offered the big one. I ventured further. "Alessio, did you know that you were hurting Giovannino, that you were hurting him so terribly?" "Sì, signora. Lo so di avergli fatto un pò male." "Yes, my lady, I know I hurt him a bit," he answered willingly. I asked him why he would want to be so violent with his little friend. Alessio looked at me full face: "Signora, siamo romani. Combattere è nel nostro sangue." "We are Romans, my lady. To fight is in our blood." Educated by the eight-year-old gladiator, I could only shake his hand, then shake the hand of Giovannino and walk back to our table.

Fernando told me quietly that a Roman boy could never be Huckleberry Finn.

During the lunch, I noticed that Alessio, now sitting on a bench between two people who were likely his grandparents, kept looking at me, waving once in a while, smiling at me with sympathy for my unworldliness. He strolled by the table a little later and asked if we were going to taste the gelato di fragole. It's made with basil and pepper and vinegar, he proclaimed, as though that composition might be as difficult for me to comprehend as was his penchant for rough sport. He went on to assure us it was the best gelato in Nemi. We asked him if he might like to join us. He said he couldn't, but thanked us, bowed rather smartly, and walked off toward his own Sunday lunch. We sat for a long time, eating Alessio's gelato and musing over him. Surely he'd been right about its goodness, its tint a sort of pale, silky green from its affair with the basil, the tiny berries left whole, studding the cream like iced rubies, the scent of it pepper-spiced, its dark sugariness playing voluptuously with the hushed bittersweetness that was the vinegar. Surely the beautiful little Roman had also been right about the gelato.

3 cups heavy cream

1 cup whole milk

3 tablespoons dark honey (chestnut, buckwheat, etc.)

½ cup dark brown sugar

1 cup torn basil leaves

1 teaspoon freshly ground pepper

3 cups very ripe strawberries, rinsed, hulled, and lightly crushed
   (if the berries are the tiny wood strawberries, half can be left
   whole, the other half lightly crushed)

2 teaspoons balsamic vinegar

In a heavy pot, bring the cream, milk, honey, brown sugar, basil leaves, and pepper just to a simmer, stirring a moment to dissolve the honey and sugar.

Cover the pot and permit the cream and milk combination to steep for an hour or so. Strain the mixture, discarding the basil and any remnants of the pepper. Stir in the prepared strawberries and the vinegar.

Cover the mixture and chill it for several hours before proceeding to freeze it in an ice cream maker according to the manufacturer's instructions.

ABRUZZO

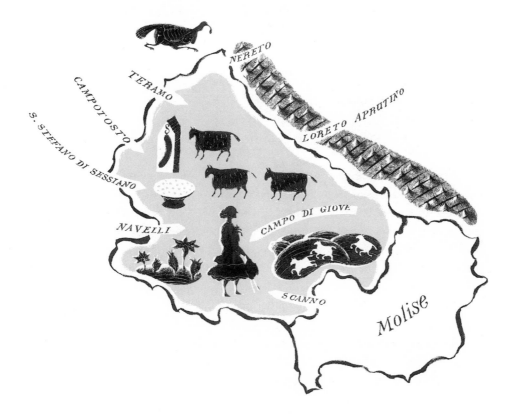

The Abruzzo has a terrible magnificence. Savage, frozen faces of echoless mountains, ramparts heaving up from the sea, with narrow, curling throats the only passages into the villages that hang from their stony cheeks. Too, she has gentler faces of russet earth smoothed by sympathetic hands into sheepfolds and meadows and shelves of high plains, places with no noises save the stretching of the grain and the shivering of a sunset wind, the chink of a bell on a newborn lamb.

In the mid-1800s, a few high-spirited English, seeking refuge from the gloss of Rome and Florence, wanted to know what strangeness lay only two days' carriage ride away or a scant week's trek over the edges of civilization into the darkness of the Abruzzo. They thought to find a land of ungallant men—desperadoes or pagans, all of them. What they found was much as what one finds now. The Abruzzo is of sweet peace, of people chiseling out chivalrous lives and moving, joyously, from canon to magic, both colors becoming them. It is a land and a consciousness rapturously adrift. Her insularity is the issue of uninviting confines and more, perhaps, from thick, cherished moorings to the rites and rhythms of an agrarian, pastoral life, of an unshouted and mystical faith.

She is still the Abruzzo over which those long-ago English rhapsodized. It was for her that came poet and chronicler and those who would paint her, saving, sealing her images against some eclipse. They needn't have worried. She is the old whispering muse who sifts moonlight on a road where one might expect a blackguard on horseback, but where one finds, rather, a lady, besweatered and of voluminous black skirts, a great sheaf of twigs her headdress, walking home to feed a fire.

About the Cuisine

*M*ore than in any other region of the south, the Abruzzo's cuisine reflects both *la vita signorile*, the high-born life, and *la vita povera*, the life of the poor. Her dishes are gracefully, assiduously faithful to the old writs. Most often her foods are pure and undisguised, yet they are never artless. When her dishes are more complex, they are still restrained, illuminating, always, the genuineness of each component. Elegance is not a function of wealth. The food of the Abruzzo is elegant in its fantasy, its dignity. Often a people's pride asks more of them in times of misery than it does when life is prosperous. It was, is, still that way in the Abruzzo. And she will not trump up her menu to comfort you or any other traveler coming to visit.

Her gastronomy is as much a part of her as are the mountains and her memories, as is her mysticism. She likes it the way it is, no matter what century, what millennium happens to be passing by. It is not so everywhere in Italy.

Maccheroni alla Mugnaia con Peperoncini Dolce Forte

HANDMADE PASTA WITH SWEET AND FIERY DRIED CHILES

Serves 4

The transumanza is all but a faded pastoral ritual in the Abruzzo. Once three million sheep and lambs were guided each year from summer mountain pastures to the winter lowlands and back again, but now—with the flocks reduced to several hundreds of thousands—they are transported in huge, canvas-roofed vans. And thus the pastoral life is in suspension, lulled into a smaller, less dramatic sort of existence that permits the shepherd to stay fixed, to have some dwelling or other as a home. Before, he lived with only the sky as refuge. His nobilities and his indignities, his dreaming and sleeping and, often, his dying, were fulfilled in the open air. But to hear stories from old men who, as boys, were raised to be shepherds, whose youth, nomadic and primitive, was spent in the waning epoch of the transumanza, one thinks it might hardly have been a life of desperation. Its very solitude was often its gift, say the old men. In his aloneness, the shepherd honed a curiously grand capacity to listen and discern. He became a piper of sorts, free to move about from village to village, and thus to transport to the hungry ears of each place his accumulation of stories. He was a folkloric hero, an exotic who lived by the graces. The old men smile deep in their eyes when they speak of they who live and die hanging tight to the fancy that security is palpable as a jewel.

And, so, having heard the dusty memoirs and the swollen legends recounted by the old shepherd romancers, of the austere dishes they recall being cooked out in the open over their fires or under the shelter of some ruin, we wondered if someone, somewhere, might be cooking them still.

Having just billeted ourselves at a modest hotel, La Bilancia, in the environs of Loreto Aprutino, spurred by the repute of its kitchen and cellars, we approached our host. Sergio is a gallant man with a burly sort of gentility. He said how strange it was that the circle had closed so quickly, that in his own lifetime, foods representing poverty had come to be of historical, gastronomic, interest to a stranger. We followed him into the kitchens, the parish of his wife, Antonietta. It was she—one who had every comestible at her disposal, kitchens with the square footage of a small village, four chefs at work under her soft-spoken guidance—who offered to cook the old dishes. They were, after all, her childhood food, the consoling plates of her grandmothers. She explained that the Abruzzesi, even when their means invite them to eat more extravagantly, still cook the old dishes at home. "They still comfort," she said. "They are cherished, they are our nostalgia." Too, she mused, this was not so true in some other regions where the foods a people ate when they were poor were fast set aside in better times.

And so, because her clients partake of these dishes at home, it is other foods they long for when they sit in her dining room. Hence, it was a somewhat singular occasion for Antonietta to prepare the old foods. She set to making her lists, dispatching us on a mission to the nearby town of Penne to find a certain flour, a certain dried bean. Antonietta cooked two of her own preferred dishes from the traditions of the transumanza, from la cucina povera. And that evening, the immense room filled with guests vanquishing great hefts of roast lamb and fricasseed veal and saddle of hare and generous plates of maccheroni alla chitarra with a sauce of *wild boar. She sat with us, her impeccable white cook's bonnet always in place, eating the simple food with an unembarrassed appetite. We, too, loved the dishes, as much for their own goodness as for the images they lit.*

The rough pasta dough is made from three flours and hand-rolled. Cut into rustic strings, this is not the ethereal pasta of the refined cucina *whose destiny it is to linger about with shavings of white truffle or the belly of some poached lobster. It is the coarse stuff that is homey sop for simple yet luscious sauces, the two fusing into one soft, sensually pungent taste.* Maccheroni alla chitarra, *made from* farina di grano duro, semolina, *and eggs and lopped into thin strings as it is rolled over a wooden box fitted with six thin wires, is the classical pasta of Abruzzo and, though it is good, the* mugnaia *seems more interesting to prepare.* Maccheroni alla chitarra *can be found dried quite readily, exported by good, artisinal Abruzzesi houses to American specialty shops.*

The Sauce

    1 cup extra-virgin olive oil
    4 to 6 fat cloves of garlic, peeled, crushed, and minced
    1 tablespoon sweet ground paprika
    1 to 2 small, dried red chiles, crushed, or ⅓ to ⅔ teaspoon dried
       chile flakes

In a small saucepan, warm the oil and soften the garlic for several minutes, permitting it to take on a little color. Add the paprika and the crushed chiles, stirring them about. Remove from the heat, cover the oil, and let it stand for ½ hour or longer. Reheat the oil slightly before saucing the *mugnaia*.

La Mugnaia

    1 cup all-purpose flour
    1 cup fine semolina (sometimes labeled "pasta flour"), plus addi-
       tional as needed
    ¼ cup stone-ground whole wheat flour
    1 teaspoon fine sea salt
    2 large eggs
    2 to 3 tablespoons water
    2 tablespoons coarse sea salt

On a large wooden board or a pastry marble or in a large bowl, place the flours with the fine sea salt in a flat mound and form a well in the center. Break the eggs directly into the well, add 2 tablespoons of water to the well, drawing the flour from the inside wall of the mound gently into the eggs and water.

Using your hands, continue to work the elements into a rough paste. Should the paste be too dry, add the additional tablespoon of water—or even a few drops more, if necessary—and work it vigorously. Should the paste be too wet, add a few tablespoons more of the all-purpose flour and work it with the same vigor.

Flour is never the same, even if it comes from wheat harvested from the same field and ground at the same mill on the same day by the same miller. Age and humidity act upon it, changing its structure so that it will drink in more or less moisture.

Knead the dough, then, deliberately and rhythmically, for 8 to 10 minutes or more, until it is smooth and resilient to your touch. Wrap the dough in plastic wrap, permitting it a 20-minute rest to relax its hard-worked glutens.

Don't bother with a pasta machine for this rustic dough. I suppose the shepherds just patted it out on a flat stone. You'll find it easy enough to roll by hand. Begin by dividing the dough into thirds, covering two of the pieces to prevent their drying while you work with the first.

Lightly sprinkle semolina over the work surface and, wielding a long, heavy wooden rolling pin, roll out the dough in one direction, using an outward motion. Roll the dough into a circle, rotating it often as it stretches and grows thinner. When the dough is rolled and stretched to a somewhat uniform ¼ inch, roll it up, strudel fashion, and, with a sharp knife, cut it into ¼-inch ribbons. Unroll the ribbons, dusting them lightly with semolina, and place them on metal sheets or trays, lined with clean kitchen towels. Proceed to roll and cut the remaining portions of dough.

The *mugnaia* will be ready to cook after ½ hour or so or will keep nicely, tucked in under the kitchen cloths, overnight. Do not refrigerate the pasta.

To cook the *mugnaia*, bring abundant water to a rolling boil, add 2 tablespoons coarse sea salt and the pasta. Cover the pot. As the water returns to the boil, begin counting. *Mugnaia* will usually take 4 to 5 minutes to cook, but test the texture after 3 minutes and cook it just to al dente.

Drain the pasta, leaving it somewhat wet, and return it to the still-warm cooking pot.

Add the sauce and coat the *mugnaia* very well. Serve the *mugnaia* in shallow bowls and offer the bottle of *olio santo* (see page 155). Cheese is not a classic adornment to this dish. I imagine the shepherds grew weary, once in a while, of even their own good pecorino.

La Fracchiata

A PUREE OF DRIED FAVA BEANS WITH FRIED SEMOLINA BREAD

Serves 4

This is a substantial soup classically made from fresh fava beans and a dried sort of bean/pea hybrid called la cicerchia, *whose taste and texture are very like that of the fava when it is dried. This version, asking only for the dried favas since* la cicerchia *is not readily found in America, yields a rich, smoky flavor that is wonderful against the comfort of the warm crunch of the bread.*

8 ounces dried fava beans

2 tablespoons fine sea salt

½ cup extra-virgin olive oil

3 fat cloves garlic, peeled, crushed, and minced

1 small, dried red chile pepper, crushed, or ⅓ to ½ teaspoon
   dried chile flakes

3 ounces pancetta, diced

4 thick slices semolina bread or other sturdy-crumbed, country
   bread, crusts removed and cut into small cubes

Place the dried favas in a large soup pot, cover them with cold water, add 1 tablespoon of sea salt and bring the beans to a simmer. Cover the pot and let the beans rest for 1 hour.

Drain the beans, covering them with fresh, cold water and adding another tablespoon of sea salt. Bring the beans to a simmer again, cooking them over a gentle flame for 1 hour or until very tender. Drain the beans, reserving 2 cups or so of their cooking water, and set them aside.

In a medium sauté pan over a medium flame, warm ¼ cup of the olive oil and soften the garlic for a minute or two, taking care not to let it color. Add the chile and the pancetta, sautéing over a gentle flame until the pancetta has given up its fat and the oil is perfumed.

In the work bowl of a food processor, pulse the favas, adding some of their cooking liquors to obtain a pourable but not too liquid puree. Add the aromatic oil and the pancetta and process for another minute to blend the components. Turn the puree out into a medium saucepan and set aside.

Heat the remaining olive oil in a sauté pan and sauté the cubes of bread, turning them about in the oil until they are browned and crisped.

Reheat the puree for a minute or two, adding its cooking liquors if the soup seems too thick. Ladle the soup into shallow, warmed bowls, strewing each with the bread.

Polenta con Sugo Piccante di Maiale e Peperoni alla Spianatoia di Elisabetta

POLENTA WITH BRAISED PORK AND ROASTED RED PEPPERS SERVED ON
A WOODEN BOARD IN THE MANNER OF ELISABETTA

Serves 6

Abruzzesi women seem congenitally beatific. They endure, they temper, they are faithful to their own notion of life and betray none of the gnashing dramatics of those Italian women who seem to burlesque passion, who remain in pain eternal, fanned if only by the postino's tardiness. The Abruzzesi are intrinsically more dignified than those.

As wives and mothers, the Abruzzesi seem more revered than leaned upon. Not the archetypal massaia, farmwife, a woman of the Abruzzo historically worked the fields, made bricks, and piled them up into rude buildings with the same good sentiments with which she told fables to her children and suckled her baby. There are many stories, in fact, of women of the Abruzzo that I might tell you. I could tell you about Francesca Cipriani.

Well into her seventies, slender, of fine bearing, her long, silver hair pinned up under a kerchief, she speaks eloquently of what it is to live in an isolated mountain village at the end of this millennium. She knows very well that hers is the last generation with the will to stay there inside the small rhythms of its solitude. She is of the village of Campotosto, long and still famed for its plump, rough-textured sausages. She is one of the last artigiani—artisans—who build, by hand, the mortadelline di Campotosto. We were hard put, though, to talk her into selling a few of them to us. She said that this last batch had not yet had time to age properly and that she simply would not sell them in their unfinished condition. We told her that we had a wood-shed much like hers and that we lived, not so high up as she, but nevertheless, in the mountains and that we would promise to hang the little sausages there in our own crisp, cold, oak-scented air. She consented. As we were driving away, she raced after the car, counting on her fingers and calling to us, "Lasciatele appese fino al giorno di Pasqua e a quel punto saranno perfette"—"Leave them to hang until the day of Easter, at which point they will be perfect." We did exactly as she said, taking Francesca's mortadelline from the woodshed on Easter morning, slicing them thickly, and eating them with a soft, buttery pecorino bread for our Easter breakfast. And then I could tell you about Elisabetta.

We found her in the countryside between Anversa and Cocullo. We saw a sign fixed to a tree, penned in a child's hand, we thought, that read, LA VERA CUCINA ABRUZZESE. COME ERA UNA VOLTA. THE TRUE COOKING OF ABRUZZO. AS IT ONCE WAS. It was, after all, nearly noon, and the invitation was, indeed, irresistible. We pointed the car, as the sign's arrow indicated, down the narrow, scraggly lane. We stopped in front of the only house. There was a puppy sitting among the weeds and wildflowers, a starched, white napkin laid before him like a tablecloth and beset with various little dishes. After wishing him a buon appetito, we turned to the door. Another sign, in the same child's hand, invited us to ring the bell if we were hungry. We rang the bell. And there came Elisabetta. A rosy wool skier's cap pulled low over her brow, her thin, tiny body swathed in long skirts—one piled over another for warmth—and scuffed black boots composed her costume, all of it ornament to her caffè-latte-colored skin and the great, gray sparklers she had for eyes. Elisabetta, now seventy, began her career as a restaurateur at sixty-one. She was just coming into her stride, she told us.

Since we had arrived much too early for lunch, she sat us down in the kitchen in front of an old whisky bottle filled with cerise-colored wine and two tumblers. She puttered about, chopping and stirring and such, talking about her life, her adventures, how, when her then twenty-year-old son was sent to Sicilia for his military service, she went along. Because she feared the boy would miss her too much and because she feared, too, she might not otherwise ever see the island, it seemed right to go with him. She found work as a cook in a monastery and taught the monks a thing or two about good food, she assured us. Of course, she brought baskets full of pasta with lamb sauce and newborn breads and sweets to the barracks several times a week, taking her pay from the monks only in food. Soon other people began to arrive. All of them were as familiar to her as we were strangers. They huddled in the kitchen, lifting lid covers, washing a dish or a pot, tasting a sauce, as though they were her family who had come to Sunday dinner. She finally shooed us all into the dining room with its mismatched trappings and thick yellow dishes and began serving lunch.

She had spread a great wooden board (called a spianatoia) with polenta and poured over it a sauce made from pork and roasted peppers and tomatoes and red wine, all of it spirited with crushed chiles. She portioned the polenta with a length of string whose ends she wound around her hands, each of us sliding a heft of it onto our plates with a spatula. She waltzed through the funny little room as though it were a grand salon, furnishing us with more sauce, more pink wine. It was a beautiful lunch.

Elisabetta lives upstairs over her osteria with the puppy who likes to eat on a tablecloth. She shops, cooks, serves, washes up, and plays briscola (a popular card game) in the late evenings with the townsmen, sitting in the chair where her husband sat for longer than half a hundred years.

The Sauce

4 ounces pancetta

½ cup flat parsley leaves

4 fat cloves garlic, peeled and crushed

½ cup extra-virgin olive oil

1½ pounds pork shoulder, well-trimmed of its fat and cut into
    1-inch dice

3 teaspoons fine sea salt

1 medium yellow onion, peeled and minced

1 tablespoon fennel seeds

1 small, dried red chile pepper, crushed, or ⅓ to ½ teaspoon
    chile flakes

2 cups good red wine

2 14-ounce cans crushed plum tomatoes, with their juices

2 medium red bell peppers, roasted, peeled, seeded, and diced

2 teaspoons good red wine vinegar

With a mezzaluna or a sharp knife, mince the pancetta with the parsley and the garlic to a fine paste.

In a large sauté pan over a medium flame, warm the olive oil with the pancetta/parsley/garlic paste and add the pork—only half at a time—browning and sealing the meat well. As it is browned, remove the pork to a holding plate. Sprinkle the pork generously with about 2 teaspoons of the salt.

Soften the onion in the remaining fat for several minutes. Add the fennel seeds and the chile and sauté for another minute. Add 1 cup of the wine, stirring and scraping at the residue and permitting the liquid to reduce for a minute or two. Add the remaining wine, the tomatoes, the peppers, and 1 teaspoon of the sea salt, bringing the sauce to a simmer. Over a medium flame, permit the sauce to reduce and thicken for 20 minutes. Lower the flame, add the pork and, covering the pot with a skewed lid, gently simmer the meat for 30 minutes or until it is soft and fork-tender. Remove from the heat and stir in the red wine vinegar. Permit the sauce to rest for several hours or overnight.

The Polenta

3 cups water

1½ cups whole milk

6 tablespoons sweet butter

1 teaspoon light brown sugar

2 teaspoons fine sea salt

1½ cups polenta

Generous grindings of pepper

Just-grated pecorino

Olio santo (page 155)

In a large, heavy saucepan over a lively flame, combine the water, the milk, 4 tablespoons of the butter, the sugar, and the sea salt and bring the whole to a simmer.

Lower the flame and, with one hand, slowly shake the polenta from its cup into the simmering mixture while energetically stirring with a wooden spoon in the other hand. Adjust the flame to its lowest setting, stirring constantly, and cook until the spoon will stand up by itself, about 30 minutes.

Remove from the flame, grind over the pepper, and dot the polenta with the remaining butter. Have your board or marble—your *spianatoia*—at the ready.

Pour the polenta out onto the flat surface, smoothing it, urging it into a somewhat rectangular form with a spatula or a wooden spoon. Permit the polenta to cool and firm up a bit. Cover it lightly with a clean kitchen towel.

Reheat the sauce, have the pecorino nearby, and call everyone to the table. Pour half the sauce over the slightly cooled polenta and dust it very generously with the just-grated cheese. Carry it to the table on the board. Using a long length of butcher's twine—its ends wrapped several times around each of your palms—"cut" the polenta into squares while someone else deftly slips a spatula under each piece and serves it. Pass the remaining sauce and a bowl of just-grated pecorino. Of course, Elisabetta went round the table blessing everyone's plate with *olio santo*.

Scamorza alla Brace

SCAMORZA GRILLED OVER A WOOD FIRE

Serves 2

There is a simple sort of glory about handmade scamorza *(a semifresh cow's milk cheese very much like mozzarella) charred over a wood fire, all plumped, swollen, its skin blistered black and gold and barely able to contain its little paunch of seething cream. Anointed with* olio santo *and taken with oven-toasted bread, it can make for a fine little supper, a sublime one, even, if the cheese is genuine.*

> 2 whole *scamorza* or *caciocavallo*, smoked or unsmoked (approximately 8 to 10 ounces each)
> *Olio santo* (page 155)

Build a wood fire—indoors or out—and when the embers are red/white-hot, place the cheeses, cut in half, over an oiled grate. Grill the cheeses until a golden skin forms before turning them gently with a spatula and roasting the other side to a dark, golden color. Transfer the roasted cheeses to a plate and anoint them with tears of the *olio santo*, presenting them with chunks of good bread that were toasted alongside them. The light of a candle and a jug of good red wine finish the tableau.

Coniglio Arrostito sotto le Foglie di Verza

RABBIT ROASTED UNDER LEAVES OF CABBAGE

Serves 4

The Abruzzesi have long feasted on wild rabbit and hare. The formula for their preparation traditionally employed some version of al coccio—the braising of the rabbit in a terra-cotta pot. They might first brown it in olive oil with garlic, then cook it quietly with rosemary in white wine, perhaps enriching the dish with a dose of tomato conserve and finishing it with a handful of stoned olives.

The peasants typically cooked rabbit in this mode, as it was a carne secca—a dry flesh— and hence deemed inappropriate for roasting. But in the late fifteenth and sixteenth centuries, the brigade of serfs who cooked in the castles and villas of the nobility in the province of Pescara soon learned from their masters that all it took was a blanket of some sort—a quilt of buttery crust, a rasher or two of fat prosciutto or pancetta, even a few leaves of cabbage would do—to keep the scant juices of the little beast from becoming vapors in the heat of a wood oven.

The Rabbit

1 3½- to 4-pound rabbit, cleaned, its liver reserved
Fine sea salt
Freshly cracked pepper
Freshly grated nutmeg

Rinse and pat dry the rabbit, rubbing its flesh and its cavity with the sea salt, pepper, and nutmeg.

The Stuffing

4 ounces plus 4 thin slices pancetta
3 fat cloves garlic, peeled and crushed
1 tablespoon rosemary leaves
4 tablespoons flat parsley leaves
5 tablespoons extra-virgin olive oil
2 teaspoons fennel seeds
The rabbit's liver, rinsed, trimmed, and coarsely chopped
¼ cup Cognac
Fine sea salt
3 ounces prosciutto, minced

4 ounces fresh, Italian-style pork sausage, removed from its
  casing
1 cup dry white wine
3 ounces freshly made coarse bread crumbs
3 ounces just-grated pecorino
4 ounces green Sicilian or Greek olives, crushed lightly with a
  mallet, stones removed, the flesh chopped coarsely
1 extra-large egg
4 or 5 large leaves Savoy cabbage, rinsed and dried on
  absorbent paper towels

Preheat the oven to 375 degrees.

With a mezzaluna or a very sharp knife, mince the 4 ounces of pancetta, garlic, rosemary, and parsley to a thick paste. In a sauté pan over a medium flame, warm 3 tablespoons of the olive oil, heat the aromatic paste in it, adding the fennel seeds and sautéing for a minute until lightly colored. Add the liver, rolling it about in the perfumed fat and pour over the Cognac, shaking the pan, permitting flames to ignite and disperse. Salt the liver lightly and add the prosciutto and the sausage, sautéing until the sausage has taken on a bit of color. Turn the mixture out into a large bowl.

Rinse the still-hot sauté pan with ½ cup of the wine, stirring and scraping at the residue and permitting the wine to reduce for a few seconds. Pour the reduced wine over the mixture in the bowl. Add the bread crumbs, pecorino, the olives, and the egg, combining all to form a loose, light stuffing. Sauté a spoonful of the mixture, tasting it for salt and adjusting it with a sprinkling, if necessary.

Place the stuffing inside the cavity of the prepared rabbit and sew or skewer the rabbit closed.

In a large terra-cotta or enameled cast-iron casserole, heat the remaining 2 tablespoons of the olive oil and, over a high flame, brown the rabbit on all sides. Lay the slices of pancetta over the rabbit and cover it with the leaves of Savoy cabbage. Transfer the casserole to the preheated oven and roast the rabbit, uncovered, for 40 minutes. Remove the leaves of the cabbage and discard them. Permit the rabbit and the pancetta to take on a good, golden color for 10 minutes. Test the rabbit by piercing the flesh of its legs, which should be tender. Roast it for only 5 minutes more if you must, as it is sure to be sufficiently cooked by then.

Remove the rabbit from the casserole to a serving plate and rinse the casserole with the remaining wine, scraping and stirring at the residue and permitting the wine to reduce for 2 minutes. Pour the casserole juices over the rabbit and carry it to the table. Carve it and serve it with the stuffing and spoonfuls of the juices.

Intinglio di Agnello allo Zafferano di Campo di Giove

A BRAISE OF SAFFRONED LAMB IN THE MANNER OF CAMPO DI GIOVE

Serves 6

⅔ cup extra-virgin olive oil

3 fat cloves garlic, peeled, crushed, and minced

2 tablespoons fennel seeds

3 pounds lamb, cut from the leg, well-trimmed of its fat and cut
   into 3-inch chunks

Fine sea salt

Freshly cracked pepper

1 14-ounce can crushed plum tomatoes, with their juices

1½ cups dry white wine

¼ teaspoon saffron threads

2 tablespoons warmed white wine

In a small saucepan, warm ⅓ cup of the olive oil and soften the garlic in it for 2 minutes, without coloring it. Add the fennel seeds and permit them to perfume the oil for 1 minute. Place the prepared lamb in a large bowl, pour the warm oil over it and rub it well into the flesh of the lamb. Cover the bowl with plastic wrap and let the lamb rest for 1 hour or up to 4 hours, in a cool place but not in the refrigerator.

In a large sauté pan, heat the remaining olive oil and in it brown on all sides the chunks of marinated lamb. Cook at one time only those pieces that will fit in the pan without touching. Salt and generously pepper the meat. As the lamb is browned, remove it to a holding plate.

Add the tomatoes and wine to the still-warm sauté pan, scraping, stirring at the residue and permitting the liquids to reduce for 5 minutes. In a small pan, toast the saffron threads lightly over a low flame for 1 minute. Dissolve them in the warmed white wine. Add the saffroned wine and reduce for another 30 seconds. Lower the flame, return the lamb to the sauté pan, and bring it to a gentle simmer. Cover with a skewed lid and braise the lamb for 1 hour or until the meat is soft.

Permit 1 hour's rest before serving the lamb in shallow bowls with oven-toasted bread, or presenting it as a sauce for polenta (page 43). Or use some of its juices as a sauce for pasta before serving the lamb itself as a second course.

Agnello da Latte in Tegame sul Forno a Legna

SUCKLING LAMB BRAISED IN A SEALED CASSEROLE IN A WOOD-FIRED OVEN

o r

Agnello Piccino, Piccino, Picciò

DELICATE, MORE DELICATE, THE MOST DELICATE LAMB OF ALL

Serves 6

Just outside the village of Campo di Giove—Field of Jove—southeast of Sulmona, there lives and works a butcher who is also a chef of sorts, roasting and braising, as he does, some of his wares in a great, old stone bread oven that sits behind his pristinely stuccoed shop. His clients come sometimes to buy their lunch or their supper still warm and fragrant, readied for the table. Though it was achingly cold on that February morning when first we came upon the butcher at work in his outdoor kitchen, we joined the long, decorously kept line that wound its way from his ovens down the country road. We offered our good-days to the mostly women in whose midst we now stood, women typically Abruzzese, with serene, high-boned faces. They carried their pots and casseroles in sacks or against a hip and, when they felt our interest, they talked to us a bit about the dishes for which the old butcher was celebrated. Mutton braised overnight with tomatoes and onions and red wine; pork braised with bay leaf and garlic and peperoncino in Trebbiano d'Abruzzo; tripe and pancetta with tomatoes and yet more peperoncino; kid roasted with centerbe (an artisanly distilled liqueur made with mountain herbs). Long and reverent was their litany, but when one of them spoke of his agnello da latte—of suckling lamb that he braised only with butter in a sealed copper pot—there came a swift agreement that it was his piatto prelibato—his dish of greatest refinement and delicacy.

As the gods would have it that day, the butcher had not prepared agnello da latte but intinglio di agnello allo zafferano (page 47), which, when it came our turn, he packaged for us in a little plastic tub and on which we later lunched in the car with the motor running. It was luscious. We returned in the afternoon, forsaking the day's program, to beg its formula and to know when the mythical angello da latte might be forthcoming. Il macellaio, the butcher, shook his head on both counts. The suckling lamb in the sealed casserole he prepared only when he found lambs of just the right plumpness and age whose mothers fed only on certain grasses. He turned to the next question. "Una ricetta è una questione di cuore, signora mia; è molto personale," he said. "A recipe is a thing of the heart, my lady; it is most personal." I simply looked at him, neither beseechingly nor with delusion, and proceeded to tell him how I thought it had been accomplished. I spoke for a long time, I suppose, he never interrupting even as clients accumulated around his cold white cases. I sealed my discourse by asking why he'd used imported saffron rather than the milder one harvested locally up near Navelli. By now, he was laughing, mostly at my accent, I thought, which is distinctly Northern and often unpleasant to southern ears. At a point much later, after we knew each other longer, he confessed it was only my determinazione—determination—that had made him laugh.

The butcher, at least with words, never told me if my understanding of his beautiful lamb stew was correct, but each time I make the dish, I know that the pungent, melting result is a fine tribute to him. And so, when Campo di Giove sits even remotely on our route, we visit, happy to see our friend and hoping to find agnello da latte. *We are always a day too late, a week too early. Someday our timing will be divine. Curiously enough, though, the butcher, without my asking for it, one day told me its formula.*

3 to 4 pounds of milk-fed lamb, cut from the leg into 3-inch
   chunks
4 tablespoons sweet butter
1 medium yellow onion, left whole, peeled, and pierced with
   2 cloves
Fine sea salt
Thick trenchers of country bread, oven-toasted

The casserole used there is of primary importance. The stuff of its composition—copper, ceramic, terra-cotta, enameled cast iron—is less critical than its lid, which must fit tightly, hermetically. Should this equipment not be in your battery, seal a less-precise cover with a thick paste of flour and water.

Place the lamb in the casserole with the butter and the onion, sprinkling sea salt generously over all. Cover or seal the casserole and place it—lacking a wood-burning stove—in a 400 degree oven. Do not disturb the lid, even momentarily, during the 1 hour it will take for the lamb to cook. About halfway through the cooking, remove the casserole from the oven and, holding it on either side with protective gloves, give it a few firm shakes to turn the lamb, preventing it from adhering to the pot or cooking too long on one side.

After about 1 hour, remove the casserole from the oven, break its seal or lift its lid, discard the onion, and serve the lamb—now of a wonderfully silky texture—and its juices over the slices of oven-toasted bread.

Coscia di Agnello Schiacciata sotto i Mattoni

LEG OF LAMB PRESSED UNDER THE HEAT OF WOOD-FIRED BRICKS

or

La Coscia della Sposa

THE BRIDE'S THIGH

Serves 6

Once upon a time, the panarda was a rustic sort of feast hosted by a farmer for his neighbors and friends, for his tribe. A feast whose substance was bread and lard—pane e lardo— the words meshed, dialectically, as panarda. Lard was a precious comestible, a potent winter fuel that could keep a body whole up there in the mountains. Thus, if a family had a pig to slaughter, it was a family blessed. And if this family was wont to share its sainted beast, even if only the herb-scented renderings of his fat spread on a trencher of honest bread, it was a festival cheered.

Time and greater plenty swelled the proportions of the panarda, it growing into a flushed reveling, a Pantagruelian episode staged by one who desired to give thanks for some plague disarmed, some spiritual wound soothed. The panarda became a gastronomic pageant, a devout rite of Christendom quickened with mystical invocations—a duality, then and now, with which the Abruzzesi are at their ease. A wake, a wedding, a generous harvest, an homage—all these became motives to unfurl the festival, to illuminate, throughout its thirty courses, the inextinguishable Abruzzese ebullience. So fraught is the feast with the host's honor and the honor of his forebears that guests at his panarda must take to heart the intricacies of the culture into which they have entered. He who does not is imperiled. Stories are recounted of one or another unwitting stranger, who, by the twenty-fifth or twenty-eighth plate, begged his leave from the table. It was then that the barrels of primitive muskets were leaned against the temple of the blunderer, these inspiring, pell-mell, the rediscovery of his appetite. Still, today, when one sits at a panarda table, one is bound to partake of any and all that is set before him. To this, I make personal testimony.

Our induction into the rites of the panarda was at a country wedding near the city of L'Aquila, its thirty-two courses presented to nearly two hundred celebrants. Here follow the two dishes I loved best, the first for its straightforward symbolism and display of the ticklish Abruzzese humor, the second for its pure, seminal goodness.

½ cup olive oil

4 fat cloves garlic, peeled and crushed

3 tablespoons minced fresh rosemary leaves

1 small, dried red chile pepper, or ⅓ to ½ teaspoon dried chile
   flakes

2 tablespoons fennel seeds, crushed

1 5- to 6-pound leg of spring lamb, boned, well-trimmed of its
    excess fat, tied at several intervals with butcher's twine

1 cup dry white wine

2 tablespoons good red wine vinegar

1½ tablespoons fine sea salt

Several large branches of rosemary

In a small saucepan, warm the olive oil and scent it with the garlic, rosemary, chile, and fennel, leaving it on a gentle flame for a few minutes, taking care not to color the garlic.

Place the prepared lamb in a large, noncorrosive baking dish and pour the warm oil over the lamb, rubbing it well into the flesh. Mix the wine with the vinegar and add it to the dish, rolling the lamb about in the liquids. Cover the lamb with plastic wrap and permit the lamb to rest in the marinade overnight at room temperature.

Preheat the oven to 450 degrees. Build a wood or charcoal fire. When the oven is hot, heat two pizza stones or half a dozen quarry tiles for ½ hour. Remove the lamb from the marinade, drying it with absorbent paper towels and salting it generously.

When the embers of the fire are red/white-hot, place the lamb on a rack, place the rosemary branches over it, and immediately place one of the heated stones or half of the tiles over the lamb. Keep the remaining stone or tiles hot in the preheated oven.

Grill the lamb for 15 to 18 minutes. Remove the stone or the tiles and the rosemary branches, turn the lamb, add fresh rosemary branches and the reserved hot stone or tiles, and grill an additional 15 to 18 minutes or until the flesh is rosy and still dripping with its juices.

Remove the lamb to a board that will hold its juices and carve it at table, serving it with thick slices of roasted onions dressed in good oil, oven-toasted bread, and cold white wine.

Il Rituale delle Virtù del Primo Maggio

THE RITUAL SOUP FOR THE FIRST OF MAY

Serves 30 (yes, 30)

Perhaps until the beginning of this century, there came always, in the severe mountains of the Abruzzo, a haunting desperation with the first days of May. Bankrupt of the thin stores conserved to abide the incompassionate winter—their handkerchief-sized patches of earth sown a few weeks before—the contadini (farmers) waited then for the land to give up its first nourishment. Often it came too late and many died. And even as time brought more mercy, these terrible days were remembered, the pain of them soothed by a simple ritual.

The story says that on the first of May, sette fanciulle virtuose—seven young virgins—went from house to house in a village in the Marsica, the area that suffered most in the past, and begged whatever handful of the winter food that might remain in the larders. And, then, in the town's square over a great fire in a cauldron, the fanciulle prepared a beautiful pottage to share with all the villagers, to bring them together, to warm them, to keep them safe. The potion was known as la virtù—the virtue. The soup is still made, ritualistically, faithfully, each first of May in many parts of the Abruzzo—most especially in the environs of Teramo, as well as in the Marsica—now more extravagantly, brightening the humble dried beans with spring's new harvests.

Employing even a handful or so of all the ingredients results in a great potful of the soup, assigning it thus as a festival dish. On some sweet day in May, invite twenty-nine or so good people and make the soup for them. The tail of a pig and one of his ears, though they are traditional to the soup, seem optional to me.

Total of 2½ pounds dried legumes, which may include: fava
    beans, cannellini beans or smaller white navy beans, cran-
    berry or borlotti beans, chickpeas, small brown or black lentils

2 tablespoons fine sea salt, plus additional for cooking legumes

8 ounces fat prosciutto, minced

4 ounces pancetta, minced

½ cup extra-virgin olive oil, plus additional as needed

2 large yellow onions, peeled and minced

Hearts of 2 bunches of celery, minced

1 head fennel, its fronds trimmed, its bulb and stalks sliced thin

6 small or 3 large leeks, trimmed of all but 1 inch of their green
    stems, split, rinsed, dried, and sliced thin

1 large bunch of flat parsley, its leaves minced

6 ounces spring peas, shelled

6 ounces fresh fava beans, shelled

12 small new red- or white-skinned potatoes, washed, unpeeled,
  and diced

12 small carrots, scraped and sliced

12 baby artichokes, trimmed and sliced

2 14-ounce cans plum tomatoes, with their juices

1 pound chicory, young spinach leaves, or red chard, rinsed,
  dried, and shredded

Several large leaves sage, torn

2 branches of rosemary, the leaves minced

1 large bunch of fresh mint, its leaves torn

1 large bunch of basil, its leaves torn

1 teaspoon ground cloves

1 pound dried ditalini or other small soup pasta

Just-grated pecorino

Rinse, searching for stones and such, each variety of legume, then soak them in separate bowls of cold water overnight. Drain the legumes and cook each variety in its own pot of simmering, sea-salted water until they are al dente. As each of the legumes is cooked and drained, place them together in a large holding bowl.

In the house's largest soup pot (or one purloined from a restaurant just for the festival), heat the prosciutto and pancetta in ½ cup of the olive oil and sauté the onions, celery, fennel, leeks, and parsley, sautéing the aromatics until transparent without coloring them. Add the spring peas, the fresh fava beans, the potatoes, carrots, and artichokes, rolling the vegetables about in the scented fat. Add the tomatoes and about 6¼ quarts of water to the pot with 2 tablespoons of the sea salt and bring to a simmer, cooking the vegetables gently over a medium flame for 10 to 15 minutes or until they are nearly soft. Add the mixture of cooked legumes to the pot and simmer for 5 minutes before adding the shredded greens, the herbs, and the cloves. Gently simmer the soup for 5 to 7 minutes more to soften the greens and the herbs.

Cover the pot and permit the soup to rest while you cook the pasta in abundant boiling, sea-salted water just to al dente. Drain the pasta and add to the pot, stirring it in well and bringing the soup once again to a quiet simmer for several minutes.

Though the soup should be thick, some liquids should remain. If necessary, thin the soup with a bit of stock or water. Taste the soup for salt, adding a bit more if you think it necessary. Ladle the soup into warmed bowls or into several tureens and serve it with threads of good, green oil and generous dustings of pecorino.

Scrippelle 'mbusse alla Teramana

CREPES IN BEEF BROTH IN THE STYLE OF TERAMO

Serves 6

The raffinatezza—refinement—of the food of Teramo is legendary. And the Teramani propose that it was, indeed, among them that crepes—called crespelle or scrippelle in dialect—were first fashioned. It was much later, they say, that their delicate, eggy secrets traveled to France via the gastronomic exchange during the epoch of the Bourbons.

Often one finds the scrippelle plumped with a stuffing of mushrooms or a truffled paste of some sort, then gratinéed. Sometimes, they are composed into a timballo—a lovely molded cake, its layers spread with savory filling. Though they are luscious and a genuine part of the culinary heritage of the region, these fall too far, for me, from the ingenuousness of la cucina Abruzzese. The following, though, is a version of scrippelle that is more homespun, the one we eat always at a lovely Teramana osteria called Sotto le Stelle, Under the Stars.

Our ritual is this. At about eight o'clock, we stop by at the Bar Centrale (the place most intelligently furnished with the splendid labels and vintages of Italian and French wines in all of Italy south of Rome, all of it accomplished with Abruzzese grace and humility by a man called Marcello Perpentuini). There we chat with Marcello and take an aperitivo. A bit before nine, Marcello telephones Antonio, the restaurant's owner, orders a bottle of wine for us and tells him we're on our way. We walk the few blocks through the quiet streets of Teramo to the little restaurant. Our wine has been opened, some lush plate of local salame and fresh, sweet pecorino laid on our table with warm breads, and, perhaps best of all, someone back in the kitchen is making our scrippelle.

The Broth

   10 cups good veal or beef stock, preferably homemade
   1 cup good red wine
   Sea salt

In a large soup pot, bring the stock to a boil, reducing it over a lively flame for 10 minutes before adding the wine and reducing it for 5 minutes more. Taste the stock, sprinkling it with a bit of sea salt, if necessary. Cover the broth and let it rest while you make *le scrippelle*.

Le Scrippelle

1⅓ cups all-purpose flour
⅔ cup plus 2 tablespoons whole milk
⅔ plus 2 tablespoons cold water
3 extra-large eggs
⅔ teaspoon fine sea salt
3 tablespoons extra-virgin olive oil, plus additional as needed
Just-grated pecorino

Place the flour in a medium bowl. Combine the milk and water. With a wire whisk, stir the liquids into the flour, beating constantly to form a smooth batter. Whisk in the eggs with the salt, again beating constantly and vigorously before beating in 3 tablespoons of the oil. Cover the batter and permit it to rest for an hour or so in the refrigerator.

Stir the rested batter, thinning it with drops of water or milk should its consistency be thicker than good heavy cream.

Heat a heavy, 6-inch crepe pan over a lively flame. When the pan is hot, brush its surface with olive oil and ladle or pour in a scant ¼ cup of batter, tilting, maneuvering, the pan so that its bottom is completely covered. Cook the *scrippelle* for 30 to 40 seconds, turning it over gently with your fingers, or a spatula, and cooking the other side for 20 seconds. Remove the crepe to a holding plate, brush the pan with more oil, pour in the batter, tilt the pan, and while the second *scrippelle* is cooking, quickly dust the cooked *scrippelle* with pecorino, rolling it up tightly and setting it aside. Proceed with the pouring, tilting, cooking, flipping, dusting, and rolling until all the *scrippelle* are ready.

Now bring the broth to a simmer. Place two or three or more rolled *scrippelle* into each soup plate, cutting them in half should they fit better that way. Ladle over the hot broth and dust the dish generously with pecorino.

Tacchino Natalizio alla Neretese

A CHRISTMAS TURKEY ROASTED WITH WALNUTS, LEAVES OF BAY, ROSEMARY, AND GARLIC IN THE STYLE OF NERETO

Serves 8 to 10

An old Longobard town in the north of Abruzzo's province of Teramo, Nereto grows walnuts and breeds turkeys. And when the turkeys grow fat on the walnuts, their just-dressed flesh, roasted with aromatics, indeed tastes of the sweet, smoky nuts. A classic dish for Christmas there, I fix it for our Tuscan version of Thanksgiving. And because our local turkeys, as is likely the case with yours, do not feed on walnuts, I gift the bird with a luscious paste of them smoothed under the skin of its breast. I like the Neretese-inspired turkey infinitely better than the more famous tacchino alla Canzanese, *turkey in the manner of Canzano, which typically asks that the bird be relieved of his bones and poached with a calf's foot and knuckle, then cooled and presented in its jellied broth.*

12 ounces walnuts, roasted

6 to 8 fat cloves garlic, peeled and crushed

Extra-virgin olive oil

1 10- to 12-pound turkey, cleaned, rinsed, and dried

Fine sea salt

Freshly cracked pepper

Large branches of rosemary

1 large bay leaf

Zest of 2 lemons, removed in large pieces with a vegetable peeler

3 cups dry white wine

2 tablespoons plus ¼ cup *nocino* or other walnut or hazelnut liqueur

Preheat the oven to 450 degrees. In the work bowl of a food processor fitted with a steel blade, pulse the walnuts with the garlic. When the walnuts are processed to a fairly fine texture, drop in tears of oil through the feed tube—only enough to form a thick paste of the nuts, less than 2 tablespoons' worth. Loosen the breast skin of the turkey by gently slipping your fingers between it and the flesh. Carefully spread the walnut paste thickly over the flesh and under the skin of the breast, as evenly as possible. Sprinkle sea salt and freshly cracked pepper in the bird's cavity and over its skin, and stuff it with several whole branches of rosemary, the bay leaf, and the lemon zest. Massage the bird generously with olive oil, trussing it then, if you wish. Place the turkey on a rack in a large roasting pan into which you have poured 1 cup of the wine. Roast it on a rack in the hot oven for 1 hour, basting with the accumulating juices and an additional cup of the wine mixed with the ¼ cup of

walnut liqueur. Reduce the oven's heat to 325 degrees and roast the turkey for an additional
1½ to 2 hours or until a thermometer inserted into the thickest part of the breast registers
165 degrees. Baste faithfully every quarter of an hour. Transfer the bird to a holding plate,
and remove the aromatics in the cavity. Over a lively flame, heat the accumulated juices in
the roasting pan, stirring, scraping at the residue, and adding the remaining cup of wine and
the remaining 2 tablespoons of walnut liqueur. Reduce the pan juices for 4 or 5 minutes.
Carve the turkey and present it with the warmed pan juices, great chunks of charred,
roasted polenta, and poached Savoy cabbage that has been sautéed in olive oil and spiced
with *olio santo* (page 155).

Salsicce di Agnello alla Brace

WOOD-GRILLED LAMB SAUSAGE

Serves 6

Another dish often prepared for the panarda *(page 50), the sausages are rubbed with* olio santo, *wrapped in
Savoy cabbage leaves, and grilled over wood. Because lamb fat can give up an aggressive, even disagreeable,
flavor, overpowering the savor of the lamb itself, pork fat is recommended to keep the sausages full of juices and to
support their intricate spicing.*

> 12 leaves Savoy cabbage
> 1 tablespoon fine sea salt, plus additional as needed to cook
>   cabbage
> 2 pounds lamb, cut from the leg, finely minced
> 10 ounces fresh pork fat, finely minced
> 2 fat cloves garlic, peeled, crushed, and finely minced
> 1 1-inch cinnamon stick, freshly grated
> 1 tablespoon fennel seeds, toasted
> Generous grindings of pepper
> ¼ cup good red wine
> *Olio santo* (page 155)

Build a wood fire.

Remove the hard cores from the Savoy cabbage. Blanch the leaves for 1 minute
in boiling sea-salted water and drain.

In a large bowl, combine all the elements save the *olio santo* and the cabbage leaves. Form 12 plump oval sausages from the paste, brushing each of them generously with *olio santo*. Wrap each sausage in a cabbage leaf, securing it with a toothpick.

Place the wrapped sausages on an oiled grill over red/white embers and roast them for 3 to 4 minutes on each side. Depending on your taste, you can either discard the leaves of cabbage or serve the sausages in their charred cabbage "casings," drizzling them with more tears of *olio santo*. Either way, the sausages will be lush, succulent, wonderful with thick slices of wood-roasted potatoes, oven-toasted bread, and cold white wine.

Minestra di Lenticchie e Zafferano di Santo Stefano di Sessanio

A SOUP OF SAFFRONED LENTILS IN THE MANNER
OF SANTO STEFANO DI SESSANIO

Serves 6

Il Gran Sasso is the highest peak of the Apennines, surging up from the sea, a beast longer than twenty miles, a great-winged harpy, petrified, iced in flight and leaving only a slender shelf of coastal plain in its wake. And hitched halfway up its magnificence sits the medieval fastness of Santo Stefano di Sessanio. One meets few of its two hundred folk on a Wednesday evening's sunset walk through its catacombs and labyrinths, peering into the unbarred doors of abandoned houses that spirit up invention and half-light musings. Inside the bar—there is always a bar—a Medici crest embellishing its door, the briscola squad is hard at play. Curious at what could bring us forty-five hundred feet up into the January cold that afternoon, we told them we were looking for lentils. Sometimes I can still hear their laughing. But they found us some lentils, the last of that year's harvest, they told us, and they convinced us to stay the evening, the night, in a little locanda, an inn, closed for the season but of which one of them was the owner. Of course we stayed and of course we cooked and ate the beautiful black lentils that looked so like a great bowlful of glossy jet beads and of course we drank beautiful wine. And afterward we slept close by the fire. Though it is hardly traditional to adorn this humble soup with cream, when our host offered it with the willowy dollops melting into its warmth, it tasted like a dish as old as the mountains' secrets. And I would never again eat it any other way.

The ennobling of the soup with saffron is common in many dishes of the region but only for these last half a hundred years. Fields of crocus have flourished, though, for centuries in the peculiar micro-climate of the high plains of Navelli and Civitaretenga, since a curious village monk, when sojourning in Spain, folded a fistful of their dried seeds in his handkerchief and tucked them in a prayer book. The monk sowed the *seeds first in the monastery gardens, and when the flowers bloomed and he harvested their pistils according to the rites he learned in Spain, he and his brothers planted whole fields of the sweet flowers, desiring to use the saffron as a pharmaceutical and as a colorant for ceremonial vestments. Still, the old monk's is the only saffron cultivated in Italy.*

> 1 pound lentils (preferably the black lentils of Santo Stefano,
>   the brown lentils of Castelluccio in Umbria, or the green-
>   brown *lentilles de Puy* from the Auvergne in France)
> ¼ teaspoon saffron threads
> 3 tablespoons Cognac
> 2 tablespoons extra-virgin olive oil, plus additional as needed
> 3 ounces pancetta, diced
> 2 fat cloves garlic, peeled and crushed
> 1 bay leaf
> 1 14-ounce can crushed plum tomatoes, with their juices
> Fine sea salt
> 1 tablespoon good red wine vinegar
> 6 to 8 ½-inch slices sturdy country bread crusts removed, cut
>   into 2-inch squares
> 1 cup heavy cream
> Generous pinch of ground cloves

Rinse the lentils and soak them in cold water for ½ hour. If you are using a variety of lentils other than those recommended, leave them to soften in the cold water overnight.

Lightly toast the saffron threads, then dissolve them in 2 tablespoons of warmed Cognac.

In a large soup pot over a medium flame, warm 2 tablespoons of the olive oil and heat the pancetta. Scent the fats with the garlic, softening it but taking care not to color it. Add the bay leaf, the lentils, six cups of cold water, the saffron, the tomatoes, and the sea salt. Over a moderate flame, bring to a simmer and cook the lentils for ½ hour or until they are soft but not collapsing. Remove from the heat, add the red wine vinegar and stir it well into the soup.

Permit the soup to rest, uncovered, while you warm a little olive oil in a sauté pan and sauté the bread well on all sides. In a small bowl with a wire whisk, beat the cream with the cloves and the remaining 1 tablespoon of Cognac just until it begins to thicken.

Ladle the soup into warm bowls, add a few bits of the sautéed bread, and float a spoonful or two of the perfumed cream over each. Drink good red wine and continue to drink it after the soup with thick shards from a fine, aged pecorino.

Insalata di Baccalà e Carciofi

A SALAD OF DRIED CODFISH AND ARTICHOKES

or

Insalata di Pesce Dove il Mare Non C'è

A SALAD OF FISH IN A PLACE WHERE THERE IS NO SEA

Serves 4

Though the Teramani, in truth, live not so far from the sea, their cuisine is one of the interior, of the highlands, with sea fish playing an insignificant part. And so when we were served this divine little salad in a backstreet osteria in Teramo, it proved a light, breezy surprise for an early spring lunch. When we asked the old chef why he had made such an unexpected dish, he answered that sometimes, even in a place where there is no sea, one can have a desire to eat some good, bracing, and briny-tasting fish.

8 tiny artichokes, preferably the purple-lipped variety, or 4 small,
    very young artichokes, several inches of their stems still intact

1 1-pound fillet of *baccalà*, skinless and boneless

1 cup whole milk

Juice of 1 lemon

1 small head red lettuce, radicchio or red oak leaf, washed, spun
    dry, and coarsely shredded

4 ounces large green Sicilian or Greek olives, crushed lightly
    with a mallet, stones removed, the flesh coarsely chopped

⅓ cup extra-virgin olive oil

2 fat cloves garlic, peeled, crushed, and finely minced

1 small, dried red chile pepper, crushed, or ⅓ to ½ teaspoon
    dried chile flakes

1½ tablespoons good red wine vinegar

Fine sea salt

Prepare the artichokes, trimming just a snip from their still-tender leaves and leaving them whole if they are tiny, slicing them in two, or even in fourths, if they are a bit larger, cutting out the choke should it have begun to develop beyond an innocent embryo.

    Soften the *baccalà* a bit with a mallet and soak for 24 hours in cold water (change the water three times, adding 1 cup of milk to the final water), rinse the *baccalà* in cold water, cover again with cold water, and poach for 15 minutes. Drain and set aside.

    In a large bowl, acidulate the artichokes with the juice of a lemon, add the shredded lettuce, the chopped olives, and the poached *baccalà*, cut into 1-inch pieces.

Make a simple warm vinaigrette by heating the olive oil, softening the garlic without coloring it for a minute or two, and scenting the oil with the crushed chile. Remove from the heat, add the vinegar and a whisper of sea salt. Beat the dressing with a fork and pour it over the elements in the bowl, tossing them about and combining them well.

Present the salad with a young, cooled red wine that will do its best to stand up to both the artichokes and the *baccalà*.

$\mathcal{S}$*capece*

SAUTÉED FISH CONSERVED IN VINEGAR
WITH GARLIC AND SAFFRON

Makes about 3 pounds

An ancient practice to conserve some windfall of fish or vegetables is to fry them in good olive oil and tuck them under coverlets of bread crumbs into a vinegary bath. The addition of saffron is a fillip only half a century old, when the golden pistils began to be prized beyond their value as a pharmaceutical (page 58). A dish made traditionally also in Puglia, I think the Abruzzesi hands fashion the most luscious versions. Zucchini or eggplant may be treated in the same way as the fish.

> All-purpose flour
> 3 pounds fresh sardines, fresh anchovies, smelts, or other small,
>   whole fish, scaled, cleaned, and filleted
> Extra-virgin olive oil
> Fine freshly made bread crumbs, pan-roasted in olive oil
> 2 heads garlic, the cloves peeled, crushed, and finely minced
> 1 teaspoon saffron threads
> 5 to 6 cups plus 2 tablespoons good white wine vinegar

Lightly flour the fish and, in a large sauté pan over a lively flame, sauté them until deep gold in abundant, bubbling olive oil, removing them to absorbent paper towels. Continue with the procedure until all the fish are sautéed.

In a large ceramic vessel, preferably one that is deeper than it is wide, place a layer of the fish. Dust the fish generously with the sautéed bread crumbs and strew over a bit of the minced garlic. Repeat the process until all the fish, the bread crumbs, and the garlic have been utilized.

Now make their preserving bath. Lightly toast the saffron threads, then dissolve them in 2 tablespoons of warm vinegar. In a large pitcher or bowl, mix the remaining vinegar with the dissolved saffron and pour the potion over the layers of fish, immersing them in the bath. Should you run short of the vinegar mixture, make another one-quarter or one-third of the recipe, as necessary. If your preserving vessel is narrow enough, the suggested amount will be sufficient.

Cover the fish with a lid of some sort, even baking parchment tied with butcher's twine or several thicknesses of aluminum foil and permit the fish to rest in their bath for a day or so in a cool place before presenting them as an antipasto. Serve with good, warm bread to take up the juices and rivers of cold white wine. The *scapece* will only improve in flavor as they rest for up to a week or ten days.

Ciambelline al Vino Scannese

THE SWEET OLIVE OIL BISCUITS OF SCANNO

Makes about 3 dozen

Beautiful breakfast biscuits with hot anisette-sparkled milk, caffè, *or* cioccolata calda.

3 large eggs
⅔ cup sugar
¼ cup extra-virgin olive oil
2 cups plus 2 tablespoons all-purpose flour
1 teaspoon baking powder
1½ tablespoons aniseeds

Preheat the oven to 350 degrees.

In a large bowl with an electric beater, beat the eggs with the sugar until they are light and form a ribbon as the beaters are lifted. Add the oil and beat for 30 seconds.

Sift the flour with the baking powder and add it and the aniseeds to the batter, mixing with a wooden spoon to form a soft dough.

Pinch off small pieces of the dough and with your palm roll them into rough lengths of about 5 inches long and ½ inch in diameter. Form the ropes into circles, pressing the ends together firmly.

Place the *ciambelline* on parchment-lined sheets and bake them for 15 to 18 minutes or until they are golden and crisped.

Pepatelli all' Arancio Scannesi

THE ORANGE-PERFUMED PEPPERED BISCUITS OF SCANNO

Makes about 4 dozen 2-inch cookies

The town of Scanno is bedded quaintly on a valley floor near the tortuous Gole del Sagittario—a mountain road called the "Throat of Sagittarius," on the fringes of the Parco Nazionale degli Abruzzi, a national park and nature reserve. Bespeaking eloquently its Late Renaissance and Baroque past, its little streets and alleyways are warmed by artisans working in gold and silver and lacemakers with their small wooden hoops. The women—many of them, rather than only an archaic few—toddle through the enchanted tableau of the old village on Sundays garbed in long black skirts that rustle their arrival, their hair swept up in gorgeous and ornate headdresses of lace and velvet, their arms comforted in black woolen capes. Theirs is no quaint, historic burlesque. They are wearing the clothes that please them, that are faithful to their images of themselves, that honor their heritage. They are at their ease.

A poetically costumed nonna (grandmother) admonishes her young grandson—in jeans and a T-shirt, his hair falling in soft brown curls below his shoulders—to be neither late nor in a hurry for Sunday dinner before she disappears through the small, humble portal of her home. Scanno, if one watches her carefully, will give view to a life inviolate. And these are her traditional biscuits, all chewy and full of spiced Renaissance perfumes and savors, lovely with good red wine, especially when it's warmed and spiced with pepper and cloves, or, in summer, a little goblet of sweet, iced moscato.

> 3 cups dark honey (chestnut, buckwheat, etc.)
>
> ⅓ cup freshly squeezed orange juice
>
> 6 ounces almonds, blanched, chopped, and lightly toasted
>
> 6 ounces pine nuts, lightly toasted
>
> 6 ounces walnuts, crushed and lightly toasted
>
> 3½ ounces extra-bittersweet chocolate, preferably Lindt or
>   Valrhona 70% cacao, chopped
>
> 1 tablespoon freshly cracked white pepper
>
> 1 inch of cinnamon stick, freshly grated
>
> Generous gratings of nutmeg
>
> ¼ teaspoon ground cloves
>
> Grated zest of 1 orange
>
> 3 cups all-purpose flour
>
> ½ cup polenta flour
>
> Olive oil

Warm the honey with the orange juice and pour it into a large bowl. Add the nuts and the chocolate, stirring well. Combine all the dry ingredients and add them to the bowl, mixing well to form a thick, sticky paste.

Lightly oil a square 10- to 12-inch baking pan and spread the paste evenly in it, pressing firmly on the surface with a wet spatula to compact the paste. Cover the pan with plastic wrap and chill it for 1 hour.

Preheat the oven to 350 degrees.

Unmold the sweet onto a work surface and, with a sharp knife rinsed in hot water, cut it into shapes, approximately 2 inches by 2 inches. Place the biscuits on parchment-lined sheets and bake them for 18 to 20 minutes. Cool the biscuits on a rack and store them in a tin.

MOLISE

We have spoken nothing here of Molise, the tiny region that sidles up to the Abruzzo as well as Lazio, Campania, Puglia, and the Adriatic. A sweet and simple parish without much to trumpet, it might seem the Abruzzo's quiet third cousin, were there a more than limping affinity. Mountains less imposing, characters less well-defined and, alas, less memorable. Molise seems of her own dominions, her own poor and stony plains, her own splendid wheat fields. Certainly, she does not eat like the Abruzzesi. Molise borrows from the cuisine of Campania, when it can, or of Puglia, more than it resonates the cooking of the Abruzzo. *La gastronomia molisana* is one of simple abundance, its tables sublimely well-laden more with its masterfully wrought products—*caciocavallo, salumi,* its celebrated dried pasta, luscious sausages preserved in lard—than with characteristic potions or some long-simmered stew. Though many of the dishes presented in this chapter can be found in the *osterie* and *ristoranti* of Molise, they are intrinsically characteristic of the Abruzzo.

A region whole—Abruzzo and Molise—until 1963, when there was a political separation, it seems strange that its people express a figure so diverse. Not unlike the character of a Maine potato farmer as it counterpoints that of a Seattle fisherman, it's just that here, only a few kilometers roll out between the two.

CAMPANIA

Six hundred years before the birth of Christ, a pastoral tribe descended from Apennine huts to the edges of the Mar Tirreno to stake a refuge on the gravesite of their adored pagan goddess Partenope. A siren was Partenope, a sorceress sublime, of a force so dazzling she swallowed seething tempests and willed fish into the nets of the starving. The empress siren, the one whose laugh was the sound of a harp, Partenope staggered men's hearts with the blaze of her great, golden eyes. It was there, in her sway, that the ragged clan set their camp, trusting she and her powers to preserve them. And keep them she did.

After epochs of wars and festivals and living and dying, the little patch of seaside they named Partenope joined with adjacent villages, becoming a larger parish known as Neapolis. Close upon them came the Greeks, the Romans, then the Byzantines, the Saracens, the Normans, the Angevins, the Aragonese. The Bourbons were the last of the lords to trod upon the great city that had become Napoli, each of them injuring, enriching, imprinting it all and forever. After the passage of two millennia and six hundred years more, everything has changed as much as nothing has changed. When one looks now full face into the huge, dark, gold-lit eyes of a Neapolitan, revealed is the pain of his ancient insufficiency, a flame of rage and one of joy, all of it washed in tenderness. And one wonders if the improbable light in those eyes is not that of the old siren, unextinguished still.

Hence it is Napoli that is the Campanian lodestone, congress of the region's spirit. And the farther away from her into the provinces one moves, there is heard only plainsong, muffled echoes of her immoderate self. Napoli is Campania. And the tumult of her beckons, charming until it exasperates, shifting its hold only moments before it exhausts, seducing one back into her arms.

Sunless, laundry-spangled *vicoli* contain a life of masked sufferance—the eternal tragedy in which *allegria* and *miseria* are sung in falsetto. One wonders who is left inside the apartments of the ancient, injured black palaces. The drama is played in the streets, in the thin, oily alleyways onto which one's rooms, barely draped, one's bed, even, edge freely.

Napoli is the Baroque unleashed. One can hold tight to the Church, sanctify cunning, and stitch contradictions into seamlessness. Napoli is debauchery all sugared and fawning, its spirit ensouling and crushing with the same honeyed mouth. A Napoletano can pirate your purse while exalting your beauty or the fine cut of your coat. He is sincere, open-hearted, even, in the fulfillment of all his missions. Napoli is the brigand lover whose embrace, for all the world, one would not have, for a night, forsaken.

But in the Neapolitan pathos there is a spare, sheer sort of *commedia* at work. If the blood of their sainted Gennaro—held petrified in a vial and laid in a thirteenth-century crypt in Napoli's Duomo—fails to liquefy each May and September, thus signifying his interrupted custody of their well-being, some plague or pestilence will befall, they say. But some plague or pestilence always befalls, they say also, and so one must be alert to other impulses. Better to spend one's coins to take a number in the Saturday-evening lottery as well as to light a candle to San Gennaro. All of Napoli is prostrate before this *lotto*. It is the alleluia that permits six days of dreaming, of peace broken only by the trumpeting of the winning numbers. Delusion is a short, sharp blow blunted at noon on Sunday, when the next week's tickets are thumped onto the selling tables. With one, perhaps two, tucked away, a Napoletano can hold the roaring wolf by its ears for yet another six days. There is a wistfully worn bravado in his life's arrangement.

NAPOLI/NAPLES

Cinque Brasati di Carne con Pomodori
FIVE SLOW BRAISES OF MEAT WITH TOMATOES

Thereabouts in the sixteenth century, when sacks of them—curiosities from the New World—were first ported off the great sailing ships from the Americas, the tomato became the fruit preeminent in the *cucina napoletana*. Blushing, plump, acid-sweet, it unshackled Napoli from the spice-fatigued foods of the Middle Ages. Culinary fantasies thus prickled, the Napoletani built pungent, big-hearted dishes from the red-golden beauties and a fistful of modest, indigenous ingredients. They ate the fruits raw, out of hand, distilled them with wild herbs and aromatics into lush sauces, strewed them in terra-cotta pots with bits of meat or fish or a scuttleful of clams, braising them into potions savory and sympathetic. They dried them in the parching heat, thickening their skins and juices into sweet, salty flesh that tasted of the sun. Too, they crushed them with a few drops of good oil, smearing the poultice over rough, raw dough and cooking the resulting little pies in the reddened embers of their old wood ovens. Under the generous sun, tomatoes fairly burst from the countryside's fat, black earth, nourished by Vesuvius. So impassioned were they, and are they still, by this tomato, the Napoletani liken its form to their own hearts, its seeds to their security, its potency to their own sensuality. Here follow, then, five recipes that employ the tomato. Very particular versions of *la cucina povera*, these are languorously braised meats that soothe and titillate, their resulting juices sending up ripe, steamy perfumes and providing condiment for pasta. With a single and unfussy preparation, one makes first and second courses—humble yet refined dishes smitten, always, with some irresistible press of the baroque. They represent, I think, the most translatable, portable recipes typical of the cuisine of Napoli.

Braciole di Vitello del Portinaio

VEAL ROLLS BRAISED IN THE MANNER OF THE GATEKEEP

Serves 6

Traditionally, the gatekeep of an apartment building in Napoli is a widow or a widower of a certain age, one of whose missions, as spiritual guardian of the palazzo, is to slot the mail—after fastidious palpating of its contents, lifting it to the light of the sun, trawling it for heretical intelligence, and generally shadowing the recipient's movements by it, to diligently rouse, invent, and unbosom internal gossip. The good gatekeep only breaks from these industries to stir at or baste some one of his legendary little potions, all of which signal to the tenants as they cross the threshold what will be the old watchdog's supper.

Fine sea salt

12 thin slices of veal, cut from the leg, pounded lightly with a
    meat mallet to a fairly even thickness of ¼ inch

½ cup pine nuts, lightly toasted and coarsely chopped

½ cup white raisins, plumped in warm red wine

⅔ cup just-grated pecorino

Freshly ground pepper

3 ounces fat prosciutto

⅓ cup flat parsley leaves

3 fat cloves garlic, peeled and crushed

1 large egg

⅓ cup extra-virgin olive oil

1½ ounces pancetta, finely minced

1 large yellow onion, peeled and thinly sliced

2½ cups canned tomato puree

2 cups good red wine

Lightly salt the prepared veal, laying a few of the slices out on a work space and stacking the remaining pieces nearby. In a medium bowl, combine the pine nuts, raisins, pecorino, and generous grindings of pepper. With a mezzaluna or a very sharp knife, mince the prosciutto, parsley, and garlic together to a fine paste. Add the aromatic paste and the egg to the medium bowl and blend the ingredients. Place a generous spoonful of the paste over each scallop of veal, spreading it to cover all but the outer ½ inch of its surface. Roll up the scallop tightly, securing it with butcher's twine or toothpicks. Repeat, filling and rolling all the veal. In a large terra-cotta or enameled cast-iron casserole over a medium flame, heat the olive oil and sauté the pancetta for a minute or two before adding the onion and lightly sautéing it. With a slotted spoon, remove the onion and the bits of pancetta to a holding plate, then brown the *braciole*, crusting them well on all sides. Cook only as many at a time as will fit in the pan without touching. Remove the veal to the holding plate with the onions and pancetta. Add the tomato puree and the wine to the pan, stirring, scraping at the residue and permitting the sauce to reduce for 1 minute. Lower the flame, add the veal, the onions, and the pancetta to the casserole and bring to a gentle simmer. Cover the casserole tightly and braise the veal, its liquids barely simmering, for 1 hour. Permit the rolls to rest in the sauce for 1 hour or so before very gently reheating them, presenting them on a warmed platter with their sauce. Should you wish to serve pasta with a few tablespoons of the sauce before the veal, use the method on page 71.

La Genovese

BEEF BRAISED WITH ONIONS AND WHITE WINE

Serves 6

It seems unclear why a dish characteristic of Napoli should be called after a Ligurian port. Some say it's because a Genovese sailor cooked it for some locals and the goodness of it was hailed throughout the hungry city. Others will tell you that Genovese is nothing more than a torturing of Ginevrina—of Geneva—hence giving a Swiss chef, one from the tribe of the Bourbons' monzù, no doubt, credit for the sauce (page 84). The truth of its origins, adrift forever, holds less fascination, I think, than the patently simple recipe and the lovely, lush sort of texture the meat takes on from its long, slow dance in the pot.

> 2 ounces salt pork
>
> 1 ounce *salame*
>
> 1 ounce prosciutto
>
> ⅓ cup extra-virgin olive oil
>
> 2 pounds top or bottom round of beef, tied at 2-inch intervals
>   with butcher's twine
>
> 4 to 5 large yellow onions, peeled and sliced thin
>
> 3 medium carrots, scraped and chopped
>
> 2 stalks celery, chopped
>
> 1 cup canned tomato puree
>
> ½ teaspoon fine sea salt
>
> 1⅓ cups dry white wine

With a mezzaluna or a very sharp knife, mince the salt pork, *salame*, and prosciutto to a fine paste. In a terra-cotta or enameled cast-iron casserole—just large enough to hold the beef and its accessories—warm the olive oil over a medium flame and soften the paste in it.

Pat the beef dry with absorbent paper towels and brown it in the fragrant fat, crusting it well on all sides—a process that takes at least 10 minutes. Remove the now deeply crusted beef to a holding plate.

Add the onions, carrots, and celery to the pot, rolling them about in the fat, softening them without coloring them. Add the tomato puree, the sea salt, and the wine, stirring, scraping at the residue in the pan and letting the sauce simmer gently for 1 minute before returning the beef to the pot.

Cover the casserole tightly and, over a low flame, braise the beef, its liquids barely simmering, for 2½ hours.

When the beef is fork-tender, it is properly cooked. Should it require longer braising, add a few tablespoonfuls more of wine, replace the lid, and let the whole continue to cook for 20 to 30 minutes more. Permit the dish a ½ hour's repose. I would never think to strain the sauce of all the lush debris remaining from the aromatics, the *salame*, and the prosciutto. I suppose, though, a classic Swiss cook might think to improve it by straining it. I'd hope for his sake that he might spread the resultant paste on a heft of warm toast and eat it for his own private lunch. Should you wish to precede its presentation with pasta, see the instructions on page 71.

Brasato di Fesa di Vitello del Carnacottaro

LEG OF VEAL BRAISED IN THE MANNER
OF THE ROVING MEAT COOKER

Serves 6

It was not often, that one was plump enough in the purse to buy a kilo or so of meat from the butcher, carry it home, and cook it up into some luscious, soulful dish. When fortune placed in one's purse a few centesimi more than were necessary for subsistence, one sought out the carnacottaro *(an itinerant seller of cooked meat).*

¼ cup extra-virgin olive oil
3 to 4 pounds leg of veal, well trimmed and tied at 2-inch intervals with butcher's twine

1½ teaspoons fine sea salt

2 ounces sun-dried tomatoes, drained of their preserving oil,
    slivered

6 ounces large green and black Sicilian, Greek, or Spanish
    olives, lightly crushed with a wooden mallet, stones
    removed, and coarsely chopped

½ cup white raisins, plumped in warm white wine

1½ cups canned tomato puree

2½ cups dry white wine

In a large terra-cotta or enameled cast-iron casserole over a lively flame, warm the olive oil and seal the veal, crusting it well on all sides. Remove the veal to a holding plate, sprinkling on the sea salt. Add the sun-dried tomatoes, the olives, and the raisins to the casserole, stirring the ingredients together for about 1 minute before adding the tomato puree and the wine and bringing the sauce to a simmer. Turn down the flame, add the veal, cover the casserole tightly, and, over the quietest flame, permit the liquids to barely simmer around the veal for 1½ hours.

Remove the cover and baste the meat, adding a few tablespoonfuls more wine if the liquids seem scant. Replace the lid and braise the veal ever so slowly for an additional ½ hour or until the meat is fork-tender.

Permit the veal to rest in its sauce, the lid in place, for 1 hour or so before reheating gently.

Use a few generous spoonfuls of the good sauce for just-cooked pasta—perhaps ziti or penne cooked to al dente, drained and tossed with a generous dollop of sweet butter and handfuls of just-grated pecorino before adding the sauce.

When ready to present the veal, remove it to a deep platter, spooning some of the sauce around it. Carve it into ⅓-inch-thick slices at table and offer the remaining sauce from a small bowl.

One might use a loin of pork or a round of beef in place of the veal, extending the braising session a bit longer.

Brasato di Maiale con Ragù Nero

PORK BRAISED IN BLACK SAUCE

Serves 6 to 8

This was and is still the dish every Napoletano wishes to come home to for Sunday lunch. There have been son-nets written to its lush sauce, to the perfumes of it curling down to the alleyways below, signaling that, at least for a day, all would be well for that family. The tomato, after its long, slow courting with the red wine, takes on a sort of rusted ebony tint, a beautiful rich color the Napoletani, with their keenness for flourish, are wont to call "black."

3 to 4 pounds boned loin of pork, tied at 2-inch intervals with
    butcher's twine
2 teaspoons fine sea salt
6 large fresh sage leaves
3 ounces pancetta
3 fat cloves garlic, peeled and crushed
⅓ cup flat parsley leaves
¼ cup extra-virgin olive oil
2 cups good red wine
2 cups canned tomato puree

Dry the pork with absorbent paper towels. Rub the meat with the sea salt and tuck the sage leaves under the twine. Permit the pork to absorb the salt and sage perfumes for ½ hour or so.

Prepare the pork's braising sauce. With a mezzaluna or a very sharp knife, mince the pancetta with the garlic and parsley to a fine paste. In a large terra-cotta or enam-eled cast-iron casserole over a medium flame, warm the olive oil and melt the aromatic paste. Brown the pork, crusting it well on all sides, a task that takes at least 10 minutes. Pour 1 cup of the wine over the pork, letting it evaporate before adding the remaining cup of wine and the tomato puree. Cover the casserole tightly, bringing the ingredients to a simmer. Lower the flame and permit the pork to braise, its liquids barely simmering, for 2 hours. Lift the lid and test the doneness of the meat—it should be fork-tender.

Permit the pork a rest while serving a bit of pasta, as suggested on page 71. Afterward, carve the pork into ⅓-inch-thick slices and present it with spoonfuls of the sauce.

Coniglio all' Ischitana

RABBIT BRAISED IN THE STYLE OF ISCHIA

Serves 4

An island off Napoli's great bay is Ischia. Wild rabbits thrived there once and some still do for a while, before the clever Ischitani sack them, whipping them into old terra-cotta pots, flattering their dry, scant flesh into rose-maried silk.

1 3½- to 4-pound rabbit, cleaned, its liver reserved
⅓ cup extra-virgin olive oil
1½ teaspoons fine sea salt
Freshly cracked pepper
3 fat cloves garlic, peeled, crushed, and finely minced
3 large ripe tomatoes, peeled, seeded, and chopped
1 large branch of rosemary
1½ cups dry white wine
2 tablespoons good red wine vinegar
½ cup torn fresh basil leaves

Cut the rabbit into 8 pieces. Rinse and dry on absorbent paper towels. In a large terra-cotta or enameled cast-iron casserole over a lively flame, heat the olive oil and sauté the rabbit—cook only those pieces at a time that will fit without touching—browning the pieces well on all sides. Sprinkle on the sea salt and generous grindings of pepper. Remove the rabbit to a holding plate.

Add the garlic to the pan and permit it to soften a minute or two, taking care not to let it color. Add the tomatoes, the rosemary, and the wine to the casserole, bringing the mixture to a gentle simmer. Return the rabbit to the casserole, cover it with a slightly skewed lid, and, over a low flame, braise the rabbit for 1 hour.

Mash the liver with the vinegar and add to the casserole, blending it well into the sauce. Continue to braise for an additional 10 minutes.

Remove from the heat, stir in the basil leaves, and present the rabbit, in its casserole, warm or at room temperature. Should you wish to precede it with pasta, follow the instructions for its presentation on page 71.

73

Le Cozze delle Due Rivali
THE RIVALS' MUSSELS

Half a millennium ago, in the curve of a tiny spur on the Bay of Napoli, shouldered by Vesuvius and a great Norman castle, a band of impoverished fishermen settled the *porticciolo*—the little port—of Santa Lucia. With the sun to warm them and the sea to feed them, their village grew, so that when the twentieth century ensued, Santa Lucia was a port of modest activity, the post where fishermen docked to unload a catch, repair nets, and take sustenance before setting sail once again. It was then, amidst this idyll, that perhaps the most modern frame was captured in the sacred folkloric story of Napoli.

Two young women of Santa Lucia opened their homes as humble *osterie*, offering some reviving soup and bread and wine to the fishermen. Soon, it is told, people from the surrounding neighborhoods of Napoli came to sit at the long wooden tables of Teresa and Emilia, each on her own jot of the land that faced the sea. They came to take in the soft, salt breeze and to lunch on vermicelli and small, sweet clams spewing up garlicky vapors, or on crisped tangles of tiny fish all golden and just rescued from their baths of gurgling oil. Their rivalry grew sturdily, as did their fame, and, with the grit of buccaneers, they say, these two Lorelei did lure whomever they might from the greater village and, too, from the pilgrims and passersby who came to stay near beautiful Napoli.

Then, as it is wont to be in fables, came princes and kings to be beguiled by their sea and their genuine food. These sojourns of the royals fixed the little port on the lists of journalists and tabloid writers and foreign correspondents. The lessers and the greaters—soubrettes and cavaliers, Toscanini and Mastroianni, Pavarotti and Loren and Elizabeth the Queen came to stroll and to dine on one or the other of their then grander terraces. Before the Second Great War, Mussolini came to lunch on Santa Lucia. He chose to dine at Emilia's—La Bersagliera—rather than with Zi' Teresa. The one scorned marched into the enemy's salon. Taking Il Duce by the hand, propelling him to her entryway, she railed that wretched city codes prevented her from constructing a proper stairway and installing appropriate signage and that champion her he must or Emilia would soundly do her in. Il Duce returned to his *fritto misto*.

And thus the not-so-elegant events between the two women continued. Fuming sulks gave way to umbrage and to an imbroglio irresolute. In 1960, Zi' Teresa walked away from Santa Lucia and, unmenaced at last—but also without her oldest friend, some say—Emilia was left to carry on. And so she did, tramping imperiously through her dining rooms and kitchen, adjusting, cajoling, until the very day of her death in 1969. She was eighty-seven years old. Various of her five daughters and seven sons and their progeny have since partnered in the project and thus, La Bersagliera endures in the social/gastronomic fabric of Napoli, beckoning one to descend the tiny stairway down from the grand

Lungomare Caracciolo that hems the port, past the staid door to the rowing club and onto the terrace of Donna Emilia's old protectorate.

Here, then, are two recipes for mussels, both primitive in their simplicity, both briny symbols of the pleasure it is to eat a beautiful, nearly naked food, in celebration of past and present lives on the porticciolo di Santa Lucia.

Impepata di Cozze

PEPPERED MUSSELS

Serves 6

3 cups dry white wine
4 fat cloves garlic, peeled and crushed
8 dozen mussels, scrubbed, bearded, and rinsed
1 cup minced flat parsley leaves
Pepper

In a large terra-cotta or enameled cast-iron casserole over a lively flame, bring the wine and the garlic to a simmer and add the mussels, cooking them uncovered. As they begin to open, strew them with the parsley and grind pepper very generously over them—a tablespoon or more—so that it is quite visible in the cooking liquors. At the point when all the mussels are opened, spoon some of the cooking liquors over each one and poach them for another ½ minute.

Present the mussels in their cooking pot with a great basket of oven-toasted, olive-oil-rubbed bread and jugs of cold white wine, inviting each one to fish out his own mussels and ladlefuls of good liquor.

Cozze Piccanti Fredde

SPICED COLD MUSSELS

Serves 6

2 cups dry white wine

8 dozen mussels, scrubbed, bearded, and rinsed

⅓ cup extra-virgin olive oil

4 fat cloves garlic, peeled, crushed, and minced

4 ounces anchovies, preserved under salt

1 small, dried red chile pepper, crushed, or ⅓ to ½ teaspoon
   dried chile flakes

2 tablespoons good white wine vinegar

½ cup minced flat parsley leaves

In a large pot over a lively flame, bring the wine to a simmer and add the mussels, poaching them, and removing them to a large bowl as they open. When all the mussels have opened, reduce the cooking liquor to ¾ cup and set it aside. When the mussels are cool enough to handle, remove the flesh from the shells to a holding plate. Discard the shells.

In a very large sauté pan over a medium flame, warm the olive oil and soften the garlic, taking care not to color it. Rinse the anchovies. Remove the anchovies' heads and bones, dry on paper towels, and crush lightly with a fork. Add the anchovies and the chile, tossing them about in the oil for a minute or two before adding the mussels, the reduced cooking liquor, and the vinegar. Permit the mussels to simmer gently for a minute or two. Set the mussels aside to cool.

When the mussels have cooled, transfer them to a large bowl, cover them tightly in plastic wrap, and refrigerate for several hours or overnight. Toss with the parsley and present the mussels as an antipasto or a main dish with olive-oil-oven-toasted bread and cold white wine.

These two recipes from Napoli's cucina povera *are ministrations for the dispirited, dishes to stay the ogres. Conjured from almost nothing, yet giving forth perfumes of security and nostalgia, they promise comfort, they stimulate, revive, as might the flump of a cork being slipped from its bottle or a kiss, hung softly and low on the nape of the neck.*

Vermicelli alle Vongole Fujite

THIN STRINGS OF PASTA WITH ESCAPED CLAMS

Serves 6

This is the poorest of dishes for the days when the seas are as empty as one's belly, when even the clams have for-saken one. Fashioned from seawater—sometimes bits of seaweed—a tomato or two, some fat, firm garlic, a dried red chile, and a thread of good oil or a spoonful of sweet, rendered pork fat, hoarded from an easier day.

2 large, ripe tomatoes, peeled, seeded, and chopped

2 teaspoons fine sea salt

1 ounce salt pork or pancetta

4 fat cloves garlic, peeled and crushed

⅓ cup extra-virgin olive oil

1 small, dried red chile pepper, crushed, or ⅓ to ½ teaspoon
dried chile flakes

1 pound vermicelli or other thin string pasta

Coarse sea salt for the water

In a large, shallow bowl, toss the tomatoes with the sea salt and permit the tomatoes to give up their juices while you proceed.

With a mezzaluna or a very sharp knife, mince the salt pork with the garlic to a fine paste. In a small sauté pan over a medium flame, warm the olive oil and sauté the paste, taking care not to color it. Add the chile and set the mixture aside.

Cook the pasta in abundant, boiling, sea-salted water to al dente, draining it, reserving ½ cup of its cooking water and placing it in the bowl with the sea-salted tomatoes. Add the garlic/chile-scented fat and the still-hot, reserved cooking water, tossing the pasta over and over to coat each strand thoroughly. Present the pasta in warmed, shallow bowls. One might wish to substitute bottled clam juice for the reserved pasta cooking water, giving the humble condiment some stronger reminiscence of the sea, of the fugitive bivalves, thus diluting, though, the romance of the dish.

Maccheroni alla Carrettiere

PASTA IN THE MANNER OF THE STREET VENDOR

Serves 4

Though the ancient origins of pasta are likely Egyptian, it was inside the eternal Saturnalia of fifteenth-century Napoli where the simple stuff began its story as an everyday comfort against the hungers of the southern Italian poor. Crafted and cooked and dispatched from painted wagons spirited through the city's boisterous alleyways—they were exuberant vehicles of rescue enrobed in garlicky vapors, for nearly everyone could sport the price of a portion of il carrettiere's belly-warming wares, hence thwarting the troll for yet a few more hours.

Typically, il carrettiere prepared his long, thick cords of dried pasta by dragging them through a warmed coalescence of olive oil, ravishingly perfumed with garlic, oregano, and peperoncino. Should one have been so flush as to call for cacio, his dose would have been handsomely dusted with the piquant pecorino of Crotone in Calabria. The formula stayed safe through time, its solace radiating north and south, where still some one or another version of pasta all' aglio, olio, e peperoncino prevails as cure for surfeit now as much as for want, but always, one hopes, with homage to il carrettiere.

As rudimentary as this dish is, don't mistake it for one whose elements might be collected without care. One needs crisp, sharp, juicy garlic and a fine extra-virgin oil. That little bottle in the cupboard with the blue or red top that is older than the Flood and smells only of dust is no longer oregano. And the pure, clean fire that comes from a small, whole dried chile pepper crushed between your thumb and fingers can rarely be had from flakes of them long-ago collected in jars.

> 1 cup extra-virgin olive oil
> 1 or 2 small, dried red chile peppers, or ½ to ⅔ teaspoon dried
>   chile flakes
> 1 teaspoon dried, fragrant Greek oregano, crushed
> 1 tablespoon fennel seeds, crushed
> 4 to 6 fat cloves garlic, peeled, crushed, and finely minced
> Coarse sea salt for the water
> 1 pound bucatini or other string pasta

Over a medium flame, heat the oil in a small, heavy saucepan. Crush the chile peppers—better two than one—into the warming oil. As the oil approaches a simmer, add the oregano, fennel seed, and garlic, removing the pan from the heat. If the oil is sufficiently hot, a great sputtering will ensue. Stir, permitting the garlic to take on the palest of gold color. Anything darker will result in a bitter sauce.

Now for the pasta. In abundant, boiling, sea-salted water, cook the pasta to al dente, draining it and turning it out into a warmed, shallow bowl, tossing it about energetically with the scented oil. It needs only an honest red wine and a heel of bread to chase the smudges of oil left on one's plate.

Perhaps the most significant point of the warm-hearted rite of *il carrettiere*, though, is that one prepares it and eats it with those for whom one feels affection and whose presence at table is enriching. If they've scattered for the moment, better to perform the ceremony only for one. Its goodness would be lost in the company of buffoons.

Peperoni Arrostiti Ripieni
ROASTED STUFFED PEPPERS

Serves 4

This illuminates the pervasive Napoletano mastery over vegetables, the charred, sweet flesh of the peppers invigorated by the brine of the capers and olives, excited by the potency of the garlic and the pecorino, all of it hushed, then, by the raisins and the bread.

> 4 very large, fleshy yellow or red bell peppers
> Fine sea salt
> 2 cups just-made fine bread crumbs, lightly toasted
> ½ cup capers preserved under salt, rinsed and dried
> ½ cup golden raisins, plumped in warm red wine
> 4 ounces black and green Sicilian or Greek olives, lightly
> crushed with a mallet, stones removed, and coarsely chopped
> 4 fat cloves garlic, peeled, crushed, and finely minced
> 1 cup just-grated pecorino
> 6 tablespoons extra-virgin olive oil
> 1 cup good red wine
> 2 tablespoons good red wine vinegar

Roast the peppers—over a wood fire, under a broiler, in a hot oven, over a gas flame—until their skins are blackened and charred, their flesh tender. Place the roasted peppers immediately into a paper bag, folding it down tightly over them. Leave the parcel in a bowl, to catch the juices that will likely escape.

Preheat the oven to 375 degrees.

When the peppers have cooled thoroughly, relieve them of their charred skins, which will slip off like pajamas. Take care to leave the stems intact and the peppers

79

unwounded. Slit the peppers with a small, sharp knife, along a horizontal edge—about a 4-inch incision—and carefully scoop out their seeds. Sprinkle a generous pinch of sea salt into the interior of each and set them aside.

In a large bowl, combine the bread crumbs, capers, raisins, olives, garlic, pecorino, and 2 tablespoons of the oil, working the ingredients into a well-amalgamated paste. With your hands or a small spoon, fill the peppers with the paste, dividing it equally among them, urging it into the far reaches of each pepper.

Position the peppers, reclining, in a shallow terra-cotta or enameled cast-iron casserole. Combine the wine and the vinegar and douse the peppers. Place the peppers in the oven and braise them for ½ hour, basting with their juices twice during the process. Remove the peppers from the oven and permit them to cool to room temperature. They can wait up to 24 hours, covered and left in a cool place—not in the refrigerator.

When you are ready to present them, drop threads of the remaining olive oil over them and carry them to table in their braising dish. Offer good bread for the irresistible juices and jugs of red wine. The peppers will support a very slight reheating should one wish to serve them tepid, but it is at cool room temperature that they are most gorgeous.

Panzarotti

DEEP-FRIED MOZZARELLA-STUFFED DUMPLINGS

Makes 10 savory pastries

Historically the Napoletani have been able and brilliant friggitori—*fryers of food. Until only a few years past and sometimes, still, in the quarters of the poor, the very air was thick with the scents of food being crisped to a light gold in boiling oil. The humble kiosks of the* friggitori, *traditionally wagons fitted with cauldrons, were wheeled about the dank alleyways, the* friggitori *wailing out the worth of their salty wares, promising them to be "nuvole ricoperte d'un manto dorato"—"clouds mantled in gold." Sometimes, the offering was a nugget of simple bread dough stretched out and fried, then dusted in sea salt and anointed with oil, other times there might be little croquettes of rice and cheese or fritters of broccoli or artichokes. Often, though, the* friggi-tori *brought forth lusciously crunchy half-moons of dough plumped with mozzarella and known as pan-zarotti. Our favorite kiosk sits, still, in front of the Pizzeria Bellini, just down the street from the Accademia delle Belli Arti in Via Costantinopoli, a tiny quiver of space where one can stand, at nine in the morning, even, to bite at hot, too hot, savories while listening to two violins, a viola, a violoncello, and a Baroque guitar working through Boccherini.*

Here follows a version of panzarotti *made from course dough rolled thin, laid with mozzarella, pecorino, and bits of salty meat or tomato or anchovy, folded over and cast into whorls of bubbling oil.*

> 1 tablespoon plus 1 teaspoon active dry yeast or 1½ small cubes
>   fresh yeast
>
> 2 cups warm water
>
> ⅔ cup extra-virgin olive oil
>
> 1 tablespoon plus 1 teaspoon fine sea salt
>
> ⅔ cup whole milk
>
> 7 cups all-purpose flour
>
> ½ cup polenta meal
>
> 10 ounces very fresh cow's milk or buffalo milk mozzarella, cut
>   into ¼-inch cubes
>
> 1 cup just-grated pecorino
>
> 5 ounces finely shredded *salame* or prosciutto
>
> OR
>
> 3 ounces finely shredded sun-dried tomatoes
>
> OR
>
> 3 ounces anchovies preserved under salt (rinsed, heads and bones
>   removed, dried on paper towels, and lightly crushed with a fork)
>
> Pepper
>
> 1 liter (about 1 quart) olive oil

In a small bowl, soften the yeast in the water, permitting it to rest and dissolve for 15 minutes. In another small bowl, combine the olive oil, the salt, and the milk. Measure out the flour and the polenta meal into a large bowl, add the yeast and the olive oil mixtures, forming a rough dough of the ingredients. Turn the dough out onto a work space and knead the dough to a smooth resiliency, a task that takes at least 6 minutes. Place the dough in a lightly oiled bowl, cover it tightly with plastic wrap, and permit it to rise for 35 to 45 minutes or until it has nearly doubled.

Divide the dough in two. Roll out the first piece into a large rectangular shape about ¼ inch in thickness. With a biscuit or a pastry cutter, cut 5-inch rounds from the dough. Reroll the scraps and cut again. Repeat the process with the remaining half of the dough. Cover the disks with a clean kitchen towel, permitting them a 10-minute rest.

Place one-tenth of the mozzarella over one side of each disk. Dust the mozzarella with the pecorino, adding your choice of either the meat, the tomatoes, or the anchovies. Grind pepper generously over the filling. Fold the uncovered half of the disk over the filling, pressing down on the edges, sealing them well, then pinching the ends and forming a half-moon of the pastry.

Cover the *panzarotti* with a clean kitchen towel while the oil heats in a deep, heavy pan. Choose the pan so that the liter of oil will yield a depth of at least 5 inches. When the oil is very hot but not yet smoking, add a few of the *panzarotti*, browning them well before turning them over with tongs and browning the other sides.

Remove the *panzarotti* to absorbent paper towels, transferring them to a plate in a 150-degree oven while they wait the crisping of the others. Better yet, present them pan to plate to mouth right in the kitchen, as long as someone is dutiful about the furnishing of cold white wine.

There's nothing to do but go out to dinner after the triumph of the *panzarotti*. There will seem few dishes with which one might follow these. Better to compare them to someone else's work than your own.

Grappoli di Pomodorini con Mozzarella di Bufala

STILL-ON-THEIR-STEMS MINIATURE TOMATOES
WITH BUFFALO MILK MOZZARELLA

Serves 2

Perhaps the essence of Campania is this, of the countryside, of the pastoral innocence of the good, pure foods one eats there. Search, beg, grow, procure these few ingredients, first eating them with your eyes, dashing all record of plastic mozzarella and dusty-fleshed fruit masquerading as a tomato. This is not a recipe as much as it is quiet illustration of one fine way to eat in Italian.

As many of the tiniest red or yellow or green tomatoes, preferably still on their stems, that you and one other might desire
1 pound very fresh cow's milk or buffalo milk mozzarella
1 dozen or so large fleshy leaves of fresh basil
Extra-virgin olive oil
Pepper
Fine sea salt

Rinse the tomatoes, shaking them gently dry, and lay them to the side of two very large plates. Place a few slices of mozzarella across the plate from the tomatoes, laying the basil leaves between them. Drop tears of the oil over all the ingredients. Grind pepper lightly over the mozzarella.

Have a dish of sea salt and a tiny jug of good oil at table, along with a beautiful bread and a cooled bottle of Mastroberardino's Greco di Tufo.

La Vera Pizza
THE REAL PIZZA

The truth is that by the end of the eighteenth century, the Napoletani had embraced the homey rite of stretching out hunks of the dough they prepared to make bread, spreading it with an unctuous salve of olive oil or the rendered fat from some part of a pig, making it savory with a fistful of wild herbs and a plump clove of garlic, smashed with the flat of a knife. The smeared dough was heaved into the smoky environs of the bread oven, whose high heat cooked it in a minute, two minutes, crisping its surfaces, charring its edges, the fat having seeped inside it, leaving a soft, chewy crumb between the darkened crusts. And it was this that was the antecedent of *la pizza*.

Though Napoli was then already in love with the tomato, the sassy, juicy fruit figured not in the components of the flat pie until a bit later. In fact, it was not until the mid-nineteenth century that *la pizza*, finally rubbed with crushed tomato and dusted with pecorino, became the rage of Napoli.

Food of the poor, the *borghesi*, the artists, the nobles, even the king and queen of Savoia, who were escorted one historic spring evening through the backstreets of the city to a place where one Raffaele Esposito had been commissioned to cook *la pizza* for their majesties, Umberto and Margherita. The royals were said to have been enchanted. The place was under the patronage of *la famiglia* Brandi and still, now, it is there in the Salita Sant'Anna di Palazzo, its walls all agloss in certificates and photos and paintings and press releases, testimony to the authenticity of the family as the creators of *la pizza Margherita*. But it is not there that one eats the finest pizza in Napoli. Nor is it at Ciro a Santa Brigida nor at Lombardi a Santa Chiara nor even at Port' Alba nor Umberto that waits the most luscious of all the world's tomato pies. *La vera pizza napoletana* is presented in Via Cesare Sersale, da Michele. Quite simply, there is no other like it.

It is a primitive, wood-baked bread, a blistered, scorched communion splendid with tomatoes and oil and a crush of herbs. It is unforgettable. Even the place itself, there for more than a century—its proprietors the sons and brothers of the sons and brothers of the founder—is honest, uninjured by its own quiet celebrity. The only recipe for it that I can give to you is to impel you to go there. Eat a *pizza napoletana* or a *pizza marinara*. Drink a beer. There is no wine. Know that, at Michele, you will have a whiff, a taste, of a food pure, a food sincere enough to warm a poor heart, a rich heart, an old one, a baby one. And don't ever confuse this true one with some other one, mattering not who made it where or with what arrangement of stuffs. After Michele's pie, there is no other.

Timballo di Maccheroni alla Monzù

A MACCHERONI PIE IN THE MANNER OF THE MONZÙ

Serves 6 to 8

When Napoleon lifted up his brother-in-law Joachim Murat to the throne of Napoli in the early nineteenth century, he wittingly rubbed the gastronomic culture of the city to a high French polish. As the governor of Paris, Murat fixed for himself a popular reputation as gourmand, having conducted the business of his offices more often than not midst the ever-sumptuous, sometimes not-meant-to-be-eaten bas-relief of his banqueting tables.

And trailing Murat to Napoli marched legions of French chefs. The great toques were an outlandish platoon, striding about the city's marketplaces and food shops like so many swells among the rabble and answering only to the title monsieur. The irreverent Napoletani soon punished the word into monzù. But even without the genuflection of the masses, the French masters left rich, culinary impress. In the embrace of their hyperbole, there was nothing too spangled, their dishes mostly unredeemed paroxysms of the baroque in both component and construction. And one of their glory dishes was the timballo— the drum—recalling the high-sided round or oval forms in which the chefs built great, towering pies, as much for table architecture as for their eventual service as dinner. One version of the timballo asked for a deep mold upholstered in sweet short pastry, layered with pasta stuffed with veal sweetbreads, layered with the livers of game and whole fat, musky truffles, all of it robed in a salsa besciamella—béchamel—spiced with cinnamon and nutmeg and cloves. The timballo was roofed then in more pastry, painted with egg wash and baked golden as amber. Here follows a version less awkward to make, less fantastic, perhaps, but no less sublime for its relative restraint.

When preparing any one of the cinque brasati di carne con pomodori (page 67), increase the amount so that some might be saved, then used to flavor the timballo.

The Pastry

2¼ cups all-purpose flour, plus additional as needed

1 teaspoon fine sea salt

12 tablespoons sweet butter, cut into small cubes and placed in
   the freezer for 15 minutes

⅓ cup iced dry white wine

1 large egg, slightly beaten

In a medium bowl, mix the flour with the sea salt and rub the very cold butter into the flour/salt mixture with your fingertips or a pastry blender until it resembles very coarse crumbs. Mix the iced wine with the beaten egg and add these to the bowl, stirring with a fork to form a rough paste. Turn out onto a very lightly floured work space and blend the mixture, with a few short strokes, into a dough.

Flatten the dough into a disk, wrap it tightly in plastic wrap, and place it in the freezer for 20 minutes. Unwrap the dough and divide it into two pieces—one-third and two-thirds. Wrap the smaller piece and place it in the refrigerator while you roll the larger piece out into a circle approximately ⅛ inch in thickness.

Butter the inside surfaces of an 8- or 9-inch springform pan and fit the pastry into it, permitting its edges to overhang a bit. Cover the pastry-lined pan with plastic wrap and place it in the refrigerator while you deal with the pie's lid.

Remove the smaller piece of pastry from the refrigerator and roll it out into an 8- or 9-inch circle. Gently fold the pastry circle in half, wrapping it in plastic and refrigerating it. The pastry will wait an hour or so while you proceed with the *maccheroni* and the mushrooms, or it can wait overnight should you wish to spread out the procedure over two days. In any case, the next task is to prepare the fillings.

The Fillings

4 cups beef or veal stock, preferably homemade

12 ounces *maccheroni*—ziti, penne, or rigatoni

1 tablespoon coarse sea salt

4 tablespoons sweet butter, slightly softened

1 cup just-grated pecorino

Freshly ground white pepper

3 tablespoons sweet butter

1 tablespoon extra-virgin olive oil

1 pound fresh, wild mushrooms (porcini, cèpes, chanterelles, portobelli, etc.), cleaned with a soft, damp cloth and thickly sliced

Fine sea salt

⅓ cup dry white wine

2 cups sauce with bits of meat from any one of the five braises (page 67)

1 large egg yolk beaten with 1 teaspoon of extra-virgin olive oil

In a very large pot over a lively flame, bring the stock and 3 quarts of water to a boil. Add the *maccheroni* and the coarse sea salt and cook the *maccheroni* almost to al dente. Drain the *maccheroni*, turn it out into a large bowl, and toss it with the butter, the pecorino, and generous grindings of white pepper. Set the *maccheroni* aside.

In a large sauté pan over a medium flame, heat the butter and the olive oil and soften the mushrooms, permitting them to give up their juices. Sprinkle on the fine sea salt and freshly ground white pepper and add the wine. Cover the pan with a skewed lid and simmer for 15 minutes or so, allowing the mushrooms to plump, to take back their juices and to drink in the wine. Set the mushrooms aside.

When you are ready to assemble the pie, preheat the oven to 375 degrees and remove the pastry-lined pan from the refrigerator, spooning a layer of the *maccheroni* into it Add several spoonfuls of the mushrooms and then some of the *brasato*, both meat and sauce. Repeat until all the components are nicely bedded down. Unfold the pastry lid and place it over the pie, crimping the edges of the bottom crust and top crusts together, taking care not to let any pastry drape over the edges of the form. With a pastry brush, paint the pie with the egg wash—the egg yolk beaten with the oil—and bake it for ½ hour or until the crust is a wonderful yellow-gold. Cool the pie on a rack for 15 minutes before removing it from the springform pan. Present the pie on a pedestal dish, cutting into it at table with some cere-monial knife, serving it forthwith some drama and a worthy, if not noble, red wine.

Zuppa di Soffritto di Maiale

A RED WINE TOMATO SOUP WITH SPICED PORK

Serves 4

In the thirteenth century, when the Angevins reanchored their royal seat from Palermo to Napoli, the latter was illuminated, transformed, by the influx of a luxe new citizenry. Royals, nobles, and government bigwigs were followed by a cadre of the epoch's great artists. Giotto and Petrarch and Boccaccio ensconced themselves in Napoli. And as they are wont to do, the masses, too, followed, hoping to stay warm, a little warmer even, inside the echoes of the city's great, new noise. And as much as she did flourish then, also did the misery of her increase. In great part, Napoli starved under the reign of the French kings. While obscenely cinematic festivals were being staged inside the lustrous salons, the Napoletani waited outside each evening for the cooks to wallop out over the castle walls to them the viscera of the lords' sheep and cows and pigs and goats. And from these mean stuffs did the women and men of Napoli invent their suppers. Among the dishes that became tradition during this time was zuppa di soffritto, a high-spiced potion made from the heart, spleen, and lungs of the pig and still prized by the Napoletani. Here follows a version of the good soup that asks for less exotic parts of the pig.

    4 ounces pancetta
    1 ounce salt pork
    2 tablespoons rosemary leaves
    3 fat cloves garlic, peeled and crushed

2 large yellow onions, peeled and sliced thin

1 small, dried red chile pepper, crushed, or ⅓ to ½ teaspoon
   dried chile flakes

1 pound tenderloin of pork, minced

1 teaspoon fine sea salt

2½ cups good red wine

1½ cups canned tomato puree

About ½ cup extra-virgin olive oil

4 ½-inch-thick trenchers of good country bread

With a mezzaluna or a very sharp knife, mince the pancetta, the salt pork, the rosemary, and the garlic to a fine paste. In a large terra-cotta or enameled cast-iron casserole over a medium flame, heat the paste and soften the onions to translucence, taking care to sauté them only slightly. Add the chile.

Brown the pork now in the casserole, crusting it a bit and sprinkling on the sea salt. Add 1 cup of the wine, letting it evaporate before adding the tomato puree and the remaining wine, and bringing the soup to a gentle simmer. Cook the soup uncovered and over a low flame, for ½ hour.

Heat the olive oil and brown the bread, letting it rest a moment on absorbent paper towels before placing it in a napkin-lined basket. Present the soup in its casserole along with the basket of fried bread, each guest ladling the hot, thick soup over a golden trencher laid at the bottom of his bowl.

The Caffè Culture of Napoli

"*Quant' è buono il babà!*" "How good a *babà* is!" This is a happy phrase one hears bandied about mornings and more, at teatime, in the grand *caffès* of Napoli, affirming the people's penchant for the little rum-drenched breads. Though the *babas* are luscious at Gambrinus and, too, at the Professore, it is at Scaturchio in Piazza San Domenico Maggiore that they are most splendid.

And lovely it is to stand there in the tiny polished area of Scaturchio, taking a cappuccino, nibbling first at a *sfogliatella*—a shell-shaped crisp of pastry plumped with ricotta—then the baba and, perhaps, just one tiny pistachio tart fluffed with coffeed cream. This is a nine-thirty ceremony for us so as to pace the morning for a stop at Gambrinus in Piazza Trieste e Trento at eleven.

The barman will tell you the story of them while he pumps and presses at the great, hissing coffee machine, of how a desultory Austrian prince sat, one evening, wetting the edges of his Kugelhopf in a cup of hot rum while reading *A Thousand and One Nights*. The prince, aroused from his sulks by the sweet concoction of rum and cake, pronounced it *Ali Baba*, in romantic homage to the fable.

And lovely it is to stand there in the tiny polished area of Scaturchio, taking a cappuccino, nibbling first at a *sfogliatella*—a shell-shaped crisp of pastry plumped with ricotta—then the baba and, perhaps, just one tiny pistachio tart fluffed with coffeed cream. This is a nine-thirty ceremony for us so as to pace the morning for a stop at Gambrinus in Piazza Trieste e Trento at eleven.

Perhaps my favorite *caffè* in all of Italy, the pale green and gold of Gambrinus, the chandeliers dripping their quiet light, the waiters in morning coats, the old nobles at peace behind the pages of *Il Mattino di Napoli* and in front of some tall, pink *aperitivo*, is a tableau without time. I love to sit there of an early evening, too, in a brown velvet cloche, smoking Gitanes and drinking tea while I wait to rendezvous with my husband. There as well as in any other bar or *caffè*—luxurious or humble—into which one might wander in Napoli, a simple espresso or a glass of wine seems always to be offered with some sort of bonhomie, with a generosity of spirit rarely risked in another Italian city

La Mitica Torta d' Arancia di Anacapri

THE MYTHICAL ORANGE TART OF ANACAPRI

Serves 10 to 12

A while ago, I'd heard from a friend about a tart made with oranges from the groves on the island of Capri, it, once an idyll and now mostly a tourist ruin just seventeen kilometers across the bay from Napoli. Specifically, it was the island's village of Anacapri that was the scene of my friend's tart story. She told me that the confection was barely sugared, so perfect were the oranges of its making. She said it was all of a cool cream in the mouth, each little bite of it a sensual, sweet/pungent explosion. She said that even the crust was scented with oranges, perhaps with some locally distilled liqueur of the fruit, and that, too, the crust gave up some soft breath of herb, like wild mint or rosemary. But where in Anacapri, I begged, never having seen the sweet in any pasticceria nor read of it on any menu nor found it perched on any dessert cart. Worse, everyone I asked about the tart shook their heads. "Non c'è una cosa del genere qui, signora." "There is nothing of that sort here, madam." This bantering betwixt my friend and I has endured several years. She insists that the tart, indeed, exists. I think it some citrusy half-dream of hers, a tart that should have been, perhaps, but one that never yet was, at least not in Anacapri.

And so I baked it, hearing her gurglings and swoonings in my mind at every step. Though I've yet to make it for her—she living in Oregon while I'm here in Tuscany—I offer it here and tell you, humbly, of its goodness, of its simple sort of persuasiveness. I think it is the pastry I would make and share and eat on the last day of the world.

The Pastry

2 cups all-purpose flour, plus additional as needed

½ teaspoon fine sea salt

1 cup confectioners' sugar

2 teaspoons very finely minced fresh rosemary leaves

Finely grated zest of 1 large orange

12 tablespoons sweet butter, very cold, cut into small cubes

1 large egg

1 large egg yolk

2 tablespoons very cold Cointreau or Grand Marnier

Place the flour, salt, sugar, rosemary, and the orange zest in a medium bowl and rub the cold butter into it with fingertips or a pastry blender until it resembles very coarse crumbs. Combine the egg, the egg yolk, and the liqueur and, with a fork, stir it all into the bowl with the flour mixture, forming a rough paste.

Turn it out onto a lightly floured work space and, with a few short strokes, form the mixture into a dough. Flatten the dough into a disc, wrap it tightly in plastic wrap and, place it in the freezer for 20 minutes. Press the rested, chilled dough over the surfaces of a buttered 12- to 14-inch tart pan with a removable bottom. Cover the pastry-lined tin in plastic wrap and chill it again, for 20 minutes, in the freezer.

Preheat the oven to 400 degrees.

With a fork, prick the chilled pastry over its surface and bake it for 10 minutes. Lower the temperature to 375 degrees and continue baking the pastry for an additional 5 or 6 minutes or until it is firmed and barely beginning to take on some color. Cool the pastry thoroughly on a rack. Proceed with the orange cream.

The Filling

1¼ cups just-squeezed orange juice
Finely grated zest of 1 large orange
⅓ cup dark brown sugar
½ cup mascarpone
7 large eggs
3 tablespoons Cointreau or Grand Marnier
Confectioners' sugar

If the oven is not already hot, preheat it to 400 degrees.

In a medium bowl, beat together the orange juice, the zest, the sugar, and the mascarpone, amalgamating the ingredients well. Add the eggs, one at a time, beating vigorously, incorporating each before adding the next. Add the liqueur and beat thoroughly.

Pour the orange cream into the prepared pastry and bake the tart for 20 to 25 minutes or until the cream is just firmed and has taken on patches of burnished skin and the crust is deeply golden.

Cool the tart on a rack for 15 minutes before removing its ring and permitting it to cool thoroughly. Thickly dust the tart with confectioners' sugar.

Present the tart on the day it was baked, never letting it anywhere near the refrigerator. Offer tiny glasses of the liqueur used in the tart, if you wish or, slipping fast away from Italia, Campania, Napoli, much less Anacapri, pass around a bottle of fine, tawny port.

LA COSTIERA AMALFITANA / THE AMALFI COAST

A forty-kilometer corniche, the Costiera Amalfitana seems a great stone curl, its slopes all of tilted terraces beset in lemon orchards. And the earth not inlaid in citrus sprouts trees of almonds and olives, mimosa and vines—all the beauties to sustain life in a Tyrrhenian fastness. Though the celebrated coast road does deliver shivery moments, it offers only profile views of the coastline. Better to come at her from the deck of a small, speeding boat, looking straight into her gorgeous face. Disembark, perhaps, at Praiano or Atrani, Maiori, Vietri sul Mare or, more probably, at Positano or Amalfi. For us, it is always at Ravello where first we stop.

A bougainvillea-scented village of peace and ravishing beauty is Ravello, for centuries culled, graced by English and Americans. Unlike Positano, which plays too much the indulged summer princess, Ravello is more lofty-minded. Neither has Ravello much in common with little Amalfi and its palmy rhythms and labyrinthine streets. Ravello is a place where the edge of the earth stops short, heaving itself in great quicksilver crags that plunge into pools of the same cold violet sea where sirens once bathed. Ravello is a place apart.

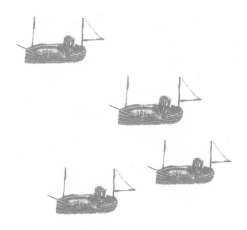

Cassuola di Vongole e Cozze all' Acqua Pazza

CASSEROLED CLAMS AND MUSSELS IN CRAZY WATER

Serves 4

Prepare it with only mussels, with only clams, with various types of clams, make it for two of you or for all of you. Carry a great, steamy pot of it outdoors to a table set with candles and backlit by the moon on a cool, almost cold evening, everyone nuzzled in sweaters but still in shorts and sandals, hungry, tired, perhaps, happy. Serve it then, just the way it is offered in the tiny taverns and six-table houses that look to the sea between Amalfi and Positano.

4 fat cloves garlic, peeled and crushed

2 teaspoons fennel seeds, crushed

⅓ cup flat parsley leaves

⅓ cup plus about 1 cup extra-virgin olive oil

1 small, dried red chile pepper, crushed, or ⅓ to ½ teaspoon
    dried chile flakes

2 large ripe tomatoes, peeled, seeded, and finely chopped

1½ teaspoons fine sea salt

1 bottle dry white wine

2 pounds clams, purged of their sand by soaking for 1 hour in
    sea-salted water, then well scrubbed

2 pounds mussels, scrubbed, bearded, and rinsed

8 ½-inch slices good country bread

2 tablespoons good red wine vinegar

With a mezzaluna or a very sharp knife, mince the garlic, fennel, and parsley to a fine paste.

In a very large terra-cotta or enameled cast-iron casserole over a medium flame, warm ⅓ cup of the olive oil and very lightly sauté the paste in it. Add the chile, tomatoes, sea salt, and the wine, bringing all to a simmer. Lower the flame a bit and continue to cook for 5 minutes, reducing the wine and softening the tomatoes. Add the clams and mussels to the simmering sauce, poaching them until they are all opened.

Warm the remaining 1 cup of olive oil and brown the bread in it, letting it drain a moment on absorbent paper towels before placing it in a napkin-lined basket.

At just the point when all the shellfish have opened, remove the casserole from the flame, stir in the vinegar, and carry it to the table along with the basket of fried bread.

Spuma di Zucchine Arrostite di Positano

A MOUSSE OF ROASTED ZUCCHINI IN THE STYLE OF POSITANO

Makes about 6 cups

A simple-to-make and delectable little paste with which to dress just-cooked pasta, to spoon into vegetable soups, to thin with milk or vegetable stock into, itself, a fine soup, to stuff into fat, ripe tomatoes, to present alongside roasted meat or fish, to spread on great chunks of olive-oil-toasted bread, to eat with a spoon while waiting for bread to bake.

> 2 pounds small zucchini
> 2 heads fresh, firm, fat garlic, the cloves separated and left
>   unpeeled
> ⅓ cup extra-virgin olive oil
> 2 teaspoons fine sea salt
> Freshly cracked pepper
> 1½ cups just-grated parmigiano
> Juice and the zest of 1 lemon
> 1 cup heavy cream
> ⅔ cup basil leaves

Preheat the oven to 375 degrees. Cut thin slices from both ends of the zucchini, slice them in half lengthwise, and lay them in a single layer on a baking sheet. Strew the garlic cloves about the zucchini, drizzle the whole with the olive oil, sprinkle on the sea salt, generously grind over the pepper, and roast them for 40 minutes or until the zucchini are very soft and nicely charred and the garlic is soft and deeply golden. Leave the zucchini and the garlic to cool a bit. Slip the skins from the garlic.

In the work bowl of a food processor fitted with a steel blade, process the zucchini and the garlic to a puree, add the cheese, lemon juice, zest, and the cream and process for 20 seconds to make a smooth paste. At the last, add the basil leaves and process a few seconds more.

Turn the paste out into a bowl. Taste it, adding more sea salt should you desire it.

Gamberoni Grigliati in Foglie di Limone

PRAWNS GRILLED IN LEMON LEAVES

Serves 6 as an antipasto

One must have a lemon tree or some harmonious acquaintance with someone who has a lemon tree, know a florist or a fruit seller who can procure untreated lemon leaves, or one can let go the idea of the lemon leaves and trump up alternate ones, such as those pulled from a grapevine or a chestnut tree. Lacking all of these, one must know how wonderful the dish will be with no leaves at all, just for grilling the fat prawns, beheaded but with their tails intact, over a good wood fire, then heaving them, all hot and sputtering, into an anise-perfumed bath. Though the lemon leaves, if they're good and fresh, do add some flavor and keep the prawns moist during the roast, they are, in the end, only a pretty and clever sort of packaging.

The Prawns

12 to 18 very large prawns
⅓ cup extra-virgin olive oil
Juice and zest of 1 large lemon
½ teaspoon fine sea salt
1 teaspoon aniseeds, crushed
Lemon, grape, or chestnut leaves (optional)

Relieve the prawns of their shells, peeling them away, leaving the tail with its bit of shell intact and pulling out the veins from the head end, rather than slitting the prawns down their backs. Place the prawns in a large bowl.

Blend the olive oil, lemon juice and zest, sea salt, and aniseeds and pour over the prawns, rubbing the mixture well into each of them.

Cover the prawns, letting them rest while you build a wood fire. If using the leaves, place 2 prawns on each leaf and, depending on the size of the leaf, either fold it over the prawns, securing it with a toothpick, or place another leaf on top of the prawns, again securing one leaf to the other with toothpicks. Place the packages on a grill over the fire and roast them for 2 minutes or less to the side, depending on their size.

If you are not using leaves, simply skewer the prawns, 2 or 3 to the stem, and roast them for a minute or so on each side, letting their edges char. In this case, immediately position the prawns, skewers and all, on a warmed, deep platter over which the warm, perfumed oil (see page 95) has been poured, presenting them at once.

If you've used the leaves, pile the roasted bundles onto a warm platter, passing them about, either already having set a small pitcher of the perfumed oil at each place or sending a larger one round the table.

The Lemon-Anise Oil

  1 cup extra-virgin olive oil
  Juice and zest of 2 large lemons
  ½ teaspoon fine sea salt
  2 tablespoons anise-flavored liqueur
  2 teaspoons aniseeds

In a small saucepan, heat the olive oil nearly to a boil, remove it from the flame and add the remaining ingredients. Cover the pan and permit the mixture to steep for ½ hour. Gently reheat the perfumed oil over the fire while roasting the prawns. It should be very warm.

La Torta Amalfitana di Melanzane e Cioccolato

A CAKE OF EGGPLANT AND CHOCOLATE IN THE MANNER OF AMALFI

Serves 6

A gastronomic heirloom of the coast, this is a humble recipe made from the bits and pieces of what was at hand, sometimes eaten as a principal dish or a contorno, *a side dish, other times as a sweet. It is still presented— though in dramatically different versions—in cherished places such as Da Gemma in Amalfi. This take, how- ever, is lighter, less vegetal than most of those with which we've been presented, the trick being the absolute thinness of the eggplant slices. This enables them to blend better with the other components, all of them then set- tling down together into a nicely married sort of flavor and texture. More eccentric than it is bizarre, this version of the ancestral dish turns out to be quite luscious.*

  3 small or 2 medium globe-shaped eggplants, smooth, tight,
      and shiny-skinned
  Coarse sea salt for the water
  7 ounces extra-bittersweet chocolate, preferably Lindt or
      Valrhona 70% cacao
  2 tablespoons cocoa powder, preferably Dutch process
  ½ teaspoon ground cloves

A few grindings of pepper

⅓ cup good red wine

5 ounces shelled pistachios, lightly pan-roasted

5 ounces blanched almonds, lightly pan-roasted

Flour

1 cup extra-virgin olive oil

1 large egg

1 large egg white

2 tablespoons sugar

Confectioners' sugar

Slice the unpeeled eggplant very thin into slices not more than ⅛ inch in thickness and nearly transparent, piling them into a large bowl of cold, sea-salted water. Permit the eggplant slices to rest in their bath for 1 hour.

In a small, heavy saucepan over a low flame, stir the chocolate with the cocoa, the cloves, the pepper, and the wine, only until the chocolate has softened and warmed. Continue to stir off the flame until the mixture is smooth. Cover the pan and set it aside.

Hand-chop or pulse the pan-roasted pistachios and almonds in a food processor to a fairly small mince. Set the nuts aside.

Drain the eggplant, squeezing the slices a few at a time. Shake the squeezed, now wrinkled-beyond-repair, slices in a paper bag with a bit of flour, coating them lightly.

Preheat the oven to 375 degrees.

In a large sauté pan over a lively flame, warm the olive oil and begin quickly sautéing the eggplant, crisping it a bit, then removing it to rest on absorbent paper towels. Repeat the process until all the eggplant slices are golden and crisped.

Very lightly oil a 10-inch springform pan and place a generous layer of the eggplant on its base. Drizzle the eggplant with a bit of the slightly rewarmed chocolate, sprinkle over some of the pistachio/almond mixture, and repeat the process until all the components are in place, ending with a thin layer of eggplant.

Beat the egg, the egg white, and the sugar together to a froth in a pitcher or a measuring cup with a spout, drizzling it carefully over and down into the cracks and crevices between the layers of the eggplant.

Bake the *torta* for 18 minutes, removing it from the oven to cool for ½ hour before unmolding. Just before presentation, dust the *torta* with confectioners' sugar. It is lovely to eat at room temperature, even better thoroughly cooled. Do not, however, refrigerate it. Obviously, one would wish to keep the *torta*'s principal component a secret, waiting to see who among them will recognize it in its sweet masquerade.

IL CILENTO /
THE CILENTO

Of an ancient quiet and an older suffering is the Cilento, a savage and rough-hewn parish whose mountains fall fast to the sea—no buffer, not the sparest littoral, even, between them. Inland from the sea, the mountains fold down with more grace, sometimes, into soft hills, the earth spreading out into high meadows and Stone Age fields where grow wild asparagus and bitter grasses and herbs full of clean, prickly perfumes. Save the Greek colony at Paestum, it is a place mostly unwashed in the colors of any epoch. Its countryside is as it was, as it shall be, one thinks, unaware of its own poignancy, not knowing how out of step it would dance with the most primitive of others. The paths to its history are open and easy to walk, they being mostly the same roadways to its present.

The descendants of those who stayed through the pests and the hungers and the wars still forage and hunt and fish as others did a hundred years ago, two or three or more hundreds of years ago, eternal antagonists in a pastoral epic. And the parts of the Cilento that grew up into villages and towns like Castellabate, Velia, and Agropoli can seem sore and crude, of an old, irrevocable hostility. There is another town nearby, called Capaccio. It is not so different from the others except that Alfonso Longo's little place is there.

His is an osteria called La Pergola, tucked off the main street in the lower part of the village. Half a hundred years ago, it was a *taverna*, his grandmother's home, the place where she bartered her stables, a plate of bean soup, and a draft of red wine with the freight carriers for a crate of Amalfi lemons or a sack of wild Cilentini artichokes.

The carriage drivers slept with their horses and, in the morning, his grandmother brewed a sort of coffee from weeds and roots and cut thick slices of her own rough bread and toasted them over the fire for their breakfast. None of them having anything of money to exchange for what they needed or desired, their mutuality, their shuffling to and fro of what each of them might gather or grow up, shoot or steal or cook or distill for some other one, was how they lived.

Time passed and pages fluttered and Alfonso, having moved about here and there in the world, returned home to Capaccio, he deciding to deliver—with no trampling on the smallest of traditions—a Cilentina osteria. And during these nearly twenty years since his quiet renaissance of the *taverna*, Longo has raised up an extraordinary house, a keepsafe for the food and the stories of his Cilento. His is the sentimental refuge of an instinctive chef, a romantic, a humanist, an incorrigible. And at a table sidled up close to his fire, one sits inside an unbroken comfort, transported amidst the vapors of nostalgia, to eat and drink of things gently divine.

Pesce Spada sotto Sale con Marmellata di Limone all' Alfonso Longo

SALT-CURED SWORDFISH WITH LEMON MARMALADE
IN THE MANNER OF ALFONSO LONGO

Serves 6 as an antipasto

In the autumn, as schools of swordfish swam south into the Bay of Policastro, the fishermen of the Cilento were often their conquerors, luring the great fish with oil-soaked bread and hauling them up from the sea—porting them like vanquished kings, high atop their heads up the steep paths from the water—to their camps to roast them or smoke them over smoldering fires of pine and olive and citrus woods. Sometimes, the Cilentini cured the fish under salt and foraged grasses and spiceberries, dousing the flesh with their own rough-made spirits. Served a dish such as this, one could think it the offering of some cultivated chef, yet, then and there, it was nothing more than the improvised handiwork of hungry men.

The Swordfish

1½ pounds swordfish, sliced thin into 12 fillets

⅓ cup coarse sea salt

3 tablespoons dark brown sugar

⅓ cup grappa or vodka

Fronds from 1 large head fennel, coarsely chopped

Prepare the fish and lay the slices in one or two large, shallow ceramic dishes. In a mortar with a pestle, pound the sea salt with the brown sugar, finely grinding the two together. Rub the poultice onto both sides of each slice of fish, baptizing the whole with grappa or vodka and strewing the lot with the fennel fronds.

Cover the dish or dishes tightly with plastic wrap and refrigerate for two days, turning the fish once or twice a day.

To present the fish, remove some of the larger pieces of fennel fronds and lay the cured slices on a large, flat platter, drizzling them with any drops of liquid that might have accumulated during the cure. Strew the fish with the fried lemon zest, passing lemon marmalade and a basket of *crostini* (see page 99 for zest, marmalade, and *crostini*).

The Lemon Marmalade

Not a terribly sweet sort of breakfast jam, not really a true marmalade, this is the rough condiment Alfonso's grandmother made when she had a few extra lemons and some even more precious sugar at hand. She served it with her home-smoked swordfish as well as the salt-cured reading. Too, he remembers her smearing it on just-baked bread for him to eat with a slice of fresh ricotta when times were flush.

> 8 large lemons
> Sugar

First weigh the lemons, or have them weighed at the fruit market, as you'll be using two-thirds their weight in sugar to make the puckery jam. Slice the lemons fairly thin and toss them into a heavy, shallow pan with the prescribed sugar and enough water to barely cover them.

Over a lively flame, stirring constantly, cook the mixture for a few minutes, then lower the flame and, still stirring, cook for 20 minutes or so, until the water has evaporated and the fruit is softened and trapped in a glossy, thick syrup.

Let the marmalade cool and then portion it out into 2 or 3 jars with tight-fitting lids to store in the refrigerator. The confection will stay nicely for a week to ten days.

The Fried Lemon Zest

> Zest of 3 large lemons
> 3 tablespoons extra-virgin olive oil

Finely shred the lemon zest. In a small saucepan, barely cover the zest with cold water and bring to a simmer. Quickly drain the zest and dry on absorbent paper towels.

Over a lively flame in a small saucepan, warm the olive oil and sauté the zest, tossing it about, letting it crisp a bit and take on a good, deep color.

The Crostini

> ⅔ cup extra-virgin olive oil
> 12 ¼-inch slices good country bread

In a large sauté pan over a medium flame, warm the olive oil and brown the bread well on both sides, cooking it until it is quite crisp.

Let the *crostini* rest a bit on absorbent paper towels before placing them in a napkin-lined basket.

Branzino Arrostito con il Mosto di Uve all' Alfonso Longo

SEA BASS ROASTED WITH GRAPE MUST
IN THE MANNER OF ALFONSO LONGO

Serves 4

Alfonso cooks a dish much like this one, invented epochs ago by the Cilentini during the vendemmia—*the harvest of the wine grapes. He tells the story of the fishermen who were also winemakers, who, after depositing the daily winemaking debris into the sea, set out their shore lines, much as they did every other evening. Serendipitously, they lured an abundance of fat, pewtery sea bass—*branzino—*the fish bewitched by the fermenting perfumes of the grape skins and seeds. The Cilentini then roasted the fish who'd fed on the grape must over cuttings from the vines. The flesh of the fish was scented, through and through, with essences of grape. Legend has it that the dish made voluptuaries of all who ate it. Stuffing the fish with cooked grapes likely gives it an even more luxurious savor than that taken on by his must-eating ancestors.*

> 3 pounds table grapes or, should they be available, wine grapes
> 1 large bay leaf
> ½ cup golden raisins, plumped in warm water
> ⅔ cup moscato or other sweet, ambered wine
> 2 tablespoons red wine vinegar
> Fine sea salt
> 1 5- or 6-pound sea bass, scaled, cleaned, and filleted
> ½ cup good red wine
> ⅓ cup extra-virgin olive oil

Stem half the grapes, never minding their seeds, and place them in a heavy saucepan, smashing at them with a wooden spoon, crushing them. Add the bay leaf, the raisins, and the wine and, over a medium flame, bring the mixture to a simmer. Lower the flame and cook until the wine has evaporated and the fruit has collapsed into a thick jam. Remove from the heat and stir in the vinegar. (Some might think to pass the jam through a fine sieve to relieve it of its debris of skins and seeds, clashing up against, though, the rusticity, the honesty of the dish.)

Preheat the oven to 375 degrees.

Sprinkle the sea salt inside the fish and then stuff its belly with the jam. With a wooden mallet or some such instrument, crush the remaining grapes that are still on their stems and place them in a shallow terra-cotta or enameled cast-iron casserole just large enough to cradle the fish. Place the fish on top of the grapes and douse it with the red wine mixed with the olive oil.

Roast the fish for 30 minutes, basting at least three times with the pan juices. As soon as the flesh is firm, the fish is cooked.

Carry the fish to table in the roasting pan, serving it with spoonfuls of the juices and perhaps a rough puree of roasted fennel and a Taurasi from Mastroberardino.

Fusilli con Vongole e Asparagi Selvatici del Cilento

FUSILLI WITH CLAMS AND WILD ASPARAGUS IN THE STYLE OF THE CILENTO

Serves 4

Six hundred years before Christ, the Greeks raised up a grand colony on the verges of the Mar Tirreno, dedicating it to Poseidon. Now known as Paestum, the whole cadence of life, as it was then and there, sits in high relief, a phenomenal diorama, traceable, floating, gleaming. The great temples, barely wounded and without a haunting, invite one inside to stay among the rests of old dreams, to race among the open pathways between them. A cordial parish, a fair Camelot, it seems, while one sits awhile on the thick tufts of grass inside the Temple of Neptune, having slipped under the easy gate to watch the sunrise, to collect armfuls of the tall, thin spears of asparagus that grow wild, treasures to take back to Alfonso to cook for lunch.

He, having spent the morning gathering clams, combined the collected booty with fusilli di Felitto—beautiful pasta, hand-rolled then wound, one string at a time, around the traditional, corkscrew-shaped wires, used and prized like jewels, by the women of the nearby village of Felitto. Dishes that marry wild vegetables with sea or shellfish are typical of the Cilentini, they thinking it a thing natural to prepare their suppers with stuffs foraged from woods that fall down to the sea.

> 2 dozen clams
> Coarse sea salt for the water
> 1 pound young, slender asparagus, stems trimmed, spears left
>   whole
> 12 ounces fusilli
> ½ cup extra-virgin olive oil
> 3 fat cloves garlic, peeled, crushed, and minced
> 1 cup dry white wine

Purge the clams of their sand by soaking for an hour or so in sea-salted water, then scrub them well.

Prepare the asparagus and drop them into a large pot of boiling, sea-salted water, poaching them for 2 to 3 minutes if they are slim as they should be, a few more if they are thicker around the middle. Drain them, reserve their cooking water, and refresh them under fresh, very cold water. Chop the asparagus roughly and set aside.

Bring a large pot of sea-salted water and the reserved asparagus cooking water to a boil and cook the fusilli to al dente, draining them and setting them aside.

While the fusilli are cooking, attend to the clams. In a shallow terra-cotta or enameled cast-iron casserole over a medium flame, heat the olive oil and soften the garlic, taking care not to color it. Add the wine and bring to a simmer. Add the clams, cooking them until they are opened. Remove from the flame, add the cooked fusilli and the poached asparagus to the casserole, tossing them about with the clams and their liquors.

Return the casserole to a low flame for a few seconds only to warm the juices before carrying the whole to table and serving it into warmed shallow bowls.

Offer a simple white wine—cold and unfazed by the challenge of the asparagus—and oven-toasted bread for the garlicky liquors.

Crema di Ricotta

A SAVORY RICOTTA CREAM

Serves 4 to 6 as a fine pasto, an end to the meal

3 ounces mild, creamy goat's milk cheese such as banon, montra-
　　chet, or boucheron from France, caprini from Italy, or any
　　one of the American-made beauties from Napa Valley,
　　Sonoma County, Wisconsin, Maine, New York, or Vermont
6 ounces very fresh, whole-milk ricotta
6 ounces mascarpone
Dark honey (buckwheat, chestnut, etc.)
OR
Marmellata di limone (page 99)

Whip the 3 cheeses together to a light, smooth cream in the work bowl of a food processor fitted with a steel blade. Turn the blended cheese out into a crock or a serving bowl, cover it tightly with plastic wrap, and hold it in the refrigerator until 1 hour before presentation.

　　　Permit the cheese to warm to room temperature and serve it with a pitcher of warmed honey or the *marmellata di limone* and a basket of oven-toasted bread. One mantles the warm, crunchy bread with the cheese, threading it with the honey or dragging it through a tiny plot of the *marmellata* on his plate, wondering why one might end a civilized supper with any other thing.

PUGLIA

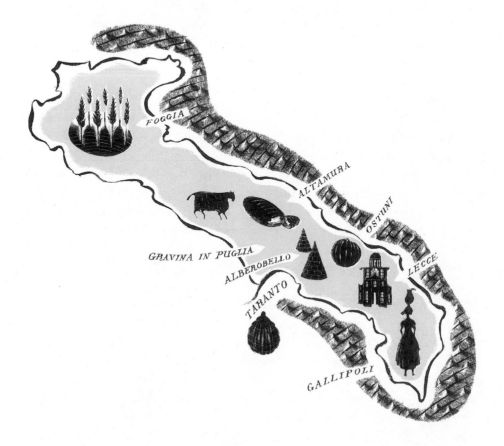

Greece marked Puglia everlastingly. After their life inside Magna Graecia, the parishes of Puglia were splintered by the cultural and political tramplings of itinerant lords. Each port, each city, inhaled the temper of a different invasion and thus remained isolated, localized, different from one another, betrothed only by a fundamental Greek sap. Taranto, Otranto, Ostuni, Gallipoli, Bari, Foggia, Brindisi, were raised up by Greece and, though physical evidences are peculiarly, unaccountably sparse—save a Doric temple at Taranto and, sometimes, a Cretanesque penchant for the piling up of its humble edifices into white-washed villages that look out to the sea—spiritual imprints are conspicuous. The dialect is mantled in Greek phrase, faces are beset with eyes *tagliati come un greco*—cut like a Greek's. How Puglia cooks and how it eats, how it thinks, some say, are all heirlooms pure, undis-guised from Greece. Also are the provinces of Puglia made kindred by their indulgent forests of olives, primeval gardens whose tribute of fat, yellow juice is common balm.

Ancient, tameless are the olive trees. Leaves dark, nearly black, and unpowdered in the pale wispiness of northern trees, they pose spookishly under the moon. Plantations of them edge onto the seas, onto the road, intrude upon the vines. Tortured, hulking grotesques, they embrace, sometimes, one reaching out to another, entwining their great, lamenting fronds for succor. Two, three, and more thousands of years have they stayed there, another kind of temple. Brave, virtuous things, one thinks. Yet they are twigs, still, in the Neolithic face of the menhir, the dolmen, *specchie*, the *trulli* of the plains and the forests of the Salento, the Murgia.

Ten-thousand-year-old witnesses are these stones—monoliths, primitive obelisks, curious tombs and towers, conical huts—sacred, magical expressions of an elf child while he waited for the trees and the vines. Puglia was already an old beard when other Italian civilities were saying matins. I suppose—it is a thing evenhanded, then—that it be there in the tiny Pugliese port of Santa Maria di Leuca, hung from the heel tap of the old boot, that Italy slips, all at once, into the waters of the Mediterranean, the Ionian, the Adriatic, as though only the force of three seas could convince her to rest, to call a truce for a while, with history.

About the Olive Oil of Puglia

In Puglia, olives are harvested from nets laid under the trees to trap the fallen, ripened fruit. One climbs up into the tree brandishing a great sort of wooden fork that one thrusts at the laden branches, loosening, compelling the black, mature fruit to fall, bruised and battered, into the nets below. The fruit is then recovered by those who, bodies folded, heads bent, race from tree to tree, separating the olives from their twigs and leaves, placing them in shallow, curved baskets and, finally, pouring them into the fifty-kilo sacks in which they will be ported to the *frantoio*—the olive-pressing mill.

Oil pressed from this ripened, fallen fruit is higher in acidity than the juice pressed from fruit hand-harvested before it is fully matured—the methodology practiced, for instance, in Tuscany. The oils that result from these dissimilar procedures of harvest and from fruit in different stages of ripeness are as unlike each other as are the cuisines to which they are fundamental.

The sober, pure, unornamented foods of Tuscany are glorified by threads and tears of its own pristine oil, often green as jade and giving up the perfume of just-crushed hazelnuts and leaving, on the tongue, the stringent savor of a crisp, young artichoke.

The often piquant, fire-spiced dishes typical of Puglia are built in concert with their harsher, more ponderous and aggressive oil. The virtues, or lack thereof, of the oils cannot be compared any more than can the dishes prepared with them. They are each of their own place, each the bounty of their own philosophical and gastronomic culture.

Though I believe that oil pressed from the fruit of the trees in the lands of the Chianti is the earth's most divine, to weave it into the foods of another region can be to dishonor it, to disperse its dimensions, its subtleties. There is greater probability that one will cook genuinely, authentically, the dishes of a given region by employing as many of its own intrinsic components as are available. If one is presenting a dish of Sicilia, a wine from the Val d'Aosta will likely not enlarge upon its goodness stylistically, aromatically, even spiritually, as will a wine made from the fruit of Sicilia's own soil. It is the same with olive oil. Hence, here cook with the oil of Puglia and with the oil of Sicilia or Toscana or Liguria or Lago di Garda when you are working with the recipes of these regions. Smell the oils, taste them raw, taste them with a bit of good, honest bread. Many of the complexities, the mysteries even, of regional cooking will be unmasked to you by this simple ceremony. A region's own oil is no less sacred to its table than is its own wine, than are its own stories.

La Cultura dell' Antipasteria
THE CULTURE OF THE ANTIPASTERIA

Washed in white and in silence and flung out over three hills is beautiful Ostuni, an Arab Casbah, sleepy and bespangled in stars. And down and up and down one of her alleyways, set in an old *forno*, a bakery, is the Osteria del Tempo Perso—Tavern of Lost Time. We climbed the steep steps into Teo Carlucci's little house and were enchanted. Every centimeter of its space is comforted with bounty of the Salento. Festoons of tiny, dried tomatoes, cheeses, *salame*, braids of garlic and violet onions and red chiles, dried flowers and drying herbs, were hung from its rafters, its rough, stone walls. Baskets of breads and handmade pasta, vinegar jugs and jars of olive oil, tubs of brined olives, barrels filled with yellow peppers and redheaded mushrooms and gnarly potatoes unwashed of their Salentine earth were there. Too, there was a great twig basket filled with *poponi*, the tiny, high-perfumed, pinky-orange-fleshed melons so celebrated in Ostuni. And there in that sort of paradisical place, under Teo's guidance, is practiced the Salentine culture of the *antipasteria*—the ceremony of bringing forth small plates, of ten or twelve or so presentations of teasing flavors that might compose a formidable meal, yet, there, perform only as lubrication for the appetite before the main courses. There were little pots of sizzling mushrooms, tiny braised artichokes, their hearts plied with anchovy, smoked sardines, aged sheep's milk ricotta, bits of savory dried sausage, vinegary vegetable marmalades, little sweet/sour chile-fired sauces and bits of just-fried bread dough all puffed, crisped, to pop-in-the-mouth, still too hot to chew, but we, chewing anyway, loved its rough, salty abuse. Here follow, then, three versions of typical *antipasti* of Ostuni.

La Rustichella

The Pastry

14 tablespoons sweet butter, lightly softened, plus 1 teaspoon
   for the pan
1 large egg, lightly beaten
6 tablespoons dry white wine
2⅔ cups all-purpose flour
½ teaspoon sugar
1 teaspoon fine sea salt
⅓ cup fine polenta meal
Flour

In a large bowl with a wooden spoon, beat the 14 tablespoons of the butter until it is soft and creamy. Add the egg and the wine and beat to blend. Add the remaining components except for 1 teaspoon butter, blending them lightly. Turn the mixture out onto a lightly floured surface, gently pressing it into a rough dough and rolling it into a ball. Flatten the ball into a disk and wrap the dough tightly in plastic wrap, permitting it to rest in the refrigerator for 1 hour or even overnight if it's more convenient.

     With 1 teaspoon of butter, grease the surface of a 9-inch tart pan with a removable bottom. Roll two-thirds of the dough—rewrapping the remaining one-third and returning it to the refrigerator—into a circle about 11 inches in diameter and transfer it to the tart pan, fitting it in snugly, permitting the excess to drape over the sides. Cover the pan tightly with plastic wrap and refrigerate it for 1 hour. Meanwhile, make the filling.

The Filling

4 ounces anchovies, preserved under salt
1 pound *baccalà* or *stoccafisso*, prepared (page 10)
⅓ cup heavy cream
⅓ cup plus 2 teaspoons extra-virgin olive oil
3 large yellow onions, peeled and thinly sliced
4 ounces large black Greek or Sicilian olives, stones removed by
   lightly crushing them with a mallet, coarsely chopped

2 tablespoons capers preserved under salt, rinsed and dried

1 large egg yolk

Rinse the anchovies. Remove their heads and bones, dry them on paper towels, and crush lightly with a fork. Set aside.

Place the soaked, rinsed, poached, drained, rinsed, skinned, and boned *baccalà* into a bowl and, with two forks, finely shred the fish. Add the cream and blend the components well. Set the bowl aside.

In a large sauté pan over a medium flame, warm ⅓ cup of the olive oil and soften the onions to transparency, taking care not to color them. Add the anchovies, the olives, and the capers and toss them about with the onions for a minute or two. Add the mixture to the bowl with the *baccalà* and blend the components well.

Turn out the mixture into the pastry-lined tin. Roll out the remaining one-third of the dough into a 9½-inch circle and place it over the filling. Turn down the edges of the pastry lining to meet the top crust, crimping them together to encase the filling. Beat 2 teaspoons of the oil into the egg yolk and, with a pastry brush, paint the surface of the tart, conserving a spoonful of it for later.

Bake the tart for 45 to 50 minutes or until the crust is deeply golden. Paint the hot, hot surface of the tart with another coat of the glaze and permit the tart to cool on a rack for 20 minutes before removing its sides and letting it cool thoroughly.

Present the tart at room temperature in generous wedges as a first course. Serve it, too, as a main course with jugs of cold white wine and a salad of bitter greens dressed in good oil and lemon juice. Also, it makes a handsome and most portable pie to accompany one on some after-dark adventure.

Insalata di Patate e Cipolle Arrositite sotto la Cenere

A SALAD OF POTATOES AND ONIONS ROASTED UNDER THE ASHES

Serves 4

A smoky char permeates the potatoes and the onions and this, fusing with the brininess of the capers and olives and anchovies, gives up luscious flavors.

4 anchovies, preserved under salt

3 fat cloves garlic, peeled and crushed

1½ teaspoons coarse sea salt

½ cup plus 3 tablespoons extra-virgin olive oil

Juice of 1 lemon

6 medium red- or white-skinned potatoes

4 medium violet-skinned onions

8 ounces large green or black Sicilian or Greek olives, stones
   removed by lightly crushing them with a wooden mallet,
   coarsely chopped

¼ cup capers preserved under salt, rinsed and dried

⅓ cup torn flat parsley leaves

Freshly cracked pepper

Rinse the anchovies, remove their heads and bones, dry on paper towels, and crush lightly with a fork.

With a mezzaluna or a very sharp knife, mince the garlic with the salt to a fine paste and place it in a large bowl. Beat in the oil, the juice of the lemon, and the anchovies, making a rough sauce. Set the bowl aside.

Wash and dry the potatoes and massage them lightly with the oil. Bury the potatoes in the embers of a wood fire.

Without peeling the onions, slice them about 1 inch thick horizontally, brush them with a bit of the oil, position them on a grate, and roast them over a wood fire, about 5 to 6 minutes on each side until they are nicely charred and softened. Slip the skins from the onions, separate the slices into rings, and place them immediately into the fragrant sauce, turning them about, coating them well.

When the potatoes are roasted through, permit them to cool a few minutes until you can almost comfortably relieve them of their skins. Chop them coarsely and add to the bowl, tossing them about with the onions before adding the olives, capers, and parsley and giving the mix another good turn.

Grind pepper generously over the salad and present it at room temperature or cold. The potatoes can, of course, be thickly sliced and roasted on the grill with the onions.

Fagottini di Finocchio e Pancetta al Forno

PANCETTA-WRAPPED ROASTED FENNEL

Serves 4

4 small or 2 larger bulbs fennel

2 teaspoons coarse sea salt

8 to 12 thin slices pancetta

2 tablespoons extra-virgin olive oil

4 ounces large black Greek or Sicilian olives, stones removed by
 crushing them lightly with a mallet, coarsely chopped

2 cups heavy cream

½ cup dry white wine

2 teaspoons aniseeds, crushed

1 tablespoon fennel seeds, crushed

Freshly cracked pepper

⅔ cup just-grated pecorino

⅔ cup just-made fine bread crumbs

Remove the fronds from the bulbs of fennel, chop them coarsely, and set them aside. Trim the stem ends of the fennel and slice the bulbs in two if they are small, or in thirds, if they are somewhat larger. Place the fennel, the fronds, and the salt in a large pot, barely covering all with cold water. Cover the pot and, over a medium flame, bring to a gentle simmer, poaching the fennel for 5 to 7 minutes or until it only begins to soften. Drain the fennel, discarding the fronds, and lay them on a work space.

Over a lively flame, sauté the pancetta in the olive oil, crisping it a bit before removing it to absorbent paper towels. Reserve the pan drippings. Preheat the oven to 400 degrees. Wrap each piece of poached fennel with a slice of pancetta, securing it with a toothpick, and lay the wrapped fennel in a single layer in a large, shallow terra-cotta or enameled cast-iron gratin dish. Strew the fennel with the olives.

In a bowl, blend the cream and the wine with the anise and fennel seeds, adding generous grindings of pepper. Pour the liquids evenly over the fennel. Dust the whole with the pecorino and the bread crumbs and drizzle the dish with the reserved pan drippings.

Roast the fennel for 40 minutes or until it has drunk in nearly all the liquids, a good burnished crust has formed from the cheese and the bread crumbs, and bits of lightly charred pancetta are poking through it all.

The perfume of this dish is a raging heartbreaker. Present it very warm with very cold white wine as an antipasto or as a first course. In any case, it deserves one's attention, to be eaten on its own.

Sei Paste del Salentino Bagnato dai Tre Mari

SIX PASTAS OF THE SALENTINO DRENCHED BY THREE SEAS

The Salento is the heel of the peninsula, a small jut of land licked by the salty effluences of the Mediterranean, the Adriatic, and the Ionion Seas. A coast of primitive, contained beauty, it is a pathway carved by fairies, one thinks. Its endless seasides, flanked as they are by low, tilting stone walls—the round, flat rocks piled artlessly—seem the work of a brigade of children staking out a playland in the wilderness. The folk themselves of Puglia seem characters lost from some ancient fable, a cast of small, swarthy rogues, sentinels against some old torment, some long-expected foreboding, they seem, as they race about the place. We went, one day, in search of more of this Salento, setting out from Lecce, past baroque villas, past the abandoned *masserie*—the stone farmhouses of the eighteenth-century feudal lords—landing at a village stilted up on the edges of the Ionian called Santa Maria al Bagno—Saint Mary of the Bath. We lunched under the gazebo at Paglialunga, a simple osteria a few meters from the sea, snuffing up platefuls of oysters and clams with a cold, stone pitcher of local *rosato* before attending to a pasta in a paste of orange-perfumed sun-dried tomatoes. We left the little house intending to walk to the nearby ruins of some fifth-century towers. Just outside the door, though, we saw a small gathering of the same people who had earlier been at table near us, they hunched round a cart of some sort, an old man in a blue beret holding court. We stood near them, watching as they scooped out and sucked at the orange flesh of the prickled sea urchins the fisherman had just harvested and had come to sell. We, too, paid his modest sums for the privilege of slipping the cool, sweet, crunchy stuff down our throats. On one after another and another of the urchins did we feast until the fisherman's buckets were bare. Almost sated, oversated, we walked down a sand path to the sea, washing our hands and faces in the briny, cerulean water. And there, laying our blowsy bodies across the pitted volcanic rocks, we slept like two plumped babies under a five o'clock sun, a soft, sibilant Ionian wind our coverlet.

Pasta alle Mandorle e Pomodorini Secchi di Santa Maria al Bagno

PASTA WITH ALMONDS AND SUN-DRIED TOMATOES IN THE MANNER OF SAINT MARY OF THE BATH

Serves 4

4 fat cloves garlic, peeled and crushed

Zest of 1 large orange, removed in strips with a potato peeler

⅔ cup extra-virgin olive oil

4 ounces blanched almonds, coarsely chopped

1 small, dried red chile pepper, crushed, or ⅓ to ½ teaspoon dried chile flakes

1 cup good red wine

4 ounces sun-dried tomatoes, drained of their oil and thinly shredded

4 ounces dried black olives, stones removed

12 ounces bucatini or other dried string pasta

Coarse sea salt for the water

1 handful of torn basil leaves

With a mezzaluna or a very sharp knife, mince the garlic and the zest to a paste.

In a sauté pan over a medium flame, heat the olive oil and add the almonds, sautéing them a minute or two in the oil, taking care not to let them get too dark. Remove from the flame and add the garlic/orange paste and the crushed chile, stirring them about and permitting them to scent the oil and the almonds. Set the pan aside.

In a small saucepan, heat the wine and add the sun-dried tomatoes and the dried olives, bringing the mixture just to a simmer. Remove the pan from the flame, cover it, and permit the tomatoes and the olives to plump up a bit for 10 minutes. Remove the tomatoes and the olives with a slotted spoon and add them to the sauté pan with the almonds. Reduce the remaining wine over a lively flame to a tablespoon or so and add it to the sauté pan.

Cook the pasta in abundant boiling, sea-salted water to al dente, draining it but leaving it somewhat wet. Transfer the pasta to a large, shallow, warmed bowl, tossing it with the just rewarmed sauce, coating each strand. Strew the pasta with a few torn leaves of basil and present it with good red wine.

Pasta Croccante e Liscia con i Ceci (Ciceri e Tria)

CRISP AND SMOOTH PASTA WITH CHICKPEAS

Serves 4

Made from handmade whole wheat or egg pasta cut into wide ribbons—half of which are sautéed until golden in garlic and chile-scented oil then, along with the poached pasta, tossed with roasted almonds and chickpeas softened in a rosemary, garlic, and bay-scented bath. It is a beauty, the crisp, garlic-scented pasta against the soft, delicate ribbons of it with the mealy, nutty little chickpeas and the bitter almonds stitching them together into a plateful of fantasy conjured from homey stuffs.

>   8 ounces dried chickpeas
>   2 tablespoons coarse sea salt, plus additional as needed
>   1 large branch of rosemary
>   1 large bay leaf
>   3 fat cloves garlic, unpeeled and crushed
>   10 ounces freshly made *pasta all' uovo*, egg pasta, cut into 1-inch
>   ribbons (or use a batch of just-made *mugnaia* (see page 38)
>   ½ cup extra-virgin olive oil
>   1 small, dried red chile pepper, crushed, or ⅓ to ½ teaspoon
>   dried chile flakes
>   3 fat cloves garlic, peeled and crushed
>   ½ cup blanched almonds, toasted and coarsely chopped

Rinse the chickpeas in cold water, place them in a large pot, and cover them with cold water. Add 1 tablespoon of the sea salt to the pot and bring the chickpeas to a simmer. Cover the pot and permit the chickpeas an hour's rest.

Drain the chickpeas, covering them anew with cold water, adding the remaining 1 tablespoon of salt, the rosemary, the bay leaf, and the unpeeled garlic. Bring to a gentle simmer and poach the chickpeas until they are tender but still holding their shape. Drain the chickpeas, conserving a ½ cup or so of their cooking liquid. Set them aside.

Cook the pasta in abundant boiling, sea-salted water to al dente. Drain it but leave it somewhat wet and return it to its cooking pot.

In a large sauté pan over a medium flame, warm the olive oil, perfuming it with the crushed chile and then softening the garlic, permitting it to take on some light color before discarding it. Let the chile remain. Sauté half the pasta in the scented oil, tossing it about until it is crisp. Remove the pasta to a large, shallow bowl. Add the chickpeas and the remaining pasta to the sauté pan, along with the reserved cooking liquids from the chickpeas, tossing the mixture about for a few seconds to warm before adding it, along with the pan juices, to the pasta in the bowl. Toss again with the toasted almonds. The dish should be quite warm when presented.

Orecchiette con Rape e Cavolfiore

PASTA WITH BITTER GREENS AND CAULIFLOWER

Serves 4

Orecchiette—little ears—are a pasta made from grano duro, *or semolina, and served often with a rough sauce of* cima di rape, *the bitter leaves of a variety of Italian turnip not always available in America. Do not mistake them for young broccoli, as some do. Should the real thing not be at hand, it is a better business to substitute dandelion or beet or turnip greens or red chard or even to make the sauce only with cauliflower, especially the grassy-green, purply-edged Roman variety.*

> 1 small head white or green cauliflower
> 2 tablespoons fine sea salt
> 1 pound *cima di rape* or dandelion greens, beet greens, or red chard
> 2 ounces anchovies, preserved under salt
> ⅔ cup extra-virgin olive oil
> 1 tablespoon fennel seeds
> 1 small, dried red chile pepper, crushed, or ⅓ to ½ teaspoon dried chile flakes
> 3 fat cloves garlic, peeled, crushed, and finely minced
> 3 ounces dried black olives, stones removed (optional)
> 12 ounces orecchiette
> Coarse sea salt for the pasta water
> 1 cup just-grated pecorino
> 1 cup just-made fine bread crumbs, sautéed in ¼ cup extra-virgin olive oil

Trim the cauliflower of its leaves and place it, whole, in a pot, covering it with cold water, adding 1 tablespoon of the fine sea salt and poaching it until tender. Drain the cauliflower and set it aside. Wash and trim the *rape* and place them in a pot, covering them with cold water, adding the remaining tablespoon of salt and poaching them for 3 minutes. Drain the *rape* very well, transferring them to absorbent paper towels. When the *rape* are cooled a bit, squeeze each piece, extracting as much water as you can before chopping them coarsely and placing them in a bowl. Add the poached cauliflower, breaking it up and blending it lightly with the *rape.*

Rinse the anchovies and remove their heads and bones. Dry them on paper towels and crush lightly with a fork.

In a sauté pan over a medium flame, warm the olive oil, scenting it with the fennel, crushed chile, and garlic, taking care not to color the garlic. Add the anchovies and the olives, if you wish to use them, stirring and blending the components. Add this hot mixture to the bowl with the *rape* and the cauliflower, smashing the whole against the sides of the bowl, permitting the vegetables to inhale the hot, spicy bath.

Cook the orecchiette in abundant, sea-salted water until al dente, draining the pasta but leaving it somewhat wet. Reserve ½ cup or so of its cooking liquids. Transfer the pasta to a large, shallow, warmed bowl. Add a few tablespoons of the cooking liquids and the pecorino to the sauce, thinning it only slightly. Add a few drops more of the cooking liquids only if the sauce is still extremely thick. Add the sauce to the pasta, tossing it and coating each little ear.

Dust the pasta with the browned bread crumbs and present the dish with a rough but honorable red wine.

Pasta alle Cozze e Capperi

PASTA WITH MUSSELS AND CAPERS

Serves 4

Mussels unfettered by garlic taste more like their own sweet, turgid selves. On the tiny porch of the seaside bar where we ate this pasta, the cook who was the mussel gatherer who was the bartender who was the pastrymaker added crushed, dried seaweed to the finished dish. He cooked the mussels and the pasta over a fire he'd built of driftwood a few meters from the bar. It was a fairly good-sized blaze, ample enough to heat an old cauldron along with the mussel pot, it bubbling with a potion of wild myrtle berries in which he immersed a great, gray fish net, tinting it, cooking it to a deep, bright blue.

12 ounces bucatini or other dried string pasta

Coarse sea salt for the water

½ cup extra-virgin olive oil

1 tablespoon fennel seeds, crushed

1 tablespoon rosemary leaves, minced

24 mussels, scrubbed, bearded, and dried

1½ cups dry white wine

¼ cup good-quality white wine vinegar

4 ounces dried black olives, stones removed

¼ cup capers, preserved under salt, rinsed, and dried

1 cup just-made fine bread crumbs, sautéed in ¼ cup extra-virgin
   olive oil

Cook the pasta in abundant boiling, sea-salted water to al dente, draining it but leaving it somewhat wet and transferring it back to its cooking pot to await its sauce.

While the water for the pasta reaches the boil, attend to the mussels. In a very large, heavy pot over a medium flame, warm the olive oil and scent it with the fennel and rosemary. Add the mussels and roll them about in the oil for a minute or two before adding the wine and the vinegar and bringing it all to a simmer. Cover the pot and steam the mussels, removing them with a slotted spoon to a deep bowl as they open. Over a lively flame, reduce the mussel-cooking liquors for 2 or 3 minutes.

Remove from the flame. Add the olives and the capers and reacquaint the mussels with their sauce. Add the cooked pasta to the pot, tossing it about with the mussels and the sauce for a few seconds only to warm it. Turn the whole out into a warmed, shallow bowl, dusting it with the golden bread crumbs.

Pasta in Nero della Consolazione

PASTA IN BLACK

Serves 4

We had been in Puglia and its environs nearly a month. Sapped from our journeys, our palates debauched into slumber from the opiate of too many chile peppers, our wits palled from nightly Circean cups, we needed redemption from the table. We asked each other what would soothe. Surely we needed to stop driving. Fernando wanted pastina in brodo— tiny pasta cooked in broth. I wanted a small custard pie, warm, soft. I wanted bread and butter. We both wanted to be in a place with not one more three-thousand-year-old olive tree. We wanted sympathy more than we wanted supper. And there we were, lost in Otranto.

When finally we asked the same giornalaio, newspaper seller, for directions to our intended destination of Melpignano for the third time and got the third different answer, we thought it a good thing to surrender our search for the unnamed, unsigned place there that had been pressed upon us by our friends in Lecce and simply brake at the next and nearest little place with even the thinnest promise about it. Finding it, we tumbled out of the car, shuffled up the drive and asked if there might be a room for us. The cheery little man took our things, showed us up the stairs, started up the heater for the bathwater and began the reverent story of his wife's genius in the kitchen. I saw Fernando's face fading a bit toward citrine. Swooning, I tried so to smile at the even cheerier little man through my narrowing vision. He began his pastoral roundelay with her pigeons braised in red wine and juniper, on to her lamb roasted with potatoes and wild mushrooms, before coming to the rhapsody of her way with goats' hearts poached in white wine and lemon. Fernando was nearly able to deflect him with an inquiry about the era of his handsome stone house before he began the lip-smacking tale of the pigs' livers roasted on branches of bay. We closed the door.

We took a bath. As we were dressing, the cheery little man knocked gently. They were waiting for us—he, his wife the cook, his son the university student, his brother the hunter, his friend the winemaker. They'd thought, since there were no other guests, we might dine together, make a real celebration of the evening. They had laid a beautiful fire and lit candles upon a narrow, wooden, unclothed table set for seven. They were so sweet, so excited by our presence, for their own clever spontaneity, for the prospect of a long winter's evening to be passed at table. Fernando rallied and began nibbling at a creamy heft of new pecorino sitting on a crisp white cloth next to our aperitivi. I followed the lady into her kitchen, unraveling our adventures in a nervous sort of monologue. Rather than sympathy, she offered her envy. "Beati voi, tutti questi giorni in giro, sempre a ristoranti." "Blessed are you, all these days running about, always in restaurants." I thought to be more direct. "You know," I said, averting my eyes from the legs of lamb she was basting, "what I would like most this evening is to eat something simple and comforting. I feel like a tired child." She looked at me for the first time, really looked at me, heard me. She wrapped her great, fleshy arms about me, crushing me to her moist, rosemary-perfumed bosom. She had understood. She marched me back to the table with instructions to sit quietly, sipping at the winemaker's best red and to wait.

After a half an hour's sashaying to and from the kitchen with the first of the feast's plates, the lady, her broad olive cheeks blushing up to the corners of her dark eyes, carried in a small, white porcelain bowl with its own cover and set it down before me. I lifted the lid, unloosing the scents of cinnamon and butter and perhaps of chocolate, which curled up through a tangle of pale yellow noodles swathed in a curiously dark sort of sauce. "Ecco la pasta in nero," she exclaimed. "There it is, pasta in black." She went on to say that here, in this part of the Salento, it was the dish characteristically offered at wakes and vigils, a dish of consolation, a balmy comfort for all the rages of childhood. The truth is, she said, growing up or growing old never meant we couldn't, shouldn't, be children anymore. I served myself from the pretty white bowl and ate, first gingerly, then with new appetite, one of the loveliest dishes imaginable. Pale, silky pasta, creamy ricotta, crisped, golden buttered crumbs of bread, all of it cheered by an almost treacly sort of taste I couldn't quite place. The cook told me it was vin cotto, cooked wine, a thick, nearly black syrup made by the slow cooking of grape must. Restored, revived, I drank some more of the winemaker's best red, and when I'd nearly drained it, I softened a few hard almond biscuits in its ruddy dregs. And so it was on that winter's night that we seven celebrated together, each one being nourished by the others' open hearts. It was what supper was always meant to be.

Here follows a version of pasta in nero, a universal cure, I think, it being warm, soft, creamy, cinnamon-perfumed, chocolated-dusted with the primitive solace of buttered toast, all in a single, encouraging dish.

1 cup moscato di Pantelleria or other sweet, ambered wine

12 ounces whole-milk ricotta

1 teaspoon fine sea salt

Zest of 1 lemon, very finely shredded

1½-inch stick of cinnamon, ground

Generous grindings of fresh pepper

12 ounces pasta all' uovo, egg pasta, cut into 1-inch ribbons

Coarse sea salt for the water

1 cup just-made bread crumbs, pan-roasted in 2 tablespoons
  sweet butter

2 teaspoons cocoa powder, preferably Dutch process

In a small saucepan over a lively flame, reduce the sweet wine, sending its vapors up to the angels. Lower the flame a bit and continue to cook it until about 3 tablespoons of dense syrup remain. Be very careful not to burn it.

In a large, shallow bowl, combine the cooked wine with the ricotta, sea salt, lemon zest, cinnamon, and pepper, blending the elements well.

Cook the pasta in abundant, boiling, sea-salted water to al dente, draining it but leaving it somewhat wet and reserving ½ cup of the cooking liquids.

Add the pasta to the ricotta mixture along with a few tablespoons of the reserved cooking liquids. Toss it about, coating each ribbon thoroughly. Dust the pasta with the buttered crumbs and sieve the cocoa over all, presenting it warm with glasses of cold sweet wine for the older children and, perhaps, some warm cocoa for the younger ones.

Una Pasta Estiva

A SUMMERTIME PASTA

Serves 4

4 ounces anchovies, preserved under salt

8 ounces canned oil-packed tuna (preferably an Italian import
    marked *"ventresca,"* signifying the flesh was cut from the belly
    of the fish), drained of its preserving oil and gently shredded

¼ cup capers preserved under salt, rinsed and dried

1 small violet-skinned onion, peeled and very finely minced

2 fat cloves garlic, peeled, crushed, and very finely minced

1½ pounds ripe tomatoes, peeled, seeded, and finely chopped

1 teaspoon fine sea salt, plus additional for the water

1 small, dried red chile pepper, crushed, or ⅓ to ½ teaspoon
    dried chile flakes

½ cup extra-virgin olive oil

Juice of 1 lemon

12 ounces penne or other short tubular pasta

½ cup fresh oregano leaves

½ cup torn flat parsley leaves

Rinse the anchovies. Remove the head and bones, dry on paper towels, and crush lightly with a fork. In a large bowl, combine the tuna, anchovies, capers, onion, garlic, tomatoes, salt, chile, olive oil, and lemon juice. Cover the bowl and let the ingredients mingle for an hour or more.

Cook the pasta in abundant, boiling, sea-salted water to al dente, draining it but leaving it somewhat wet.

Transfer the pasta to a large, shallow bowl. Toss the warm pasta with the cool sauce, carefully coating each strand. Present the pasta then or later, at room temperature. In either case, strew the pasta with the leaves of oregano and parsley just before serving it.

La Puddica Brindisina

THE FLATBREADS OF BRINDISI (SMALL SEMOLINA FLATBREADS
WITH BITTER GREENS, ANCHOVIES, AND BLACK OLIVES)

Makes 12 small breads

Brindisi, the ancient Brundisium of the Romans, is a sort of rough, emotionally bankrupt port city. Still, we like to walk and sit, sometimes, on the edges of its rickety old wharfs early of a morning to inhale the bright, briny tableau of the place. And round about eight-thirty—high noon for the fishermen, who rise before the sun—we wait to see the baker's boy running down the docks, toting a great basket of puddica—*traditional Brindisino flatbreads—just born and sending up great hungering perfumes for the fishermen's lunch. It seemed to us the highest form of ceremony left in the dour old place.*

The Dough

2½ teaspoons active dry yeast or 1 small cake fresh yeast

⅓ cup warm water

2½ cups tepid water

¼ cup extra-virgin olive oil

2 tablespoons heavy cream

1 tablespoon plus 1 teaspoon fine sea salt

3 cups *farina di grano duro* (hard durum wheat flour), which is
semolina ("pasta flour")

4½ cups all-purpose flour

In a large bowl, stir the yeast into the warm water, permitting it to rest and dissolve for 15 minutes.

In a small bowl, combine the tepid water, the oil, the cream, and the sea salt.

Combine the flours and add them, with the liquids, to the rested yeast, working the components into a rough dough.

Turn it out into a lightly floured work surface, kneading it into soft, smooth dough. The task takes at least 8 minutes. Transfer the dough to a lightly oiled bowl, cover it with plastic wrap and permit it to rise for 1 hour or until the dough has doubled.

Now, turn to the toppings.

The Toppings

1½ pounds *cima di rape*, dandelion greens, beet or turnip greens, or red
    chard
1 tablespoon coarse sea salt
6 ounces anchovies, preserved under salt
¾ cup extra-virgin olive oil
3 fat cloves garlic, peeled, crushed, and finely minced
1 small, dried red chile pepper, crushed, or ⅓ to ½ teaspoon dried
    chile flakes
6 ounces large black or green Sicilian or Greek olives, crushed lightly
    with a mallet, stones removed, and chopped coarsely

Wash and trim the *rape* and place them in a pot, covering them with cold water, adding the tablespoon of sea salt and poaching them for 3 minutes. Drain the *rape* very well, transferring them to absorbent paper towels. When the *rape* are cooled a bit, squeeze each piece, extracting as much water as you can before chopping them coarsely and setting them aside.

Rinse the anchovies. Remove the heads and bones, dry them on paper towels, and crush lightly with a fork.

In a large sauté pan over a medium flame, heat ½ cup of the olive oil, scenting it with the garlic and the chile, softening the garlic but taking care not to color it. Add the poached, chopped *rape*, rolling it about in the perfumed oil for 2 minutes before adding the anchovies and the olives, tossing it all together, permitting the components a minute or two to become acquainted. Set the pan aside.

Preheat the oven to 425 degrees.

Divide the risen dough into 12 pieces, rolling each of them into a ball. Permit the balls a 10-minute rest under a clean kitchen towel before flattening them with your knuckles, stretching them into rustic little rounds of about 5 to 6 inches in diameter. Let the breads rest under a towel once again for 10 minutes. Give the rounds a final dimpling with your knuckles, brushing each with a bit of the remaining ¼ cup of olive oil. Give each a generous dose of the topping.

Bake the breads on parchment-lined baking sheets or on preheated baking stones for 15 to 18 minutes or until they are golden-edged. Pile the *puddica* immediately into a basket and serve them hot or permit them to cool on racks to serve at room temperature. In any case, don't ask them to wait more than 1 hour.

Il Pranzo di Pasquetta all'Aria Aperta
THE EASTER MONDAY PICNIC

Not that of Palermo nor Napoli nor Roma, the grandest, most unblushing of all Baroque expression sits tenderly, ingenuously in the city of Lecce. Finer, sweeter, more fluent, more garrulous, even, are the stories carved from the soft, honeyed Leccese stones. There one feels less the sort of fencing charlatanism of High Baroque and more the shivery sentimentality of that epoch's passion. One thinks to come closer to the intentions of the work, that even some candid conference, some tête-à-tête, might be possible with the unreserved prettiness of the slant-eyed mistresses, the laurel-crowned patriarchs. One feels invited, impelled, to purloin a pomegranate from a capital of Santa Croce. Lecce seems all of happiness. And of a morning there, one celebrates life, too, in the Pasticceria Alvino.

Tucked off to the side on the Piazza di Sant' Oronzo, its little portal is the threshold to a libertine's salon. Every sort of pastry and sweet and nut and fruit drenched in slippery syrups and powdered in the dusts of yet more sugar are laid out for the taking. And it was there, over a tray of warm ricotta tarts and *caffè* beguiled with Grand Marnier, that we were summoned to partake in a most traditional Leccese event, the great exodus from the city on the day after Easter for the rite of Pasquetta—little Easter—observed with a picnic by the sea.

Frittata con Asparagi Selvatici e Mentuccia

A COLD OMELETTE WITH WILD ASPARAGUS AND MINT

Serves 4

Made with bruscandoli, *hop shoots, should their wisp of a season embrace Easter. If not, one searches out the first, slimmest shoots of asparagus.*

> 1 pound fresh asparagus, trimmed, stem ends scraped, cut into
>   2-inch lengths
> Coarse sea salt for the water
> 6 large eggs
> ½ teaspoon fine sea salt
> Freshly cracked pepper
> 1 tablespoon dry white wine
> ½ cup just-grated pecorino
> ½ cup fresh mint leaves, half of them torn, half left whole
> ¼ cup extra-virgin olive oil
> 1 fat clove garlic, peeled, crushed, and finely minced

Cover the asparagus with cold water, add sea salt, and bring to a simmer, poaching the asparagus until they are barely tender. The time will depend wholly upon the thickness of the stalks. Drain the asparagus and refresh them under very cold water to revive their color. Set them aside.

In a medium bowl, beat the eggs with the fine sea salt, generous grindings of pepper, the wine, the pecorino, and the torn mint leaves. Over a lively flame in an 8- to 10-inch skillet with an ovenproof handle, heat the oil. Sauté the poached asparagus, tossing them about in the oil for a minute or two before adding the garlic and softening it without permitting it to take on color.

Pour in the egg batter, tilting the pan to distribute it. Lower the flame only a bit and cook the frittata, lifting its cooked edges every once in a while, permitting the uncooked batter to flow beneath. When the underside is deeply crusted and golden, place the pan several inches beneath a very hot broiler, urging the top side to cook and bubble up a bit, taking on a fine bronzed skin.

Remove the pan from the oven and immediately slide the frittata onto a handsome plate. Present the frittata at room temperature or cold, ornamenting it with the whole leaves of mint.

Schiacciatine di Agnello e Patate sulle Brace

LAMB AND POTATO SAUSAGES GRILLED OVER A WOOD FIRE

Serves 4 to 6

3 fat cloves garlic, peeled and crushed

1½ tablespoons fresh rosemary leaves

1 tablespoon coarse sea salt

2 ounces pancetta

1 pound lamb, cut from the leg, finely minced

5 ounces fresh pork fat, ground

1 small, dried red chile pepper, crushed, or ⅓ to ½ teaspoon
  dried chile flakes

4 medium red- or white-skinned potatoes, boiled in sea-salted
  water until tender, peeled and mashed

1 1-inch stick of cinnamon, ground

⅓ cup dry white wine

Extra-virgin olive oil

With a mezzaluna or a very sharp knife, mince the garlic, rosemary, sea salt, and pancetta together to make a paste. In a large bowl, combine the paste with all the other ingredients save the wine and the olive oil, mixing them, kneading them with your hands, urging them into a fine, fragrant mixture. At the last, add the wine, blending it in thoroughly. Cover the mixture tightly with plastic wrap and permit its flavors to develop and mature overnight.

Shape the mixture into oval sausages, 3 inches long and 1½ inches thick. Brush them lightly with the oil and roast them over the red/white embers of a wood fire. Pan-sautéed in olive oil, they are nearly as good.

'n Capriata

A PUREE OF DRIED BEANS AND BITTER GREENS PRESENTED
WITH FRIED COUNTRY BREAD

Serves 6

Creamy evidence of how savory and seductive can be a naïve little pap made from a handful of dried beans.

8 ounces dried cannellini beans
8 ounces dried fava beans
5 tablespoons coarse sea salt
2 small branches of sage
½ cup plus ⅓ cup plus ½ cup extra-virgin olive oil
8 to 10 large sage leaves, torn
4 fat cloves garlic, peeled, crushed, and minced
1 small, dried red chile pepper, crushed, or ⅓ to ½ teaspoon
    dried chile flakes
2 teaspoons fine sea salt
2 tablespoons fennel seeds, crushed
⅓ cup heavy cream
1 tablespoon good red wine vinegar
1 pound *cima di rape* (page 115) or dandelion greens, mustard
    greens, or red chard
2 fat cloves garlic, peeled and crushed
12 ½-inch slices of good country bread

Each bean should be in its own pot. Cover the cannellini and the favas with cold water, adding 1 tablespoon of coarse sea salt and a branch of sage to each, and bring to a simmer. Cover the pots and permit the beans to soften for 1 hour. Drain the beans, again, each in their own pot, cover them anew with cold water, add another tablespoon of coarse sea salt to each pot and bring the beans to a simmer, poaching them until they are very tender and collapsing. Drain the beans, reserving a cup of their cooking liquids, combine them and set them aside.

      While the beans are cooking, you can attend to the oil that will eventually perfume them. In a small saucepan over a medium flame, warm ½ cup of the olive oil, adding the sage leaves, minced garlic, chile, 2 teaspoons fine sea salt, and fennel, rolling the components about for a minute, taking care that the garlic does not color. Set the perfumed oil aside.

      In a food processor fitted with a steel blade, process the beans, in batches if necessary, adding a few tablespoonfuls of the cooking liquids to form a thick, smooth paste.

Turn the paste out into a large bowl. With a wooden spoon, vigorously beat the perfumed oil into the paste, glossing and scenting it. Last, beat in the cream and the vinegar. Cover the paste with plastic wrap and chill it for several hours or overnight.

Wash and trim the *rape* and place them in a pot, covering them with cold water, adding 1 tablespoon coarse sea salt and poaching them for 3 minutes. Drain the *rape* very well, transferring them to absorbent paper towels. When the *rape* are cooled a bit, squeeze each piece, extracting as much water as you can before chopping them coarsely and setting them aside.

Just before serving *'n Capriata,* warm ⅓ cup of the oil over a lively flame in a sauté pan and sauté the crushed garlic, scenting the oil. Remove the garlic and discard it, add the *rape* and roll it about in the oil for a minute or two. In another sauté pan over a lively flame, heat the final dose, ½ cup, of oil and quickly sauté the bread on each side, giving it a good crust but leaving its interior crumb soft.

To present the dish, place two trenchers of the hot bread on a plate with some of the warm sautéed greens and then top the whole with generous spoonfuls of the chilled bean paste. In part, it is the play of the hot, crisp bread against the cold, smooth, lusciously perfumed puree, each of them relieved, fused, by the bitter greens between them, that makes the dish spectacular. More, though, I think it is so good for its unexpectedness.

Torta di Cioccolata Amara con Glasse di Anice della Pasticceria Alvino

AN ANISETTE-GLAZED BITTER CHOCOLATE TART
IN THE MANNER OF PASTICCERIA ALVINO

Serves 8

1 tart pastry recipe (page 216)

1½ cups heavy cream

10½ ounces extra-bittersweet chocolate, chopped, preferably
   Lindt or Valrhona 70% cacao

2 tablespoons cocoa powder, preferably Dutch process

2 large eggs plus 1 large egg yolk, lightly beaten

1 teaspoon aniseeds, crushed

1 tablespoon plus 2 teaspoons anise-scented liqueur

1 cup confectioners' sugar

1½ tablespoons milk

You will need a 10- to 12-inch tart pan with a removable bottom. It should be buttered and lined with the tart pastry. Chill it well, then bake at 400 degrees for 12 minutes. Cool thoroughly and set aside.

In a saucepan over a medium flame, bring the cream just to a simmer. Remove from the flame, add the chocolate, stirring to melt it. Permit the mixture to cool for 20 minutes.

Using a wire whip, beat in the cocoa and the eggs. Add the aniseeds and 1 tablespoon of the liqueur, whisking again. Pour the chocolate into the pastry and bake it at 375 degrees for 15 minutes or even a bit less, just until the chocolate forms a shiny skin and is beginning to firm but remains unset at its center. Cool the tart on a rack for 15 minutes, remove its sides and permit it to cool thoroughly.

Make the glaze by beating the confectioners' sugar with the milk and 2 teaspoons of the liqueur to a thin and pourable consistency. Add a few drops more of milk should the glaze be too thick. Drizzle the cooled tart with the glaze in a zigzag pattern and permit the glaze to harden. Present the tart with little glasses of anise liqueur.

La Gallipolina della Vedova

THE TRADITIONAL FISH SOUP OF GALLIPOLI
IN THE MANNER OF THE WIDOW

Serves 8 to 10

Once Kallipolis—"beautiful city" in Greek—Gallipoli is a tumult of white-chalked abodes heaped up under a feverish sun. A fishing village three thousand years ago and now—after its episodes with pirates and slavish dominions, its risings and its fallings—it is a fishing village still. Affixed to the newer town by a bridge, its oldest quarter is a quaint islet in the Ionian. And it was there that we first saw Rosaria.

It was in the pescheria (fish market). It was the late-afternoon market where the day's second catch—and what might have remained from the morning, at a smaller price—was offered. Admiring her confidence, her stroll over the slippery, sea-washed stones of the market floor, inspecting the gleanings—silently, unerringly, one thought—and transacting prices with the fishmongers only with her eyes. When she was convinced by something, she pulled coins and bills from a small pouch hung around her like a necklace, then positioned the parcels in a basket she carried atop her head, leaving her small, elegant hands free to repose on her hips, to move in agreement or discord or exclamation.

We dared to ask her the names of the more exotic offerings and, so encouraged by her gently spoken responses, we opened discourse on the celebrated fish soup of Gallipoli. Through her laugh, she told us that the allure of the soup seemed perplexing to her. It was, after all, a potful of humble fish. Nearly everyone cooked it, in one form or another, every day. "We cook what the sea gives up to us. It's our garden," she said. She told us she had cooked the soup for as long as she could remember, and that the perfumes of it being cooked by her mother and grandmother were older yet in her sensual memory. She volunteered news of her evening's program and said we might join her if we wished. She was to prepare a supper for three old friends, widows all, and molto simpatiche—most pleasant. She said we might meet her at 7:45 in front of Sant' Agata. Timid, pleased, we sealed our agreement. By then, the weak February sun was readying itself to slide into the sea, rosying the clouds in its path, bedazzling them in washes of gold. We watched her climb the curling road farther up into the old town until her narrow, top-lofty form melted into sweet lilac dusk. We looked at the last of the sunset from the terrace of a little bar, adding jackets and sweaters and scarves against the winds, sipping at red wine, imagining what would be our evening with her.

We found her in front of the cathedral and, following her the few meters to her door, were welcomed into her apartment in whose parlor we sat whilst she collected, arranged the soup's elements. Only then did she invite us into the kitchen. First, though, the ceremony of gli aperitivi—cold, pink wine poured into small, rounded crystal cups. Then was Rosaria ready to dance.

She set about by whacking the filleted fish—sea bass and red hogfish—into great chunks; she warmed oil in an old coccio, adding garlic, onion, and crushed salt anchovies. In the scented oil, she deftly browned the fish—removing it to await the second act—adding fat prawns, heads removed, tails intact, and rolled them about, flourishing her wooden spatula with a sort of spare drama and sending forth great sea-scented mists. She made the sauce by adding peeled, seeded, chopped tomatoes and white wine. After ten minutes or so, she reunited fish to sauce, rubbing peperoncini—I saw three for certain, but there might have been four—between her fingers into the pot and leaving the soup to gently simmer while she fried trenchers of rough bread in sizzling oil. I flashed a moment upon the contortions I'd suffered to build a bouillabaisse, one whose directions filled more pages than a play by Pirandello. I thought, too, to the flushed, moist faces of cooks—spent, broken-winded—who have delivered pots of zuppa di pesce to my table as though proffering the still-beating heart of an ostrich. Perhaps those soups were more sophisticated in their components, perhaps more layers of flavor were constructed into their sauces. But this one seemed to ask so little for all the goodness it sent up. In the finish, every fish soup is the same, I suppose, all of them having been born on the day when someone first came, hungry, to live beside the sea.

Rosaria's scant half hour's worth of pageantry had left her composed if not just a touch triumphant, poised, as the bells of Sant' Agata rang eight and a half, ready to welcome the chorus of widows. All of them wrapped in shawls, the ladies arrived, gathering easily for the ritual of the Thursday evening festa; one carried a plate of apples, one a bottle, rustically corked and unlabeled, and the last had a kitten tucked under her arm. They greeted us with neither surprise nor ceremony, as they might greet each other. And together we dined, speaking, in deference to Fernando, of the Venetian conquest and domination of Gallipoli, all of them significantly informed. We spoke, too, of their lives as girls and young wives. They talked of solitude, of jealously preferring it to any fraying of their serenity. Two of them had received offers to sell their homes. "A handsome German simply pulled at my bell one morning, asking what sum I would accept for the sale of my home," one said. "I asked him where in the world he thought I was going to live," she continued. "But, signora, you can buy any home, anywhere you'd like, with the money I will pay you," said the German. "I already have a home. You can buy any home, anywhere you'd like with your money," finished the signora. The concept of selling a home to buy another was nothing less than astonishing to her.

When I asked about their travels, they became uneasy, the question confounding them, as though wandering from Gallipoli would be treason. But, ah, yes, one had gone twice to Lecce (forty-two kilometers; about twenty-nine miles) to attend cousins' weddings. They spoke of gitarelle—jaunts on foot or in a borrowed carriage—into the countryside to forage for mushrooms and herbs and grasses when they were girls. One had married a man whose family extended as far away as Brindisi, and each February they journeyed the seventy-seven kilometers that separated them to visit for a few days. They had, each of them, though, often set out with their fishermen husbands, when bounty was scant, to search a catch farther out to sea. They stayed with them in their small workingmen's boats, cooking for them, helping, even, to land the bigger fish. These seemed not adventures to them but simple conventions of their lives. Rosaria had been a promising pittrice, a painter. So talented was she that her family collected to wring hands together over her future. Her grandfather offered to send her off to the fine arts academy in Naples so that she might have instruction, be inspired by other vistas. He had quietly arranged for her board and her chaperon and she cried day and night when she heard the news. "What would I have done there, even for a day, without this sea?" she asked. "Even now, it is all I ever want to look at, to paint, to listen to as I fall asleep." "How long would you have been gone?" I asked. "As long as a month," she said. Rosaria will never need to see Naples.

When the table was cleared, we walked together farther up into the nearly silent town to eat gelato di pistacchio and plump, rum-soaked almond cakes called divino amore. Exchanging our buona *notte easily, we knew we were all changed a little. We were strangers who had lived out a lifetime's worth of friendship in one evening, wrapped together in the steams of an ancient soup.*

　　3 pounds mixed white-fleshed sea fish fillets (sea bass, monkfish,
　　　　halibut, snapper, etc.), rinsed in sea-salted water
　　6 ounces anchovies, preserved under salt
　　2 cups extra-virgin olive oil
　　1 large yellow onion, peeled and finely minced
　　6 fat cloves garlic, peeled, crushed, and minced
　　16 to 20 large prawns, heads removed, tails intact
　　2 14-ounce cans plum tomatoes, with their liquids
　　2 teaspoons fine sea salt
　　1 small dried red chile pepper, crushed, or ⅓ to ½ teaspoon
　　　　dried chile flakes
　　1 bottle dry white wine
　　8 to 10 1-inch slices good country bread

Cut the fish into 4- to 5-inch chunks and pat dry.

Rinse the anchovies. Remove their heads and bones, dry on paper towels, and crush lightly with a fork.

In a very large terra-cotta or enameled cast-iron casserole over a medium flame, heat 1 cup of the oil and soften the onion to translucence. Add the anchovies and garlic, rolling them about in the oil for 1 minute, taking care not to color the garlic. Add the fish, a few pieces at a time, sautéing each lightly and removing to a plate. Next add the prawns, in two batches if necessary, turning them about until their shells turn angry red. Remove the prawns to the plate with the fish. Now add the tomatoes, sea salt, chile, and wine, bringing it all to a simmer, stirring it forcefully to loosen any bits lolling at the bottom of the pan.

Permit the sauce to cook, reducing, for 10 to 15 minutes while you warm the remaining olive oil and quickly brown the bread on both sides. Keep the bread hot in the same low oven where the bowls in which you'll present the soup are warming.

Acquaint the fish and the prawns with their sauce, permitting them to cook over the gentlest flame, the sauce barely simmering, for 3 or 4 minutes.

Carry the *coccio*—casserole—to table. Place a trencher of bread in the bottom of each warmed, shallow bowl and cover it with several pieces of fish and a pair of prawns that you've retrieved with a slotted spoon. Then ladle over all some of the good broth. Frowning faces, pouting lips coated in golden crumbs, have instructed me to sauté double or triple the amount of bread that might otherwise content my companions. It is a good thing, too, to double the wine rations for the feast.

Ostriche del Mar Piccolo

OYSTERS FROM THE COASTAL LAGOONS OF TARANTO

Serves 4

After the fast demise of Sybaris, it was Taranto that grew up, the city most splendid of Magna Graecia. And it was there that oysters were first cultivated, for the coddling, I suppose, of true sybaritic cravings. Taranto was and is quite perfectly situated for the business, sitting, rather like an island, between the mar piccolo—*the little sea—a coastal lagoon fed by both fresh and sea water and the* mar grande—*the big sea—part of the Gulf of Taranto in the Ionian Sea. And it is this very shifting in the salinity of the waters around Taranto that builds up the sweetest, fattest oysters. Nothing better can be done to a fine oyster than to slip it down one's throat, chasing it with sips of some crisp, icy white wine. But here follows a recipe for barely roasting oysters that, if not ennobling them, at the least takes nothing from their own natural goodness.*

24 oysters
Coarsely chopped fronds from a bulb of fennel
½ cup extra-virgin olive oil
2 fat cloves garlic, peeled, crushed, and finely minced
1 small bulb fennel, very finely minced
2 teaspoons fennel seeds, crushed
1 teaspoon fine sea salt
Juice of 1 lemon
1 cup dry white wine

Scrub and open the oysters, reserving their liquors. Loosen the flesh of each oyster from the lower, curved shell and position the meat and shell bottom in a shallow terra-cotta or enameled cast-iron gratin dish. Tuck a few pieces of fennel frond in each shell under the oyster. Discard the top shells.

In a sauté pan over a lively flame, warm the olive oil and soften the garlic and fennel to translucence, adding the fennel seeds, the sea salt, and the lemon juice and stirring it all about for another minute. Spoon a bit of the mixture over each oyster and place the dish several inches below a very hot broiler for a minute or two to lightly brown the topping and to barely warm the oysters.

Meanwhile, in a small saucepan, warm the wine with ⅓ cup of the reserved oyster liquor nearly to a simmer. Remove the dish from the oven and quickly, gently pour the hot wine and oyster liquor into the dish, taking care not to disturb the oysters. The hot liquids against the hot pan will send up beautiful vapors, finish warming the oysters, and build a little sauce.

Present the oysters at once with rough hunks of just-toasted bread to use as sops for the juices and jugs of cold white wine. It seems a better feast if each one takes an oyster or two at a time with spoonfuls of the sauce to his own plate, then goes back for another and another, the oysters staying warm in their cozy dish. At the last, it's a free-for-all to swoop up the last of the liquors with the last of the bread.

Pane di Altamura

THE BREAD OF ALTAMURA

Makes 2 large loaves

If I were given the task of choosing one bread from all the bakers of Italy, one that I could eat everyday and for-ever, it would be the golden-fleshed bread of Altamura, its thick skin, parched, crackled, its form a fat, crisped heart, cleaved nearly in two.

The Starter

¼ teaspoon active dry yeast or a pinch of a small cake of fresh
    yeast
¼ cup warm water
⅔ cup tepid water
1½ cups all-purpose flour

In a medium bowl, stir the yeast into the warm water and permit it to rest and dissolve for 15 minutes. Add the tepid water and the flour and stir vigorously with a wooden spoon for a minute or two. Transfer the mixture into a very lightly oiled larger bowl, cover it with plastic wrap, and permit the starter to rise at room temperature for not less than 8 hours, preferably overnight.

The Dough

1½ teaspoons active dry yeast or half of a small cake of fresh
    yeast
⅓ cup warm water
About 1⅔ cups of the starter

1⅔ cups tepid water

6 cups *farina di grano duro* (hard durum wheat flour), which is
  semolina ("pasta flour"), plus additional as needed

1 tablespoon fine sea salt

In a large bowl, stir the yeast into the warm water and permit it to rest and dissolve for 15 minutes. Add the starter and the tepid water to the rested yeast and, with your hands, break down the fibrous, stringy texture of the starter, incorporating the water and yeast into it and, finally, with a wooden spoon, beat the components into a smooth batter.

Add the flour and the salt and, with your hands, combine the components into a rough dough. Turn the dough out onto a very lightly floured work surface and knead it energetically into a smooth, resilient, wettish sort of dough. The task takes at least 8 minutes.

Place the dough in a lightly oiled bowl, cover it tightly with plastic wrap, and permit it to rise for 1½ hours.

Turn the dough out onto the work surface, divide it in two, and form each piece into a fat oval, flattening its ends a bit, pinching them into "tails." Carefully transfer the formed loaves onto baking parchment. Cover the breads with clean kitchen towels and permit them a 45-minute rest. Holding the ends of the parchment, turn the breads over onto a baker's peel or onto baking sheets. Holding one hand perpendicular to the loaf, give it a deft smash a little to the left of its center. This little rite imposes the bread's traditional clefted heart form. Shake the loaves off the peel onto a preheated baking stone, sprinkled lightly with semolina, or place the loaves, on their baking sheets, in the oven.

Bake the breads for 30 to 35 minutes or until they are deeply golden and have formed a thick, hard crust. The process of misting will help accomplish this (page 214). Permit the breads to rest in the oven with the door open for 15 minutes. Cool them thoroughly on a wooden surface.

This is the sort of bread one can break rather than slice, passing it round the table so each guest can tear off a chunk.

Caldariello

SUCKLING LAMB BRAISED IN MILK

Serves 6

A perhaps four-thousand-year-old, pre-Mosaic formula, the name of the dish is derived from its cooking vessel, caldaro—cauldron. A characteristic preparation of Gravina in Puglia, this is the ancient dish thought to be denounced in the Old Testament: "Thou shall not seethe a kid in his mother's milk," forming the Orthodox Hebrew proscription against dishes that combine meat with milk. This version sautés suckling kid or lamb until golden in fennel, parsley, and garlic-perfumed oil before its milk braising.

1½ tablespoons fennel seeds, crushed

2 fat cloves garlic, peeled and crushed

⅔ cup flat parsley leaves

½ cup extra-virgin olive oil

3 pounds suckling lamb or kid, cut from the legs into 3- to
    4-inch pieces

Fine sea salt

3 cups whole milk

1 cup heavy cream

1 large branch of rosemary

Freshly ground white pepper

With a mezzaluna or a very sharp knife, mince the fennel, garlic, and parsley together to a fine paste.

In a large terra-cotta or enameled cast-iron casserole over a medium flame, warm the olive oil and melt the aromatic paste, taking care not to color it. Add the pieces of lamb—only those at a time that will fit without touching—browning them until they are crusted well on all sides. Remove them to a holding plate. Salt the lamb generously after it has been sealed. Pour ½ cup of the milk into the hot casserole, stirring and scraping at the residue over a lively flame for a minute or two before adding the remaining milk, the cream, the branch of rosemary, and the seared lamb. Over the gentlest flame, bring the mixture to a low simmer, cover the casserole tightly, and permit the lamb to cook ever so slowly for an hour or until the meat is barely melting into its milky juices.

With a slotted spoon, remove the lamb to a deep bowl, covering it loosely while you strain the pan juices, pressing hard to get all the liquid. Rinse the cooking vessel, return the juices to it, and, over a lively flame, reduce the sauce for 3 minutes. Taste the sauce, adjusting it with a little sea salt, should you wish, and generous grindings of white pepper. Reacquaint the lamb with its sauce, immersing it well and permitting it to warm through over a low flame.

Carry the casserole to the table, serving the lamb, its juices, chunks of bread, and a good red wine with a salad of bitter greens afterward.

135

La Torta di Patate Foggiana

A POTATO TART IN THE STYLE OF FOGGIA

Serves 6

Foggia is the city studding the largest wheat fields of Italy's south—the tavoliere—*it being the ancient, present, and endless granary of the peninsula. Too, are potatoes cultivated there, soothing the Pugliese penchant for them in breads, tarts, stews.*

Our maîtresse d'hôtel *in Foggia baked a reprise of this luscious tart evening after evening, sometimes filling it with minced lamb or thin slices of poached sausage or crumbles of smoked ricotta, and presented it barely warm as our first course.*

The Sauce

3 tablespoons extra-virgin olive oil

1 fat clove garlic, peeled, crushed, and minced

1 14-ounce can plum tomatoes, with their liquids

2 teaspoons fine sea salt

1⅓ cups good red wine

¼ cup capers, preserved under salt, rinsed and dried

4 ounces large black Sicilian or Greek olives, crushed lightly
   with a mallet, stones removed, and coarsely chopped

The Potatoes

1½ pounds red- or white-skinned potatoes

2 tablespoons extra-virgin olive oil

1 small red onion, peeled and very finely minced

⅔ cup just-made fine bread crumbs, lightly pan-toasted

2 teaspoons fine sea salt

⅔ cup just-grated pecorino

⅓ cup good red wine

1 tablespoon good red wine vinegar

To make the sauce: In a large sauté pan over a medium flame, warm the oil and soften the garlic, taking care not to color it. Add the tomatoes, salt, and wine, increase the flame, and bring the mixture to simmer, permitting it to cook for 15 minutes or so and reduce to a thick, dense sauce. Remove from the flame, stir in the capers and the olives, and set the sauce aside.

To make the potatoes: Boil the potatoes until tender in sea-salted water. Drain them—then peel and mash them. In a medium bowl, mix the mashed potatoes with the olive oil, the onion, 3 tablespoons of the bread crumbs, the sea salt, the pecorino, the wine, and half the vinegar, blending well.

Lightly oil a shallow terra-cotta or enameled cast-iron casserole and spread it with half the potato mixture. Spoon half the sauce over the potatoes, cover the sauce with the remaining potatoes, finishing the whole with the remaining sauce. Dust the *torta* with the remaining bread crumbs and bake the dish for ½ hour.

Though the *torta* can be presented hot from the oven, it is a better dish served at room temperature. Baptize the *torta* with the remaining drops of vinegar, cut it into generous wedges and pour thick tumblers of the same good wine you used to make the dish.

Focaccia di Patate del Tavoliere

POTATO FLATBREAD WITH CAPERS, BLACK AND GREEN OLIVES, AND PECORINO IN THE STYLE OF THE FOGGIAN PLAINS

Makes 1 large focaccia

The Dough

10 ounces red- or white-skinned potatoes

2 teaspoons active dry yeast or ¾ of a small cake of fresh yeast

3¾ cups all-purpose flour, plus additional as needed

3 tablespoons extra-virgin olive oil

2 teaspoons fine sea salt

Cook the potatoes until tender in boiling, sea-salted water. Drain, reserving 1 cup of their cooking liquid. Peel and mash them.

In a large bowl, stir the yeast into the cup of reserved cooking water from the potatoes, cooled to tepid, permitting it to dissolve and rest for 15 minutes. Add the cooled mashed potatoes, the 3¾ cups of flour, olive oil, and sea salt, mixing the ingredients into a rough dough.

Turn the mixture out onto a floured work space and knead it into a soft, resilient dough. This takes at least 8 minutes. Place the dough in a lightly oiled bowl, cover it tightly with plastic wrap, and let it rise for 1½ hours or until it doubles in bulk.

The Topping

1½ cups ripe cherry tomatoes, halved, tossed with ½ teaspoon
    fine sea salt and permitted ½ hour's rest
½ cup capers, preserved under salt, rinsed and dried
8 to 10 ounces mixed large black and green Sicilian or Greek
    olives, lightly crushed with a mallet, stones removed, and
    coarsely chopped
4 ounces just-grated pecorino
2 tablespoons extra-virgin olive oil

Preheat the oven to 425 degrees.

Roll or stretch the risen dough out into a rather free-form oval shape. One does not strive here for symmetry. Cover the dough with a clean kitchen towel and permit it to rise for ½ hour.

Lay the tomatoes and their liquids, the capers, and the olives over the dough, dusting the whole with the pecorino. Drop threads of olive oil over all and bake the focaccia on a parchment-lined tin or on a preheated baking stone for 20 to 25 minutes. Present the focaccia very warm.

Spuma di Mele Cotogne

A QUINCE MOUSSE

Serves 6

From Lecce and its environs, quince paste—a deeply bronzed jelly molded into plump squares and tucked inside wooden fruit boxes—is our favorite Puglian treasure to take back to Tuscany. Here follows a lovely sort of pudding made from quince that, though it offers a less-dense dose of the fruit, yields one with all its beautiful, apple-wine sort of autumn savor.

>About 2 pounds quince
>14 ounces dark brown sugar
>Juice of 1 lemon
>¼ cup dark rum
>2 cups heavy cream

Preheat the oven to 325 degrees.

Polish the quince with a soft cloth, removing their down and, in a shallow terra-cotta or enameled cast-iron casserole, roast the quince whole until they are soft and collapsing, their skins just bursting.

Cool the quince only until they can be relieved comfortably of their skins and cores. Push the flesh through a sieve, transferring it to a saucepan with the brown sugar and the lemon juice and, over a lively flame, bring the ingredients rapidly to a boil, stirring all the while with a wooden spoon. Lower the flame and cook the quince, still stirring, for 5 minutes. Remove the quince from the flame and permit it to cool.

Combine the rum and the cream and beat until it forms stiff peaks. Lighten the cooled quince puree with a third of the beaten cream, then gently fold the quince into the remaining cream.

Turn the mousse out into a serving bowl, cover it tightly with plastic wrap, and chill it for several hours—or as long as 24—before carrying it to table and spooning out the ambered, rosy fruit into small coffee cups. Sip hot spiced rum with it as we did one shivery autumn evening as close to the fire as we could sit in a rough little osteria in Locorotondo.

Crostata di Fichi Mandorlati

AN ALMOND-CRUSTED FIG TART SCENTED WITH
BAY, LAUREL, AND ANISE

Serves 6 to 8

A pastry reflecting the famous half-roasted, almond-stuffed, bay and anise-perfumed figs that Puglia exports to all of Europe, the ripe sensuality of it merits a true hunger, one not dulled by the prologue of some long, winy supper. Nibble only at a plate of fresh cheeses before it. Better, present it with no prelude at all.

The Crust

½ cup blanched almonds, lightly toasted
2 teaspoons fennel seeds
2 teaspoons aniseeds
1 cup all-purpose flour, plus additional as needed
6 tablespoons very cold sweet butter, cut into small cubes
½ cup confectioners' sugar
½ teaspoon fine sea salt
1 large egg, lightly beaten with 1 tablespoon cold water
Butter for tart tin

In the work bowl of a food processor fitted with a steel blade, pulse the almonds with the fennel and aniseeds, breaking them down into coarse crumbs. Add 1 cup flour, the butter, sugar, and salt and pulse ten or twelve times until it takes on the texture of coarse crumbs. Add the egg mixture through the feed tube and pulse eight or ten times, just until the pastry begins to take on a cohesive form.

Turn the mixture out onto a lightly floured work space and gently form it into a ball. Flatten the ball and press the dough onto the surfaces of a buttered 10-inch tart tin with a removable bottom. Cover the pastry-lined tin in plastic wrap and freeze it for ½ hour.

Preheat the oven to 400 degrees.

Prick the surface of the pastry with a fork and bake it for 12 to 14 minutes or until it has firmed and is of the palest gold color. Cool the pastry thoroughly.

The Filling

1½ cups heavy cream

1 large bay leaf

1 teaspoon aniseeds, crushed

1 teaspoon fennel seeds, crushed

1 large egg, slightly beaten

1 tablespoon confectioners' sugar

12 to 14 fresh black or green figs

12 to 14 whole, blanched almonds, lightly toasted

2 tablespoons dark brown sugar

In a medium saucepan, combine the cream, bay leaf, aniseeds and fennel seeds, and, over a lively flame, bring to a simmer. Lower the flame a bit and permit the cream to infuse the aromatics and to reduce its volume by one-third. Remove the pan from the flame, cover it, and permit it to cool. Strain the cream and add the egg and the confectioners' sugar, blending the components carefully.

Starting at their bases, vertically slit the figs almost in two, leaving the stem end intact. Stuff each fig with an almond, press the halves together, and stand each fig upright over the base of the pastry.

Carefully pour the scented custard around the figs. Dust the top of the *crostata* with the brown sugar and bake it at 375 degrees for 25 minutes or until the custard is set and crusted a dark gold from the sugar, the stems of the figs are slightly charred, and the edges of the pastry nicely colored. Cool the *crostata* for 10 minutes on a rack. Remove the tin's sides and permit the *crostata* to cool an additional 20 minutes. Present it then or serve it at room temperature.

BASILICATA

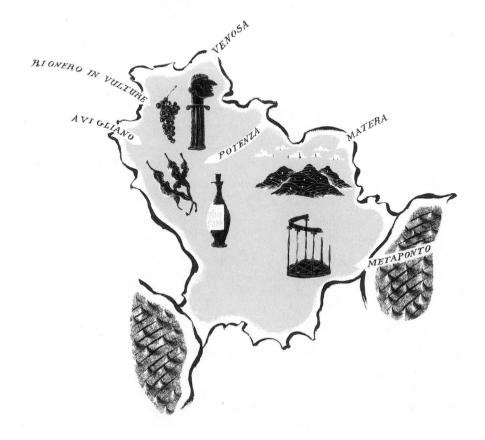

land of bitterness since the epochs before history, it was only a thousand years ago that Basilikus, king of the Byzantines, reigned over this small and lonely place, secreted by forbidding walls of mountain, its earth all of stones and despair. The old king fled quickly from the place leaving behind little more than his name. Though earlier of the lands of Magna Graecia, even the Greeks left small impress save the Doric ruins at Metaponto. When the Romans arrived, they named the place Lucania, after some indigenous tribe of the moment. But it was an all too unconsolable piece of earth to play long and grand in their scheme. One sees little of Rome in Basilicata's sad face. The Romans went from it as everyone before them and after them went from it, sucking at wounds that come from wars with desolation.

Basilicata's story is spoken neither through monuments to victory nor in thanksgiving but rather through an inexorable heap of rocks, *un rione*, a parish, inside the city

143

of Matera. The place grew up from Neolithic tribes who came to hollow refuges from the great limestone rocks hitched upon the sheer walls of a river basin. After them, there followed scores of others, each piece of each epoch bringing another anguished people, racing away from hunger or toward some sanctuary. The ancient hamlet is called *i sassi*—the rocks. The desperate continued to exist there until 1956, when the dry-eyed Philistines in Rome were enough shamed by its wretchedness to lead the people down from the rocks and to provide for their relocation.

Under the sanction of UNESCO, there are considerations at work for *i sassi*'s rebirth. People of Matera and from farther away, too, have begun to purchase small pieces of *i sassi* from the *comune*—the city hall—restructuring the ancient dwellings into studios and workrooms and apartments, their terraces beset sweetly with flower pots and happy signals of the human condition. There is a *caffè*. And there, too, in the place where is collected the pain of ten thousand years, a man called Domenico sits in the sun, carving, smoothing primitive faces from pieces of soft, yellow stone.

Once we climbed eighty-three steep, stone steps up to a small hermitage that calls itself a hotel, its few stark rooms fitted into the caves. From our single tiny window where we stayed many more days than had been our plan, we could look into the soul of the rocks, into their immensity, listening to the oldest stillness ever heard.

About the Cuisine

Basilicata well demonstrates the entanglement between gastronomy and geography. How a people eats is a symptom of its character. Its character is influenced by, among other forces—its environment. Poverty endured under a warm sun breeds a sort of bravado, the hungry knowing that one thing or another will soon be coming into ripeness. Bellies rasping in a fallow cold generate a torment that bruises, absorbs hope. These postures of a people are impressed in every corner of its civility—no less, after all, in how it feeds itself. Gastronomic tradition is then etched by the expression of this regional character. The stuffs that can be found and collected or coaxed from earth and sea are illuminated by that character. Of all Italy's regions, Basilicata has been least indulged by the gods and, until today, its tables remain the least laden, the least sumptuous. The Lucani seem content with homey plates, sated, soothed by their rough plainness, ornamented only with the fire from a handful of tiny, dried, red peppers and their honest hunger.

Un Incontro con un Cacciatore Lucano
A MEETING WITH A LUCANIAN HUNTER

A small, stark sort of place is Potenza, wounded, pummeled by earthquakes for more than two thousand years and now, all patched up and varnished, she is a quietly proud but mostly anonymous village. And northwest of it, beyond the town of Avigliano, past the medieval castle ruins, past the abandoned villages whose walls oblige a goatherd and his scruffy flock, there soar the promontories, the highlands called Marmo Platano. Few paths beg entry into the primeval woods of chestnut and beech and fir, up onto aeries hung from the shoulders of clouds. These are the Lucani's hunting grounds.

Whether shoddily outfitted or all puffed up in down-filled vests, on foot, in jeeps, on muleback, the Lucani are master hunters. Hence, here follow two recipes recounted and demonstrated to us by a hunter/innkeeper in the village of Muro Lucano.

Fastened up picturesquely to a mountain face, it was here that was played out the scene of the legendary battle between Hannibal and Marcellus. So surely a hunter born here knows of what he speaks, one thinks. And since he happened to be our hunter/innkeeper and since we wanted to learn more about the Lucanian hand with game, it might be possible for him to make dishes with hare and boar during our stay with him, one begins to hope. We broached it.

"If a boar is older than one year," he began, "his flesh must be marinated for at least three days to purge it of an aggressive gaminess. If a boar is younger than one year, his flesh has no distinctive taste and so it must be marinated for at least three days to give it some character." From this, it was clear that he believed in marinating wild boar. "And as for the hare," he continued, "well, one just can't cook a hare without cooking chestnuts. In the end, it's the hare's sauce and the chestnuts that are the best parts of the meal."

And so we'd roused him. But could we convince him to go hunting? "Well, I'd had it in mind to take a little walk anyway tomorrow morning. I'll see what I can find," he said grudgingly. Alas, our hunter returned with two hare and no boar. "Why can't we just use pork," I begged. "Its flesh is not so different from that of young, wild pig, so wouldn't the long marination give it some of the character of *cinghiale?*" I asked. Our hunter/innkeeper went off to the butcher.

We cooked and feasted on both the hunter's dishes during that cold week of winter in his old stone house with the persimmon-colored walls, the thick scents of wood smoke and tobacco and apples like a serenade for us up there in his attic under our feather bed.

Brasato di Maiale alla Nicola Taurino

A BRAISE OF PORK IN THE MANNER OF NICOLA TAURINO

Serves 8

The Marinade

½ cup olive oil

1 medium yellow onion, peeled and sliced thin

1 small carrot, scraped and sliced

1 stalk celery, sliced

1 tablespoon fine sea salt

4 fat cloves garlic, peeled and crushed

2 bay leaves

2 tablespoons fresh rosemary leaves, minced

6 whole cloves

12 juniper berries

1 bottle good red wine

The Braise

4 pounds pork shoulder, well-trimmed of its fat and cut into
   3-inch chunks

⅓ cup olive oil

3 ounces pancetta, minced

1 large yellow onion, peeled and minced

4 fat cloves garlic, peeled, crushed, and finely minced

2 cups good red wine

1 tablespoon sugar

2 tablespoons good red wine vinegar

Over a lively flame in a medium saucepan, heat the olive oil and soften the onion, carrot, and celery for a few minutes, until lightly golden. Add the salt, garlic, bay leaves, and rosemary, rolling the herbs about for a minute. In a mortar with a pestle, crush the cloves with the juniper berries, adding them to the pan with the wine. Bring to a gentle simmer, lower the flame a bit, and cover the pan with a skewed lid, permitting the liquid to barely simmer for 10 minutes. Cool the marinade.

Place the pork in a noncorrosive bowl just large enough to hold it and its marinade. Pour over the cooled marinade, stirring the meat about. Cover the pork and marinade and leave it to rest for three days in the refrigerator, stirring the pork about in the marinade at least twice a day.

Remove the pork from the marinade and set it aside. Strain the marinade and, in a medium saucepan over a lively flame, reduce it to one half its volume. Warm the olive oil in a large terra-cotta or enameled cast-iron casserole and sauté the pancetta lightly. Dry the pieces of pork on absorbent paper towels. Add them to the casserole—one or two pieces at a time, so that they do not touch—and seal them well on all sides. As the meat is sealed, remove it to a holding plate and proceed. When all the pork has been sealed, add the onion and garlic to the casserole and soften it in the fat. Add the reduced marinade to the casserole, stirring and scraping up all the residue. Add the red wine and the pork and bring just to a simmer. Over a gentle flame, braise the pork, covered, its lid barely skewed for 1½ hours or until the meat is nearly melting into its sauce.

Remove the pork from its sauce with a slotted spoon and cover it to prevent its drying while you finish the sauce. Over a gentle flame in a small sauté pan, heat the sugar, rolling it about until it melts and takes on a rich, golden color. Remove from the heat, and add the vinegar. Because the vinegar will be cooler in temperature, the caramel will seize. After a few seconds over a gentle flame, though, it will melt into the warming vinegar. Pour the caramel/vinegar into the sauce, blending the components and simmering the sauce for a minute before reacquainting it with the pork.

The dish can rest for several hours or overnight or be served immediately. Some of its sauce can be used for pasta as a first course, if you wish, and the meat presented as a second course with nothing to distract from its lush flavor save great chunks of toasted country bread and jugs of the same good wine in which the pork was braised.

Lepre al Miele con Castagne Speziate alla Nicola Taurino

HONEYED WILD RABBIT WITH SPICED CHESTNUTS
IN THE MANNER OF NICOLA TAURINO

Serves 6

The Chestnuts

1½ pounds fresh chestnuts

4 ounces pancetta, minced

2 tablespoons olive oil

1 piece of ginger, 1 inch in diameter and 1 inch thick, peeled
  and crushed

Fine sea salt

1 stick cinnamon

4 whole cloves

3 whole allspice berries

1 teaspoon whole peppercorns

⅓ cup good red wine

⅓ cup dark honey (buckwheat, chestnut, etc.)

Slit the chestnuts on their flat sides with a short, sharp knife or a hook-bladed chestnut knife. Place the chestnuts in a large saucepan and cover them with cold water. Over a lively flame, bring to a simmer and poach the chestnuts for 5 minutes. Drain the chestnuts, cut away their shells, and rub off their inner skins. The task is made simpler if the nuts are still warm, so keep them under a kitchen towel while you work. One might opt to use 2 jars of vacuum-packed chestnuts, saving an hour's work and sacrificing some fun and some flavor.

Over a lively flame in a very large sauté pan, melt the pancetta with the oil. Add the ginger, permitting it to perfume the fat for a minute or two before adding the chestnuts. Sprinkle the chestnuts with sea salt and sauté them for 5 minutes.

In a mortar with a pestle, coarsely crush the cinnamon, cloves, allspice, and peppercorns and tie them up in a piece of damp cheesecloth. Add the wine to the sauté pan and enough water just to cover the chestnuts. Add the spice sachet, bring the components to a simmer and cook the chestnuts, gently, until they are tender but still holding their form—about 20 to 25 minutes. Remove the spice sachet and then the chestnuts from their bath with a slotted spoon. Strain the liquid and return it to the pan. Over a lively flame, reduce the liquid to a scant 1 cup. Add the honey, and when it has melted into the liquids, add the chestnuts, rolling them about and glossing them in the sauce.

Cover the pan and set aside. The chestnuts can be completely prepared up to one day in advance of serving them.

The Rabbit

¼ cup extra-virgin olive oil

4 ounces pancetta, minced

1 3½- to 4-pound rabbit, cut into 6 pieces, its liver reserved

Fine sea salt

2 tablespoons minced rosemary leaves

4 large leaves sage, torn

2 cups good red wine

2 tablespoons dark honey (buckwheat, chestnut, etc.)

2 tablespoons grappa or Cognac

Over a lively flame in a large ceramic or terra-cotta casserole, heat the oil and in it soften the pancetta. Rinse the rabbit pieces and dry them on absorbent paper towels. Brown the pieces well in the fat, salting them generously, sealing them on all sides and then removing them to a holding plate.

Add the rosemary and sage to the casserole, perfuming the fat with them for a minute or two before adding the wine, stirring and scraping at the residue. Reacquaint the rabbit with its bath and bring it all to a gentle simmer. Lower the flame, cover the casserole tightly, and very gently braise the rabbit for 40 to 45 minutes or until its flesh begins to fall from its bones. A gentle flame that keeps the liquids barely simmering will yield a rabbit full of juices. With a slotted spoon, remove the rabbit pieces to a holding plate.

Strain the juices and, over a lively flame, reduce them for 2 to 3 minutes. Mash the reserved liver with the honey and the grappa and add it to the simmering sauce, stirring, amalgamating the components and thickening the sauce. Return the rabbit to the finished sauce and warm them together for 1 minute. Present the rabbit from its casserole with the chestnuts, gently warmed, as accompaniment. A bowl of simply dressed bitter greens is a welcome counterpoint.

Brasato di Funghi con Aglianico del Vùlture

A BRAISE OF FOREST MUSHROOMS WITH AGLIANICO DEL VÙLTURE

Serves 4 to 6

Rionero in Vùlture, a tiny village crouched on the hem of a quiet volcano, is where Basilicata's worthy red wine is born. Ancient gift of the Greeks were the vines called Aglianico, still flourishing, somehow, stitched up nearly three thousand feet onto the shoulders of the long-sleeping Vùlture, their black-skinned fruit nourished by the volcano's ashes and the nearness of the sun. The yields of the rich fruit of the Aglianico is each year less, not for the nature of things but for the dearth of a new generation of vine workers. Even now, the production is sadly small.

Young, the wine is untamed, full of acid and tannin and potential. After five years, an Aglianico can ripen into a wine sitting on the fringes of nobility. After an all-night rain and the next morning's mushroom hunt in the forests above Rionero in Vùlture, this dish, with a 1992 Aglianico and a half-loaf of coarse, whole wheat bread taken, warm, from the village forno, made our lunch.

2 ounces lard
½ cup flat parsley leaves
4 fat cloves garlic, peeled and crushed
6 tablespoons olive oil
2 ounces pancetta
1 small, dried red chile pepper, crushed, or ⅓ to ½ teaspoon red
    chile flakes
2 pounds wild mushrooms (porcini, chanterelles, portobelli, etc.),
    wiped free of any grit, trimmed, and sliced thick
Fine sea salt
Freshly cracked pepper
2 large ripe tomatoes, peeled, seeded, and chopped
1 cup good red wine
⅔ cup freshly made bread crumbs

With a mezzaluna or a sharp knife, mince the lard, parsley, and garlic together to a fine paste.

Over a medium flame in a large sauté pan or terra-cotta casserole, warm 4 tablespoons of the oil and, in it, soften the pancetta. Add the garlic/lard paste and the crushed chile, sautéing for a minute or two. Add the prepared mushrooms to the perfumed fat, sprinkling on sea salt and grinding pepper generously, and gently sauté them, permitting them to dispel their juices for several minutes. Add the tomatoes and the wine and bring to a simmer.

Cover the pan with a skewed lid and, over a gentle flame, allow the mushrooms to reabsorb their juices and to drink in the wine. Braise them for 20 to 30 minutes or until they are plumped and have taken on the tint of the wine.

Over a medium flame, warm 2 tablespoons of the olive oil in a small sauté pan and sauté the crumbs, tossing them about. Present the mushrooms and their juices, dusted with the crumbs, as a first course. A beautiful bread and wine are all they require. Serving them as companion to some other dish is to distract from the pleasure of them.

Arrosticini alla Brace

SKEWERS OF LAMB ROASTED OVER A WOOD FIRE

Serves 6 to 8

The hefts of lamb, perfumed with aromatics and roasted over a wood fire, speak of a primordial innocence. Make a feast of them. Bake some pettole *(page 153) and offer a great wedge of young pecorino and a jug of honest red wine.*

> 3 tablespoons good red wine vinegar
> 1 cup extra-virgin olive oil
> 1 tablespoon fine sea salt
> 1 small, dried red chile pepper, crushed, or ⅓ to ½ teaspoon
>   dried chile flakes
> 2 fat cloves garlic, peeled and crushed
> 1 large branch of rosemary
> 1 tablespoon fennel seeds, toasted and crushed
> 4 pounds lamb, cut from the leg into 3-inch chunks
> Dry white wine

In a small saucepan, combine all the elements save the lamb and the wine and heat the mixture, removing it from the flame before the oil reaches the boil. Cover the pot and permit the aromatics to infuse the oil for ½ hour or so.

Place the lamb in a large, noncorrosive bowl and pour the perfumed oil over it, massaging it into all sides of the lamb. Cover the lamb and let it rest while you build a wood fire.

Skewer the perfumed lamb onto well-soaked grapevine twigs, olive wood twigs, thick branches of rosemary, or wood or metal skewers and roast it over red and white embers, turning the skewers and basting the lamb with a few drops of white wine now and then, until the meat is crusted outside and still very pink inside. Present the lamb, on its skewers, over 2 or 3 just-sautéed *frittelle di fagioli bianchi* (page 154), a fine sop for the luscious juices.

Pasta alla Pecoraio

A SHEPHERD'S PASTA

Serves 6

An inordinately rustic dish, it asks so little of the larder and the cook and gives up good, potent flavor. The Lucani are wont to add another crushed chile to the pasta at table or under a tree, as the case may be.

3 ounces *ricotta salata* (aged, salted ricotta), grated
3 ounces aged pecorino, grated
6 ounces whole-milk ricotta
1 small, dried red chile pepper, crushed, or ⅓ to ½ teaspoon red
  chile flakes
Generous grindings of freshly cracked pepper
2 teaspoons fennel seeds, toasted
2 tablespoons olive oil
⅔ cup freshly made bread crumbs
16 ounces bucatini or other thick, string pasta
Fine sea salt
Olio santo (page 155)

In a medium bowl, combine the cheeses with the crushed chile, the pepper, and the fennel seeds, mixing the components well.

Over a medium flame, warm the oil in a small pan and sauté the crumbs, tossing them about.

Cook the pasta in boiling, sea-salted water to al dente, draining it but leaving it somewhat wet and reserving 1 cup of the cooking water. Return the pasta to the still-warm cooking pot. Beat a few tablespoons of the pasta cooking water into the cheese mixture, thinning it a bit. Pour the sauce over the pasta and toss it about, coating it well. Transfer the pasta to a warmed bowl and dust it with the crumbs. Each one can drop a few tears of *olio santo* over his own plate.

Le Pettole

SMALL BAY-SCENTED BREADS

Makes 12 small breads

Traditionally, pettole are fried in bubbling oil, but here follows a version of the gloriously bay-perfumed breads—their faces glossed with diabolical olio santo—that are simply baked. The fat little breads are wonderful to serve with the Lucanian sausages (page 157) or some great platter of dried sausages, salame, and piquant cheeses. Even unaccessorized, they are wholly absorbing, their warm, crunchy goodness complemented by some cold white wine.

2½ teaspoons active dry yeast or 1 small cake fresh yeast

1¼ cups warm water

3 cups unbleached flour, plus additional as needed

⅔ cup fine, stone-ground yellow cornmeal

3 tablespoons olive oil

1 tablespoon fine sea salt

Olio santo (page 155)

Bay leaves

In a large bowl, soften the yeast in the water, permitting it to rest for 10 minutes. Add 3 cups of the flour, cornmeal, olive oil, and sea salt to the yeast and form a soft dough. Turn the dough out onto a lightly floured surface and knead the mass until it is smooth and elastic, about 8 minutes, dusting it with a fistful of flour, should the dough feel wet. Place the dough in an oiled bowl, covering it with plastic wrap and allowing it to double, about 1½ hours.

Turn the risen dough out onto a floured work space and cut the dough into 12 pieces. Roll or press, with the flat of your hand, each piece of dough into a rough oval and paint it lightly with the *olio santo*. Position a bay leaf over one side of the oval, folding over the opposite end and enclosing the leaf. Press the ends of the little bread together firmly and place it on a parchment-lined metal sheet. Proceed with the remaining breads, leaving at least 4 inches between them.

Preheat the oven to 400 degrees.

Cover the breads loosely with clean kitchen towels and permit them to rise for 20 minutes. Paint the top surfaces with more *olio santo* and bake the breads for 18 to 20 minutes or until they are golden and crisped.

Cool the breads on a rack for a few minutes or, better, lay them in a basket lined with bay branches and pass them at table, still warm.

Frittelle di Fagioli Bianchi

WHITE BEAN FRITTERS

Serves 6

2 cups dried white cannellini beans

1 large branch of rosemary

2 tablespoons coarse sea salt

1 small yellow onion, peeled, cut in half, each half stuck with a
    whole clove

5 fat cloves garlic, peeled and crushed

1 small head Savoy cabbage

3½ teaspoons fine sea salt

2 tablespoons fresh rosemary leaves

1 small, dried red chile pepper, crushed, or ⅓ to ½ teaspoon
    dried chile flakes

Generous grindings of pepper

2 tablespoons plus ¾ cup extra-virgin olive oil

1 large egg

About 2 cups freshly made fine bread crumbs

In a large pot, cover the beans with cold water and add the rosemary branch, 1 tablespoon of the coarse sea salt, the clove-stuck onion, and 1 clove of the crushed garlic. Over a lively flame, bring the mixture to a boil, remove the pot from the flame, cover it tightly, and permit it to rest for 1 hour.

Core and roughly chop the cabbage and poach it in sea-salted water (using 2 teaspoons of fine sea salt) until tender. Drain the cabbage and set it aside. Drain the beans, discarding all the aromatics, cover them with fresh, cold water, add the remaining 1 tablespoon of coarse sea salt, and bring the beans to a simmer, cooking them gently, so they do not dry out, for 1 hour, until they are soft and creamy. Drain the beans, reserving a cup or so of the cooking water, and cool them for a few minutes.

In the bowl of a food processor, puree the beans, in two batches if necessary, adding a few drops of their cooking water to form a smooth paste. Transfer all but ½ cup of the paste to a large bowl.

Process the poached cabbage with 4 cloves of crushed garlic, rosemary leaves, and chile pepper, adding it to the bean paste. Generously grind pepper over the dish and add the remaining 1½ teaspoons of fine sea salt, blending the components well with a wooden spoon.

In a small bowl, beat 2 tablespoons of the oil with the egg and mix into the beans. The paste should be soft but of a moldable texture. Should it seem too soft, add the ¾ cup of reserved bean paste. (If you do not need the bean paste for the *frittelle*, it makes lunch for the cook spread on oven-toasted bread.)

Form the paste into plump ovals, 3 inches by 2 inches, and roll them about in the bread crumbs, giving them a good, thick coating. In a large sauté pan, warm ¾ cup of the oil and crust the fritters well on both sides. Sauté at one time only those that will fit into the pan without touching. As the fritters are sautéed, remove them to drain on absorbent paper towels and then transfer them to a warming plate set in a 200-degree oven while you proceed.

Though the fritters are a wonderful first course, they are also luscious companions to the *arrosticini alla brace* (page 151).

Olio Santo
SAINTED OIL

The Lucanian hand with *peperoncino* is generous, extravagant, sometimes oppressive, almost as though to restrain some ephemeral longing for delicacy or to redeem, somehow, the sameness, the insufficiency of his stores. His weapon, often, is a bottle of his own good olive oil inspirited with a fierce dose of chile peppers that he calls *olio santo*—sainted oil. And with it, he gives benediction to nearly everything he cooks and eats. He has no recipe for its composition, only the counsel to crush as many of the little red *bestie* (beasts) as one can fit into a liter or so of warmed oil. A more serene prescription for it is to warm 2 cups of extra-virgin olive oil and to excite it with as many as 10 crushed chiles, to pour the oil into a bottle with a tight stopper and to use it sparingly. Here follow, then, six recipes for typical, straightforward Lucanian dishes that beg the chile and/or *olio santo* and that argue the candidness of the cuisine, of the goodness that can come from "making do."

Cialledd' alla Contadina

THE FARMWIFE'S BREAD SOUP

Serves 2

A sort of Lucanian stone soup, this is from Basilicata's long repertoire of dishes built from almost nothing at all. Once the sustenance of shepherds who could concoct the dish with a handful of wild grasses and the simple stores they carried, too, it was often the family supper of the contadini—*the farmers—whose ascetic lives asked that each bit of bread nourish them. I offer it here as balm, a pastoral sort of medicine, one of the thousand historical, wizened prescripts known to soothe and sustain.*

> ⅓ cup extra-virgin olive oil
> 1 small yellow onion, peeled and thinly sliced
> 2 fat cloves garlic, peeled, crushed, and minced
> 2 medium white- or red-skinned potatoes, peeled and chopped
> 2 teaspoons fine sea salt
> 1 small, dried red chile pepper, or ⅓ to ½ teaspoon dried chile
>   flakes
> 2 cups beet greens, red chard, or spinach, rinsed, dried, and
>   chopped
> 2 cups water
> 1 small bay leaf
> 4 ½-inch-thick slices good country bread, a day or two old
> Just-grated pecorino
> *Olio santo* (page 155)

In a large soup pot over a lively flame, heat the olive oil and soften the onion and garlic without coloring them. Add the potatoes, rolling them around in the oil and the aromatics, and add the sea salt, the chile pepper, and the greens, combining the components well and permitting them to cook together for a minute or two. Add the water and the bay leaf and simmer for 15 minutes or until the potatoes are tender.

Cover the pot and let the soup rest while you oven-toast the bread. Place the bread in warm, deep bowls and ladle the soup over it. Generously dust pecorino over the soup and drop tears of *olio santo* over the cheese.

Salsicce di Lucania

THE PORK SAUSAGE OF LUCANIA

Makes about 2½ pounds

Soppressato is a dried sausage of large, oval shape, refined texture, and vivid spice, the masterwork of the salumieri lucani. This sausage is a fundamental offering on the Lucanian table and its goodness is often celebrated, imitated—in longer, more slender shapes—in all the regions of Italy, under the all-encompassing name of luganica/luganega, after Lucania. Here follows a recipe for a fresh sausage that embraces the flavors and perfumes of the traditional salsicce of Lucania.

6 fat cloves garlic, peeled and crushed

1 piece fresh ginger, 2 inches by 2 inches, peeled and crushed

3 ounces pancetta

2½ pounds pork shoulder, well trimmed of its fat and very finely
    minced

8 ounces fresh pork fat, ground

½ cup good red wine

¼ cup grappa

1 small, dried red chile pepper, crushed, or ⅓ to ½ teaspoon
    dried chile flakes

2½ tablespoons fine sea salt

½ cup olive oil

With a mezzaluna or a very sharp knife, mince the garlic, ginger, and pancetta together into a paste. In a large bowl, combine the paste with the minced pork, the ground pork fat, the wine, grappa, chile pepper, and sea salt, amalgamating the components well. Cover the bowl, permitting the ingredients to absorb flavorings and ripen for several hours or overnight, well covered in the refrigerator.

Form plump ovals—3 inches by 2 inches—and, over a lively flame in a large sauté pan, heat the olive oil and quickly sauté the sausages. Or, better, grill them, crusty and dark, on an oiled grate over a wood fire. They are fiery, sassy enough to follow *pasta alla pecoraio* (page 152) or luscious when laid, all warm and juicy, over simply dressed bitter greens.

La Pappa di Orazio

HORACE'S PORRIDGE

or

PASTA WITH CHICKPEAS AND LEEKS

Serves 4

Horace, born Quinto Flacco of freed Roman slaves in the sleepy village of Venosa in the north of Basilicata, was educated in Rome and Athens in philosophy and literature and trained as a soldier. It was his poverty, though, that piqued him to write verse. A satirist, a classicist, a romantic, Horace was also a dyspeptic. He sought cures from alchemists and magicians. He journeyed to Chiusi (an Etruscan town in Umbria, fifteen kilometers from our home) to sit his ailing bones in icy, sulfurous baths. But it was this soup of dried peas and leeks, a food of his childhood, to which he paid homage in his works as his only cure.

The folk of Venosa present, having little else to claim, make the soup in every osteria and taverna, each cook armed with at least one trucco—*trick—that makes his soup the one and only true one. Here follows mine, its only* trucco *its artlessness.*

> 6 ounces dried chickpeas, soaked in cold water for 2 hours, then
> drained
> 2 teaspoons coarse sea salt, plus additional as needed to cook
> the pasta
> 1 small branch of rosemary
> 1 branch of sage
> 1 fat clove garlic, peeled and crushed
> 4 small leeks
> 3 tablespoons extra-virgin olive oil
> 3 cups veal or beef stock, preferably homemade
> 8 ounces freshly made egg pasta, cut into wide, short lengths
> Just-grated pecorino
> Freshly cracked pepper

In a large saucepan, cover the soaked chickpeas with fresh, cold water, adding the 2 teaspoons of salt, rosemary, sage, and garlic. Over a lively flame, bring the chickpeas to a simmer and cook for 1 hour or until they are soft but still holding their shape. Drain them, reserving a cup or so of the cooking water.

Trim the leeks, leaving 1 inch of their green stem. Split, rinse, and dry them—then slice the leeks thin. In a large sauté pan, heat the oil and add the leeks, cooking them until transparent, about 10 minutes over a medium flame. Add 1 cup of stock and reduce the liquid for a minute or two.

Cook the pasta in boiling, sea-salted water for 3 minutes and drain, returning the pasta to its cooking pot. Add the cooked, drained chickpeas, the leeks, the remaining 2 cups of stock, and 1 cup of the reserved cooking liquors from the chickpeas to the pasta. Over a gentle flame, combine the ingredients.

The soup will be quite thick with the beans and pasta and leeks. Ladle the soup into warm, deep bowls, dusting it with pecorino and generous grindings of pepper.

Stinchi di Agnello alla Potentina

LAMB SHANKS IN THE STYLE OF POTENZA

Serves 4

Shanks slowly braised like these composed a winter Sunday lunch served to us in a linoleum-tiled card room snugged behind a bar on the edges of Potenza. The players were sent off precisely at one so that the cook might lay the oil-clothed tables with yellow linens and set them with blue and white china. The eight or ten tables were all reserved, as they were each Sunday, the only day when the improvised dining room was open. We had heard about the wonderful food and asked the signora if we might wait until the table of one of her fixed clients might become available. "Impossibile." She laughed. "Questi tavoli non saranno liberi prima di mezzanotte." "These tables will not be free before midnight." She explained that after lunch, the pretty linens and china would be washed and tucked away to await next Sunday, leaving the gaming tables free for cardplaying throughout the afternoon and evening. When one booked a table, one booked it for lunch and endless rounds of briscola, the high-stakes action to which even the women were invited on Sundays. A lovely and entrepreneurial program, we thought, but what about our lunch?

The sympathetic signora made room for us, tightening up the seating around a table for four, adding two more place settings and chairs. And so we dined with the priest and his mother and a retired fruit-seller and his wife, all of whom spoke only in dialect while we bumped along in Italian. The encumbrance of language soon dissolved in the mists of the signora's beautiful food. Plates of local, dried sausages and farmhouse cheeses, baskets of just-fried, bay-perfumed breads, a soup of bitter greens, great bowls of rough, handmade pasta sauced only with the rich liquors from braised lamb and dusted with pecorino and, finally, the whole, braised shanks of lamb themselves, sending up sublime perfumes of garlic and rosemary.

And as sustaining as is the memory of the company and the food on that Sunday in Potenza, it is another scene that plays more sweetly in my mind. A sort of coming-of-age for me—it was there that I learned, fast and well, the secrets of briscola.

10 ounces pistachios, shelled
4 fat cloves garlic, peeled and crushed

3 tablespoons fresh rosemary leaves

6 ounces pancetta, roughly diced

4 whole lamb hind shanks (if they are very small, use 2 for each
    serving)

⅓ cup extra-virgin olive oil

Fine sea salt

Freshly cracked pepper

1 cup good red wine

½ cup good red wine vinegar

1 pound ripe tomatoes, peeled, seeded, and chopped

Place the pistachios, garlic, rosemary, and the pancetta in the work bowl of a food processor, pulsing the elements into a rough paste. With a small, sharp knife, cut ½-inch slits over the surfaces of the shanks and massage the fragrant paste well into the cuts as well as over the whole of the meat. Cover the shanks and permit them an hour's rest.

Over a lively flame in a very large sauté pan or terra-cotta casserole, heat the oil and sauté the shanks—only as many of them that will fit at a time without touching—sprinkling on sea salt and generous grindings of pepper, sealing, crusting, them well on all sides. Remove the shanks to a holding plate.

When all the shanks have been sealed, pour off any remaining oil and rinse the sauté pan with the red wine, stirring and scraping at the residue and permitting the wine to reduce for 2 minutes before adding the red wine vinegar, the tomatoes, and 1 teaspoon sea salt. Bring to a simmer and add the shanks with their accumulated juices. Cover with a skewed lid and very gently braise the shanks over a quiet flame for 1 hour or more, until the flesh is just falling from the bones. The size of the shanks will dictate the time. Should you have chosen to use the larger foreshank portion of the lamb, the braising session will, of course, be longer.

Trota Arrosto con Olive Nere e Verdi

ROAST TROUT WITH BLACK AND GREEN OLIVES

Serves 6

The jots of coast and whatever sea fish they might offer have little embellished the Lucanian cuisine, yet the fat, brown trout from her rivers and lakes are coveted, stalked. The most characteristic prescription for their cooking is to scent them with the wild herbs one finds near the water, stuff them with a few crushed olives, wrap them in a slice of pancetta, and roast them, on site, over a beech or chestnut wood fire.

> 2 tablespoons extra-virgin olive oil
>
> 1 tablespoon minced fresh rosemary leaves
>
> 3 fat cloves garlic, peeled, crushed, and minced
>
> 10 ounces large black and green Sicilian or Greek olives,
>   crushed lightly with a mallet, stones removed, flesh chopped
>   coarsely
>
> 6 cleaned, skinned, filleted trout
>
> 12 thin slices pancetta

Go fishing. Build a wood fire. Warm the olive oil in a small pan over the fire before it gets too hot and soften the rosemary with the garlic. Combine the aromatics with the olives and spoon it over the insides of the opened trout. Lay a slice of pancetta over the olive mixture, close the trout, and wrap another slice of pancetta around the trout's belly, securing it with a toothpick.

Roast the trout, in a wire fish griller or on an oiled grate, over the fire for 2 or 3 minutes to the side. Drizzle the roasted fish with a few tears of good oil and eat them with oven-toasted bread and a red wine. Though the trout can be sautéed in olive oil, it would seem to smudge the whole idea of their rusticity.

Frittelle di Ricotta e Rhum alla Lucana

RUM AND RICOTTA FRITTERS IN THE MANNER OF LUCANIA

Makes 3 dozen fritters

So unlike the exquisitely wrought sweetmeats of other southern pasticcerie, *pastry in Basilicata is often in the form of some rustic fried fritter, its batter honey-sweetened and studded with raisins or nuts. The most luscious version, though, is the one that asks for ricotta and dark rum. We found them being made in a small shop with an even smaller selling counter on a little street off the Via Pretoria, just before one reaches Piazza Mario Pagano in Potenza. On more than one iced winter's morning have we stood outside its doors and waited for the sugar-dusted, crisp-crusted warmth of them.*

> 20 ounces fresh whole-milk ricotta
> 5 eggs, separated
> ¼ cup dark rum
> 2 tablespoons sugar
> 1⅓ cups all-purpose flour
> 3 teaspoons baking powder
> Peanut oil
> Confectioners' sugar

In the work bowl of a food processor, pulse the ricotta until it is smooth and creamy. Turn the ricotta out into a large bowl and add the lightly beaten yolks, the rum, and the sugar, beating the ingredients well. Sift together the flour and the baking powder and add it to the ricotta mixture. Beat the whites to stiff but not dry peaks and fold them, gently and thoroughly, into the ricotta mixture.

In a large, heavy-bottomed pan over a medium flame, slowly heat at least 4 inches of peanut oil and, before the oil reaches the smoking point, form the fritters by dropping scant tablespoonfuls of the batter into the bubbling oil. Cook the fritters until golden, turning them and cooking the other side.

Remove the fritters from the oil with a slotted spoon to drain a moment on absorbent paper towels before dusting them with confectioners' sugar. Serve the fritters warm on a Sunday morning with a pot of hot chocolate with rum.

Torta di Riso Nero

A BLACK RICE TART

Serves 6 to 8

Riso nero—black rice—is the dramatic name for a nursery dish offered to children as a light supper or as a sweet after a bit of broth or soup. It is most often just made with rice poached in milk that has been scented with cinnamon and mixed with a few shards of chocolate, the latter giving the dish its name as it melts and turns the rice a deep, dark color. Surely there are lovely similarities between it and pasta in nero della consolazione (page 118). Here I offer its comfort in a more adult version. The same prescriptions apply, though, as this is best presented after a light, reviving soup or, better, after no soup at all, so one can justify slipping one's fork into the spiced, chocolate depths of a second or third piece of the sweet little pie.

        4½ cups whole milk

        ½ cup sugar

        1 3-inch cinnamon stick, crushed

        Generous gratings of fresh nutmeg

        1 plump vanilla bean

        2 tablespoons cocoa powder, preferably Dutch process

        ½ teaspoon ground cloves

        ¼ teaspoon fine sea salt

        1¼ cups *superfino* rice (arborio, vialone nano, carnaroli)

        ¼ cup *liquore di caffè* (Tía Maria or Kahlúa)

        3½ ounces extra-bittersweet chocolate, preferably Lindt or
           Valrhona 70% cacao

        ⅓ cup mascarpone

        ⅔ cup pistachios, shelled, roasted, and coarsely chopped

        2 large eggs, separated

        2 tablespoons sweet butter, slightly softened

        2 egg whites

        Tart Crust (page 216)

        Heavy cream (optional)

In a medium saucepan, heat the milk with the sugar, the crushed cinnamon stick, nutmeg, the vanilla seeds and pod (slit the bean with a sharp knife and scrape its seeds directly into the milk), the cocoa, the cloves, and the sea salt, bringing the ingredients to a simmer. Stir in the rice, lower the flame, cover the pan, and cook it for 35 minutes or until nearly all the liquid has been absorbed. Remove the vanilla pod and any larger pieces of the cinnamon stick that might remain. Cool the rice for 10 minutes in a large bowl.

Meanwhile, in a small, heavy saucepan over a gentle flame, warm the *liquore* and melt the chocolate and the mascarpone in it. Add the chocolate/*liquore*/mascarpone mixture to the rice, along with the pistachios, the two yolks, lightly beaten, and the softened butter, stirring to combine the components. In a large bowl, beat the four egg whites to stiff but not dry peaks and fold them, gently and thoroughly, into the rice.

Turn the black rice out into a partially baked tart crust in a buttered 10-inch tart pan with a removable bottom. Bake the tart at 375 degrees for 25 to 30 minutes or until its center is set but still very creamy. Do not overbake the tart.

Cool the tart for at least 1 hour and present it with fluffs of barely whipped, unsweetened cream to those with hearts who can still get excited over a chocolate pie.

CALABRIA

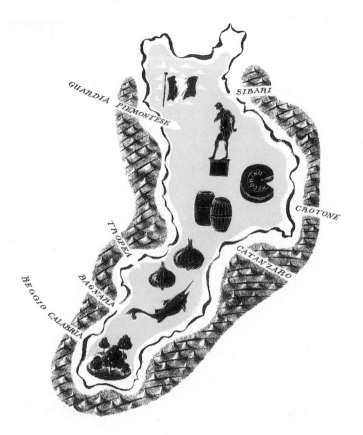

The Scylla screams no more as one passes, *adagio, adagio,* through the straits under a moon of opal glass. Rock crags crowd the ship like a bellicose cave and one feels the rasp of their ancient roughness. Only the color of the water, purling, husky under the rudder, the same hollow and lightless blue of the six-headed she-monster's eyes, recalls her. The Scylla's roars were none but the wind's voice strangled inside the caves, begging. Time freed the winds to race and whirl and whine and the Scylla's voice was hushed. Some say she lives there still, her lair jutting out where the straits curve toward land, raging at her own terror-lessness. And then there is *fata morgana.* A sorceress of purposes chaste and pure as are the Scylla's horrid. Morgana will grant, to one who stands on the verges of the straits at Reggio and looks down into the dark waters at the moment the sun rises and the winds are still asleep, an enchanting glimpse of an undersea city. A mirage, a startling, ravishing, shimmering up of Sicily's Messina, sitting across rather than under the water, it is a small bewitching from a good fairy. Calabria needs, nourishes evidences of both bane and light to stay her. She is a land of contradiction.

She grows up delicate bergamot in the fields near Reggio, the single patch of land on all the earth where is cultivated this fruit from which is extracted the precious, essential oil that contributes to and stabilizes the fragrances of French perfumes. A fribbling caprice, it seems, in a place often still hungry. It is a land where one lunches in a mountain osteria on the roasted entrails of a sheep and then, over the next mountain, comes upon a little place in which to take supper and stay the night, where one is served a lush, embroidered dish from the seventeenth-century tomes of the Spanish courts, a dish never tasted, never dreamed of, by the cook only twenty-nine kilometers distant from the other.

A region of loose precincts, mostly uninterrupted and surely untamed by time, nearly all of her is of mountains, the villages that bestride them, fortressed one from another, unsavvy to any but its own rites and rituals, its own language. Hers is a legacy of brigands. After the unification of Italy in 1861 and Rome's decree against *latifondismo*—the holding of great parcels of land by a handful of citizens—the south was politically, spiritually abandoned. No enforcement, no intervention came from the new governors and an even more base epoch of serfdom, of insufficiency ensued. Unlike in other southern regions where the poor simply died or ran away from their hunger, the Calabresi hoisted up their own impassioned service of justice, it's known as *'ndrangheta*. (Having perfected if not refined its manners over the years, still *'ndrangheta* ministers power over Calabria, they the colleagues of the *camorra* of Campania, the *mafia* of Sicilia.) And theirs was a rebellion of unshrinking *briganti e brigantesse* who, with impulse less romantic than that of dear Robin Hood, snuffed out the knaves who stood in the way of the peasants' daily bread. This in the same place where Greece raised up Sybaris and Crotone, where there was sculpted a life of more splendid proportions than had or has been lived anywhere else in time.

About the Cuisine

Meat only from the hunt, from the barnyard pig, or, less often, from the sheepfolds is carried to the Calabrian table. In the high plateaux of the Sila, a primitive gathering-foraging culture pervades. It is a big soup for which Calabria hungers, or a rough, handmade pasta cooked not in water but in the pot liquors of some slow-braising bird. Hers is a repertoire full of *piatti unici*—one-dish meals—that comprise a supper. And, too, does Calabria traffic hard in the sting of chile.

The isolation of each province, each fraction of each province, builds a cuisine unfrayed by the influences of others. Hence, the ancient parishes once lorded over by the Spaniards still unfurl their legacy in phrase, posture, philosophy, cheekbones, sentiment, and cuisine. It is the same story with the Greeks, the French, the Albanians. Hence, the food of Calabria, though fundamentally rough and plain and poor, is ornamented here and there with elaborate ancestral dishes. Hers is less a prescribed regional gastronomy than it is a collection of factional cuisines.

Pomodori alla Brace

WOOD-ROASTED TOMATOES

Serves 4

A humble prescript that flaunts the goodness of summer tomatoes, that asks their roasting over wood, concentrating, ennobling their sweet juices. Propped, then, on crusty seats of bread with a gloss of good green oil and the grace of basil and mint, they soothe hungers for purity.

> 4 large, ripe, still firm, gorgeous tomatoes
> Fine sea salt
> 8 tablespoons extra-virgin olive oil
> 2 fat cloves garlic, peeled, crushed, and minced
> 4 ½-inch-thick trenchers of bread cut from a large loaf
> 1 fat clove garlic, peeled
> 1 generous handful of whole, fat basil leaves
> 1 generous handful of whole mint leaves

Build a wood fire. Hopefully, the fire's heat and perfumes will be put to some other delicious purposes than the roasting of the tomatoes. Cut a thin slice from the top of the tomatoes and scoop out their seeds. Sprinkle sea salt generously inside their bellies, drop ½ tablespoon of oil and minces of garlic inside each, and place the tomatoes on an oiled grate over the fire. Roast them until their bottoms are charred and soft—about 7 minutes, depending on their size, the degree of ripeness, and the force of the fire—then topple them on first one side and then the other, avoiding turning them upside down, until their flesh is hot and collapsing, nearly bursting through their charred, wrinkled skins.

During this rite, toast the trenchers of bread, too, over the grate, crusting them quickly on both sides without drying the crumb. Rub the whole garlic clove over one side of the hot trenchers, then drizzle them with big tears of oil, using about ¼ cup. Place the bread cushions on a large, warm plate to await the tomatoes. When they are roasted, place a tomato on each cushion of bread, thread the remaining oil over them, and strew them with the leaves of basil and mint. Though the dish is built of such familiar stuffs, they emerge, somehow, new, sensational even, for the tomatoes' short smolder over the fire.

Ricotta Forte

SPICED RICOTTA

Makes about 3 cups

Unlike the ricotta forte *of Puglia, prepared laboriously, asking that the fresh cheese be left to drain off its opaline waters and to acidify, the dry cheese to then be kneaded, worked each third or fourth day for at least two months until it takes on a burnt ivory sort of color and its perfumes come up stinging, pungent, this version is prepared in moments. Yielding a condiment less punishing in its aromas, the Calabrian* ricotta forte *is still of an assertive and keen savor, which when smoothed over warm, crusty bread, glorifies the richness of spiced sausages and* salame *presented as antipasto. A few dollops of it, thinned with drops of pasta cooking water and tossed with bucatini or spaghetti, make a fine dish. Tucked away in a crock in the refrigerator for a week or so, the vigor of* ricotta forte *ripens and intensifies.*

> 3 anchovies, preserved under salt
> 3 cups whole-milk ricotta
> ¼ cup grappa or Cognac
> 2 small, whole red chile peppers, crushed, or ½ to ⅔ teaspoon
>   dried chile flakes
> 3 fat cloves garlic, peeled and crushed
> ⅓ cup capers, preserved under salt, rinsed and dried

Rinse the anchovies. Remove their heads and bones and dry lightly on absorbent paper towels.

In the bowl of a food processor fitted with a steel blade, whip the ricotta with the grappa to a smooth cream. Turn the ricotta out into a bowl. In a mortar with a pestle, grind the chile peppers with the garlic and the anchovies to a paste. Stir the paste into the ricotta, blending the components thoroughly before folding in the capers.

Turn the ricotta into a large terra-cotta crock or several smaller rustic sorts of vessels, covering them tightly with plastic wrap, and permitting them an overnight rest in the refrigerator to marry their good, compatible flavors and perfumes.

Minestra Invernale di Verza e Castagne di Guardia Piemontese

A WINTER SOUP OF CABBAGE AND CHESTNUTS
IN THE MANNER OF THE GUARDIA PIEMONTESE

Serves 8

A medieval fastness above the Mar Tirreno, Guardia Piemontese is a thirteenth-century village raised up by a band of French-descended, Waldensian heretics in flight from papal justice. Pursued into the pathlessness of Calabria, they resisted the Church's soldiers then and again and again. Two hundred years had passed when, flush with the dramas of the *inquisizione*, Pius V dispatched a brigade up into their serene agrarian midst, calling for, in the names of Christ and the Holy Ghost, their massacre.

Those few who escaped the flailing of the Church's swords stayed. And those who were born of them stay, still, speaking a Provencale dialect and celebrating the traditions of French country life, gentling their patch of the earth as though time was a stranger. Too, they are true to their own and simple gastronomic heritage, having obliged no transfusion of the coarser Calabrian kitchen. Here follows a thick mountain soup, so like a Béarnais garbure (a thick cabbage soup from Béarn) even to the blessing of its last smudges with red wine as the French are wont to do à la faire chabrot—pouring a few drops of red wine into the last spoonful of soup, stirring it up and getting every last drop as both a blessing to the cook and a thank-you to God.

2 pounds fresh chestnuts

2 tablespoons fine sea salt

3 tablespoons plus ½ cup extra-virgin olive oil

3 ounces pancetta, finely diced

3 ounces salt pork, finely diced

1 large head firm fresh garlic cloves separated, unpeeled, and
    slightly crushed

2 cups good red wine

4 medium turnips, trimmed, peeled, and cut into ½-inch dice

4 small carrots, trimmed, scraped, and sliced

3 small leeks, trimmed, retain 1 inch of the green stems, split,
    rinsed, dried, and sliced

1 small head Savoy cabbage, cored and coarsely shredded

Slit the chestnuts on their flat sides with a short, sharp knife or a hook-bladed chestnut knife and boil them for 3 to 4 minutes in water with 1 tablespoon sea salt. Drain the chestnuts and peel them and rub off their inner skins while they are still warm.

In a very large, heavy soup pot over a medium flame, warm 3 tablespoons of the olive oil and sauté the pancetta and the salt pork, until they have rendered their fat and are well crusted. With a slotted spoon, remove the crisped pancetta and salt pork to a holding plate.

Add the peeled chestnuts to the pot, rolling them about for a minute or two before adding the crushed cloves of garlic and stirring the mixture together. Add the red wine and 8 cups of water and return to a simmer. Cover the pot with a skewed lid and continue to simmer for 1 hour.

In a large sauté pan over a medium flame, warm ½ cup of the olive oil and add the turnips and carrots, tossing them about in the fat for a minute or two before adding the leeks, the cabbage, and 1 tablespoon sea salt and stirring the ingredients together for another minute. Remove the vegetables from the flame. After the chestnuts have simmered for 1 hour, add the vegetables to the pot, returning to a simmer. Cook the soup, uncovered, for ½ hour or until the chestnuts are tender but still holding their shape. The soup is best when it is served without pureeing first. But, if you wish, pureeing a third or so of the soup and blending it back will thicken it into a stew, leaving its integrity unharmed. It's your choice.

In any case, turn the soup out into a warmed tureen or ladle it into warm, deep soup plates. Pass the reserved crisps of pancetta and salt pork for garnish. Add warm bread, a jug of the good red wine with which the soup was made, and supper is ready.

Minestra di Cipolle di Tropea

A SOUP WITH THE ONIONS OF TROPEA

Serves 8

It is fitting that on a most divine jot of the Tyrrhenian coast, on a promontory between the limpid gulfs of Sant' Eufemia and Goia Tauro, there would glint the small, golden precinct of Tropea. Fitting, too, that there in its rich, black fields would be raised up Italy's sweetest onions, and that they be long and oval like great lavender pearls. One peels them and sets to, with knife and fork, a dish of sea salt, a pepper grinder, and a tiny jug of beautiful oil, a perfect lunch with bread and wine. Too, we saw the folk of Tropea simply fold back their papery skins and eat them raw, out of hand, layer by layer, like a magical violet fruit. Sometimes, one finds them all softened, smoothed into a delectable potion made of garlic and bay leaves and white wine. Evident in its resemblances to French cousins, the soup of Tropea, though, is a minestra strepitosa— a magnificent soup—say the Calabrian cooks, belittling the goodness of the French soup.

Here follows a version that softens the garlic, caramelizing it into sweetness with the slow cooking of the onions, before the illumination of the soup with red wine and grappa and the finishing of it with pecorino and a heavy dusting of fresh pepper.

3 tablespoons extra-virgin olive oil, plus additional as needed

4 ounces salt pork, diced

2 pounds sweet violet or red-skinned onions or yellow-skinned Vidalia, Walla Walla, or Texas Sweet onions, peeled and sliced thin

1 large head firm, fresh garlic, cloves separated, unpeeled and slightly crushed

1 tablespoon fine sea salt

1½ teaspoons brown sugar

1 bay leaf

2 cups dry white wine

5 cups good beef stock, preferably homemade

1 cup good red wine

¼ cup grappa

8 ½-inch slices good country bread

1½ cups just-grated pecorino

Freshly cracked pepper

In a large, wide terra-cotta or enameled cast-iron casserole over a medium flame, warm 3 tablespoons of olive oil and sauté the salt pork, crusting it well, then removing it with a slotted spoon to a holding plate. Add the onions and the garlic, tossing them about in the fat until the onions are translucent. Lower the flame a bit and sprinkle on the sea salt and brown sugar, cooking the onions and garlic for ½ hour, stirring them often, until they have caramelized a bit and taken on a soft, golden color. Add the bay leaf, the white wine, and the stock, bringing the liquid to a simmer, cooking the soup for 20 minutes before adding the red wine and the grappa and simmering it gently for 5 minutes more.

Preheat the oven broiler. Lay the slices of bread over the hot soup, dust the bread thickly with pecorino, and drop thin threads of olive oil over the whole. Generously grind pepper over the casserole and place it under the broiler to toast the bread and brown the cheese.

Carry the soup, golden and sputtering, to the table, ladling it into warmed, deep soup plates. Pass a bottle of grappa should anyone desire additional benediction.

Morzeddu di Agnello delle Putiche di Catanzaro

MORSELS OF LAMB IN THE MANNER OF THE TAVERNS OF CATANZARO

Serves 4

During the sovereignty of Byzantium over southern Italy in the tenth century, it was in the workshops of Catanzaro that the silks that emblazoned the courts of Costantinopoli were loomed and crafted and tinged. Thus it was that from these handiworks, humble Catanzaro, its cheek brushing close upon the Ionian, lived its few lustrous moments after the glory days of Magna Graecia. But save the lacy Oriental architecture raised up by the Byzantines, nothing of the comforts of that epoch endured.

And so Catanzaro, as did all of Calabria, pressed on in the severest of lives. And when, late in the 1700s, an earthquake felled the city, its fierceness left but dust. Reborn then, Catanzaro is now all of eighteenth-century alleyways, the parishes of the people insinuating upon the palaces of the nobles, the whole formed of a crooked, good-natured charm. And everywhere—round each curve and set into the arms of every angle wait the beloved putiche—the taverns—of the workingmen. Small, dark-wooded dens are they, wrapped in sharp, grapy vapors breathed up from the fat, brown barrels of gaglioppo (a local red wine) over these past hundreds of years. Traditionally le putiche were the dispensaries of only three balms—honest red wine, compassion, and a hellaciously spiced mash made from the viscera of pork, veal, lamb, or goat, sometimes from baccalà, the flesh braised in tomatoes and wine with peperoncini then cradled in a leaf of soft, flat, chewy bread, folded and devoured out of hand. And these morzeddu—dialectically, morsels—made the breakfast, the later morning's merendina—snack—a consolingly juicy partner throughout the day and evening with stout doses of purply wine. Sadly, there seems of late a flurry of gentrification among the putiche, the work of those who would sophisticate them into whitewashed osterie with wine lists and menus translated into English and German. The cooks, too occupied with carpaccio and tiramisù, no longer make morzeddu. Even the compassion has perished. Enough of the old and crusty taverns endure, though, their comforts unfaded, at least for a bit longer.

Here follows a version of morzeddu made with lamb—its shoulder rather than its spleen or its lungs—and a fine terra-cotta pot of the mash and a basket of warm breads are the rustic stuff with which to open an outdoor feast while some other meat or fish might be roasting on the fire.

⅓ cup olive oil

3 ounces salt pork, minced

2 pounds boned lamb shoulder, well trimmed of its fat and cut
    into ½-inch dice

2 medium yellow onions, peeled and sliced very thin

4 fat cloves garlic, peeled, crushed, and minced

1 teaspoon dried Greek oregano

1 bay leaf, crushed

2 to 3 dried red chile peppers, crushed, or ⅔ to 1 teaspoon dried
  chile flakes

1 14-ounce can plum tomatoes, with their liquids

1 teaspoon fine sea salt

1 cup good red wine

1 cup just-grated pecorino

In a large terra-cotta or enameled cast-iron casserole over a medium flame, warm the olive oil and sauté the salt pork. Brown the lamb—perhaps only half or a third of it at a time—crusting it, coloring it well, then removing it, with a slotted spoon, to a holding plate.

When the lamb has been sealed, soften the onions and garlic in the fat for 2 or 3 minutes, taking care not to let them color. Add the oregano, the bay leaf, and the chile peppers into the pan and cook another minute before quieting the flame a bit more and adding the tomatoes, the sea salt, the wine, and the sealed lamb. Cover the casserole with a skewed lid and permit it to simmer gently for ½ hour or until the lamb has all but melted into the thickened sauce.

Off the heat, stir in the pecorino. Permit the sauce to cool, cover it, and let it rest an hour or so before a gentle reheating. Carry the casserole to table with a basket of warm, small breads, already split and readied for filling, or some good baker's best crusty rolls. Invite everyone to stuff their little loaves with the tantalizing mash and to drink rough red wine with the thirst of the Catanzarese.

Maccarruni i Casa Brasati con Maiale alla Cosentina

HOMEMADE PASTA BRAISED WITH PORK
IN THE STYLE OF COSENZA

Serves 8

Here, the Calabrian fashions a rough paste of flour, sea salt, and water and perhaps an egg and a spoonful of oil, rolling it out thin and cutting it into wide, uneven ribbons, calling it maccarruni i casa—maccheroni *made at home. It is married to a well-made sauce flavored with some precious trimmings of pork and left to braise and plump in its liquors. The whole offering, pasta, meat, and sauce, is carried to table and eaten, one hopes, with the lush hunger it deserves. Here one uses a good piece rather than a few trimmings of pork. One might choose an acquisition from a good pasta shop or specialty grocery or make the good* maccheroni alla mugnaia *(page 37) for this dish.*

2 tablespoons fresh rosemary leaves

1 piece fresh ginger, about 1½ inches long and 1½ inches wide, peeled

1 small, dried red chile pepper, crushed, or ⅓ to ½ teaspoon dried chile flakes

3 fat cloves garlic, peeled

1 tablespoon coarse sea salt, plus additional as needed for the pasta

1 4-pound loin boned pork, trimmed of all but a thin layer of fat, rolled, and tied at 1½-inch intervals with butcher's twine

¼ cup extra-virgin olive oil

1½ cups good red wine

¼ cup good red wine vinegar

1 cup canned tomato puree

12 ounces just-made egg pasta, cut into ½-inch ribbons

Just-grated pecorino

In a mortar with a pestle, grind the rosemary, ginger, chile pepper, garlic, and 1 tablespoon sea salt to a paste. With a short, sharp knife, make ½- by ½-inch slits over the surface of the pork. Rub the aromatic paste over the pork, pushing it into the slits. Cover the pork loosely with plastic wrap and permit it to absorb the paste for several hours at cool room temperature.

In a very large terra-cotta or enameled cast-iron casserole over a lively flame, heat the olive oil and brown the pork, sealing and crusting it well on all sides, a task that takes at least 10 minutes. Remove the pork to a holding plate.

Lower the flame a bit and add the wine to the casserole, stirring, scraping at the residue for 1 minute before adding the wine vinegar, the tomato puree, and the pork. Bring the mixture to a simmer, cover the casserole with a slightly skewed lid, and braise the roast gently.

Cook the pasta in abundant, boiling, sea-salted water for 1 minute. Drain the pasta and set it aside. After the pork has been braising for 1 hour, test its readiness. If its flesh is fork-tender, it is braised properly. If not, let it simmer away for another 20 minutes.

When the pork is cooked, add the pasta to the casserole, tossing it about to moisten it thoroughly with the braising liquors. Cover the casserole and continue a quiet braise for 5 minutes, permitting the pasta to finish cooking and absorb the good juices. Let the dish rest for 5 minutes before carrying it to table.

Carve the roast into thick slices there, laying one over each serving of the pasta, with spoonfuls of the good sauce. Pass the just-grated pecorino.

A hamlet hung on the bluffs of the Sila Grande at Calabria's heart, is San Giovanni da Fiore, a sylvan realm of ancient pine and beech and fir, woods crystalline with snow for longer than half of every year, kingdom of the great Sila wolves, the place where falcons swoop and eagles weave their nests onto the steeps. Here is the twelfth-century monastery where the Cistercian seer Gioacchino da Fiore meditated. Here, too, are the deer and the boar, the woodcock, wild hare, pheasant, and quail, that absorb the Calabrian cacciatori. More docile quarry for them are the fat, loamy mushrooms that push up from the damp, black earth on the skirts of the old oaks. Here follow, then, two typical hunters' versions that glorify the bounty of the Sila forests.

Pasta con i Funghi Selvatici di San Giovanni da Fiore

PASTA WITH WILD MUSHROOMS IN THE MANNER OF
SAN GIOVANNI DA FIORE

Serves 4

4 fat cloves garlic, peeled

1 small dried, red chile pepper, or ⅓ to ½ teaspoon dried chile flakes

1 bay leaf

2 teaspoons coarse sea salt, plus additional for the pasta

3 ounces salt pork

⅓ cup extra-virgin olive oil

1½ pounds fresh wild mushrooms, such as porcini, cèpes, chanterelles, portobelli, etc., thinly sliced

2 cups good red wine

1 cup canned tomato puree

12 ounces just-made egg pasta

½ cup pine nuts, lightly pan-roasted

½ cup just-made bread crumbs, lightly pan-roasted in ¼ cup extra-virgin olive oil

1 cup just-grated pecorino

With a mezzaluna or a very sharp knife, mince together into a paste the garlic, chile pepper, bay leaf, 2 teaspoons sea salt, and salt pork. In a large terra-cotta or enameled cast-iron casserole over a medium flame, heat the olive oil and sauté the paste for a minute or two before adding the mushrooms, tossing them about in the perfumed fat, permitting them to give up their juices. Lower the flame, add the wine and the tomato puree, bringing the ingredients to a gentle simmer. Cover the casserole with a skewed lid and braise the mushrooms for ½ hour, permitting them to plump and turn velvety as they slowly reabsorb their juices and inhale the good wine and tomato liquors.

Cook the pasta in abundant, boiling, sea-salted water for 1 minute. Drain the pasta and add it to the casserole with the mushrooms, tossing the ingredients about thoroughly. Cover the casserole and permit the whole to cook over a low flame for 3 or 4 minutes, just so that the pasta finishes its cooking and absorbs the braising liquors.

Combine the roasted pine nuts, the olive-oil-roasted bread crumbs, and the pecorino and give the pasta a thick dusting. Carry the casserole to the table, offering more oven-toasted bread and good red wine.

Pasta Brasata con le Quaglie di San Giovanni da Fiore

PASTA BRAISED WITH QUAIL IN THE MANNER OF SAN GIOVANNI DA FIORE

Serves 4

A dish a hunter might prepare for his family even if his sack holds only a few birds, the quail are pan-roasted, pasta is added to its good liquors, the whole roasted in the oven, and carried to table as a piatto unico— *one-dish meal.*

4 farm-raised quail, cleaned, their livers reserved
6 juniper berries
6 whole white peppercorns
3 whole cloves
1 fat clove garlic, peeled
1 teaspoon coarse sea salt, plus additional as needed for the
    pasta
4 thin slices pancetta
8 large leaves sage
3 tablespoons extra-virgin olive oil
1 ounce salt pork, minced

1 teaspoon fine sea salt

2 cups dry white wine

2 tablespoons good white wine vinegar

12 ounces short tubular pasta, such as ziti, penne, rigatoni

Rinse the quail in cool water and dry them, inside and out, with absorbent paper towels.

In a mortar with a pestle, grind to a paste the reserved livers, the juniper berries, the peppercorns, the cloves, the garlic, and 1 teaspoon of coarse sea salt. Spoon a bit of the aromatic paste into the cavity of each quail. Wrap each quail in a slice of pancetta, securing it with a toothpick and slipping two leaves of sage between its breast and the pancetta.

In a large terra-cotta or enameled cast-iron casserole over a lively flame, heat the olive oil and sauté the salt pork. Place the quail in the casserole and brown them on all sides. Lower the flame, sprinkle on the fine sea salt, add the wine and the vinegar, bringing the quail and its liquids to a gentle simmer. Cover the casserole tightly and braise the quail for 12 minutes.

Preheat the oven to 475 degrees.

Cook the pasta in abundant boiling, sea-salted water for 4 minutes. Drain the pasta and set it aside.

After the quail have cooked for 12 minutes, add the pasta to the casserole, stirring it about in the braising juices and repositioning the quail so that they nestle in the pasta. The pasta and the braising liquors will protect the scant flesh of the frail little birds while the casserole roasts, uncovered, for 8 to 10 minutes. This will permit the pasta to finish cooking and to absorb the braising juices, for the quail to char and crisp prettily while they complete their roasting.

Carry the casserole to table, serving the pasta and a quail to each one.

nce the shimmering beauty of Magna Graecia was Crotone. Wrapped in fog lumbering in off the Mar Ionio, it was the place where the epoch's thinkers mused, where the old gods rested. Alas, that Crotone is no more, most of the place now occupied with the building of its fine, whiffy cheeses—the pecorino of Crotone. Here follow two heirloom dishes of la cucina delle ricorrenze—the festival cooking of Calabria. Still simple, their goodness is lit by the peppered, piquant pecorino that is stagionato—aged—for as long as two years.

Schiaffettoni di Pecorino di Crotone

SAUSAGE-STUFFED CREPES WITH PECORINO IN THE STYLE OF CROTONE

Serves 6

For the Stuffing

2 cups spring peas, shelled

Coarse sea salt for the water

¼ cup extra-virgin olive oil, plus additional as needed

1 pound fresh Italian-style sausages, casings removed

2 cups just-grated pecorino

Freshly cracked pepper

3 fat cloves garlic, peeled, crushed, and finely minced

2 large eggs, lightly beaten

1 cup dry white wine

Cook the peas in simmering, sea-salted water until they are tender. Drain and refresh them under cool water and place them in a large bowl. Alternatively, one could use asparagus or spinach rather than the peas. Raw *rucola*—arugula—also works nicely.

In a sauté pan over a lively flame, warm ¼ cup of the olive oil and brown the sausage, crushing it until it crumbles and crusting it darkly. Add the sausage to the bowl with the peas. Add 1 cup of the pecorino, very generous grindings of pepper, the garlic, and the eggs to the bowl, blending all thoroughly.

For the Schiaffettoni

Follow the directions on page 54 for *le scrippelle*, through the cooking of the little pancakes, leaving out the step that asks them to be dusted with cheese and rolled.

Preheat the oven broiler.

Place a generous tablespoon of the stuffing over each *schiaffettone*, spreading it out evenly, rolling it up tightly, and placing it, seam side down, in a large, shallow terra-cotta or enameled cast-iron casserole. Repeat, filling and rolling the *schiaffettoni*, positioning them in a single layer, employing a second casserole if necessary. Pour over the white wine, dust the stuffed *schiaffettoni* with the remaining pecorino, and drop threads of olive oil over all. Slide the casserole under the broiler, cooking the *schiaffettoni* until they are golden and bubbling.

Carry the casserole to table and serve the *schiaffettoni* onto warmed plates, spooning up some of the winy juices over each.

Carciofi Arrostiti di Crotone

ROASTED ARTICHOKES IN THE STYLE OF CROTONE

Serves 4

8 small globe artichokes, with several inches of their stems
    intact
Juice of 2 lemons, divided in half
4 fat cloves garlic, peeled, crushed, and minced
2 teaspoons fine sea salt
1½ cups just-made bread crumbs
1¾ cups just-grated pecorino
1 cup minced flat parsley leaves
Zest of 2 lemons
½ cup plus 2 tablespoons extra-virgin olive oil
½ cup dry white wine

Preheat the oven to 375 degrees.

Peel the stems of the artichokes to reveal their tender cores. Tear away the coarser petals, trim the softer petals, and remove the chokes. Immerse the artichokes in very cold water acidulated with the juice of 1 lemon for ½ hour. Drain the artichokes and slice them in half.

Combine the garlic, sea salt, bread crumbs, 1½ cups pecorino, the parsley, and the lemon zest.

Rub the 2 tablespoons of oil over the surfaces of a large, shallow terra-cotta or enameled cast-iron casserole and position half the artichokes in it. Dust the artichokes generously with half the aromatic crumbs, laying the remaining artichokes on top and ending the process with a thick layer of the crumbs. Pour the ½ cup of oil over the casserole in thick threads. Combine the juice of 1 lemon and the wine and carefully pour it down the sides of the casserole, not disturbing the top layer. Roast the artichokes for ½ hour, spooning the juices over them every 10 minutes.

Dust the casserole with the final ¼ cup of pecorino and put it under a hot broiler, until the cheese turns golden and crisp.

Carry the casserole to table then, serving the artichokes with oven-toasted bread and very cold white wine as a first course, as a main course, but never as an accompaniment, so good are they all alone.

Tiana di Agnello della Suore di Polsi

LAMB BRAISED IN THE MANNER OF THE SISTERS OF POLSI

Serves 6

Deep in the Gothic tangles of the Aspromonte sits the fourteenth-century Santuario della Madonna di Polsi, a refuge culled by an ancient order of cloistered sisters dedicated to the honor of the Madonna, through a life of acetism. Once a year, though, in the early spring, when pilgrims from faraway parishes walk over Monte Montalto to the sanctuary to celebrate the festival of the Madonna, the nuns sacrifice a flock of newborn lambs to the glory of her, braising their flesh in old, shallow coppers and feeding the faithful at long, rough-hewn tables set out on a meadow floor.

⅓ cup plus 3 tablespoons extra-virgin olive oil

1 large yellow onion, peeled and minced

3 ounces pancetta, minced

2 pounds spring lamb, cut from the leg in 3-inch chunks

Flour

1 teaspoon fine sea salt, plus additional to salt lamb

2 cups dry white wine

3 small globe artichokes, with several inches of their stems left
    intact

Juice of 1 lemon

3 medium new white- or red-skinned potatoes, peeled and sliced
    in ¼-inch rounds

1½ cups spring peas, shelled

½ cup torn fresh mint leaves

1 fat clove garlic, peeled

6 whole white peppercorns

In a very large terra-cotta or enameled cast-iron casserole over a medium flame, warm ⅓ cup of the olive oil and soften the onion and the pancetta. Remove the onion with a slotted spoon to a holding plate.

Dust the lamb very lightly with flour and seal the flesh in the fat—brown only those pieces at a time that will fit without touching. Sprinkle on sea salt, crusting the lamb well on all sides, then remove it to a holding plate.

Turn up the flame, add 1 cup of the wine, stirring and scraping at the residue, and permit it to reduce a minute or two. Lower the flame and add the lamb. Bring the combination to a quiet simmer, cover the casserole with a skewed lid, and braise the lamb for 1 hour.

Peel the stems of the artichokes to reveal their tender cores. Tear away the coarser petals, trim the softer petals, and remove the chokes. Immerse them in very cold water acidulated with the juice of 1 lemon for ½ hour.

To the casserole with the lamb, add the softened onion, the potatoes, the artichokes, drained and sliced in half, the peas, the remaining cup of wine, and 1 teaspoon of the sea salt. Bring to a quiet simmer once again. Cover the casserole with a skewed lid and continue the braise, very quietly, for an additional 20 minutes, until the lamb is very soft and the vegetables are completely cooked.

In a mortar with a pestle, pound the mint, garlic, and peppercorns to a paste, thinning and emulsifying it with 3 tablespoons of the olive oil, beaten into the paste drop by drop. Stir the mint paste into the finished casserole, blending it thoroughly.

Carry the casserole to table, serving it with crusty, warm bread and cold white wine.

Here follow two ancestral dishes, versions of heirloom recipes. I present them together as a curiosity. Both are treatments of pork, both lean on juniper berries and red wine, both are bathed or rubbed in spice before a gentle braising. The first is a take on a festival dish still cooked during the citrus harvest, while the second is illustrative of the Spanish court cuisine as it was practiced in the mountain fastness of Calabria. I find it fascinating that their fundamental sameness gives forth dishes so distinct from the other.

Maiale alla Zagara

PORK BRAISED WITH LEMONS AND ORANGES

Serves 8

Zagara—flower, in Greek—is the name farmers call their precious agrumi, *they, it seems, likening the sweet, spicy perfumes of their oranges and lemons to the scents of blossoms. Thus, citrus fruits are Calabrian flowers. One farmer dared me to try to cook this luscious dish with bergamot rather than oranges and lemons, assuring me that it was the one and only fruit with which the* massaie (housewives) *braised pork long-ago. Finding none to beg or buy, I cannot tell you how the dish might have been with the ambered flesh and juices of the mysterious bergamot. One day I will.*

> 2 cups good red wine
> Juice and zest of 1 large orange
> Juice and zest of 1 lemon

1 tablespoon whole black peppercorns

1 tablespoon juniper berries

6 whole cloves

3 bay leaves

1 5-pound loin of boned pork, trimmed of all but a thin layer of
fat, rolled and tied at 1½-inch intervals with butcher's twine

½ cup brown sugar

¼ cup extra-virgin olive oil

Fine sea salt

½ cup good red wine vinegar

3 large oranges, peeled of both their zest and their bitter white
pith and sectioned

2 lemons, peeled of both their zest and their bitter white pith
and sectioned

In a saucepan, warm the wine with the citrus juices and the zests just to a simmer.

In a mortar with a pestle, grind the peppercorns, juniper berries, and cloves to a coarse powder. Remove the wine from the flame and add the spices and the bay leaves. Cover the pot and permit the liquid to absorb flavor from the spices for 1 hour.

Place the pork in a noncorrosive bowl just large enough to contain it. Pour the cooled liquid over the pork, cover the bowl tightly with plastic wrap, and permit the pork to rest for two days in the refrigerator. Turn it several times each day.

Remove the pork from its bath—reserving the marinade—and dry it with absorbent paper towels. Pat the brown sugar over the surfaces of the pork. In a terra-cotta or enameled cast-iron casserole over a lively flame, heat the oil and brown the pork, sealing all its surfaces. Permit the flesh to caramelize and take on a dark crust without burning it—a task that will take at least 10 watchful minutes. Remove the pork to a holding plate and salt it generously.

With the flame still high, add the vinegar to the casserole, stirring and scraping at the residue and permitting the vinegar to reduce for 2 or 3 minutes. Strain the reserved marinade and add it to the casserole and, again, permit the liquid to reduce for 2 or 3 minutes. Lower the flame and add the pork to the casserole. With the liquid barely simmering, cover the pork with a skewed lid and braise it for 45 minutes.

Add the sectioned oranges and lemons to the casserole, rolling them about in the sauce. Bring again to a quiet simmer and cover the casserole with a skewed lid, continuing the braise for an additional 20 minutes or until the pork is fork-tender. Permit the whole to cool, uncovered, for 1 hour. Very gently reheat the pork in its sauce. Carve it into thin slices, presenting them on a shallow, warmed platter with the braised fruit and spoonfuls of the braising liquors.

Filetti di Maiale Brasati dei Borboni di Spagna

PORK TENDERLOINS BRAISED IN THE MANNER
OF THE SPANISH BOURBONS

Serves 6

1 tablespoon coarse sea salt

¼ cup brown sugar

1 tablespoon juniper berries

1 tablespoon whole black peppercorns

6 whole cloves

3 pounds pork tenderloins, well-trimmed of their skin and fat

5 tablespoons extra-virgin olive oil

2 ounces salt pork, minced to a paste

1 cup moscato or other ambered, sweet wine

2 tablespoons good red wine vinegar

3 ounces pancetta

4 fat cloves garlic, peeled, crushed, and very finely minced

½ cup flat parsley leaves

⅓ cup blanched, toasted almonds, finely chopped

⅓ cup toasted hazelnuts, finely chopped

⅓ cup toasted pine nuts, finely chopped

⅔ cup white raisins, plumped in warm red wine

1½ cups heavy cream

In a mortar with a pestle, grind the sea salt, brown sugar, juniper berries, peppercorns, and cloves to a coarse powder. Rub the trimmed tenderloins with the spices and permit them to rest for 1 hour.

In a large terra-cotta or enameled cast-iron casserole over a lively flame, warm 2 tablespoons of the oil and melt the salt pork. Add the tenderloins—only those that will fit at one time without touching—and brown them, sealing and crusting the meat well on all sides. Remove them to a holding plate.

Add the moscato and the vinegar, stirring and scraping at the residue, reducing the liquids for 1 minute before lowering the flame and adding the tenderloins. Bring to a quiet simmer and braise the pork for 15 to 18 minutes, only until the meat is beginning to be resilient to your prodding finger.

While the tenderloins are braising, with a mezzaluna or a very sharp knife, mince the pancetta, garlic, and parsley together to a fine paste. In a sauté pan over a medium flame, heat 3 tablespoons of the olive oil and brown the paste in it. Add the almonds, hazelnuts, and pine nuts to the fat, rolling them about and coating them well. Remove the pan from the flame.

When the tenderloins are braised, remove them to a holding plate. Raise the flame under the casserole and add the raisins and the cream, stirring and scraping at the residue, permitting the liquids to reduce for 5 minutes.

Carve the tenderloins on the diagonal into 1-inch-thick slices, laying them on a long, shallow plate, covering them with spoonfuls of the very warm sauce and strewing the whole with the sautéed pancetta, garlic, parsley, and nuts.

Agnello Arrosto Sibarita

LAMB ROASTED IN THE STYLE OF SYBARIS

Serves 4

Raised up seven hundred years before Christ on the Mar Ionio, the resplendence of Sybaris eclipsed Athens. Tenanted by unredeemed voluptuaries who roasted songbirds, wove cloth from gold, slept upon rose petals, and indulged every hunger, even their appetite for peace, these Sybarites vanished, as if by some peevish smite from the gods. All that remains is a farming village of sweet, sleepy folk who roast lamb with lemons. Still, I think theirs is a dish upon which an old Sybarite could smile.

⅔ cup extra-virgin olive oil

2 teaspoons dried Greek oregano

2 teaspoons fine sea salt

1 teaspoon freshly cracked pepper

Juice of 1 lemon

4 whole lamb hind shanks, well trimmed of their fat (if they are
   very small, use 2 for each serving)

4 whole heads garlic

2 whole lemons

1 cup white wine

2 tablespoons good white wine vinegar

In a small saucepan over a medium flame, heat the olive oil nearly to a simmer and, off the flame, add the oregano, sea salt, pepper, and lemon juice. Cover the pot and let the oil absorb the seasonings for ½ hour.

Preheat the oven to 450 degrees.

Rub the scented oil over the surfaces of the shanks and place them in an oiled terra-cotta or enameled cast-iron casserole, just large enough to accommodate them. Slice off the top of the garlic heads, leaving the cloves intact and unpeeled, and place them in the casserole. Cut the lemons into thin slices and strew them over the shanks. Roast the shanks for 10 minutes, then reduce the heat to 375 degrees, continuing to roast for 45 to 50 minutes or more, depending on the size of the shanks, until the flesh yields readily to the thrust of a fork. Remove the shanks, the garlic, and the lemons, arranging them on a long, shallow platter.

Place the casserole over a lively flame and add the wine, stirring, scraping at the residue. Add the vinegar and permit the liquids to reduce for 5 minutes before pouring the thick juices over the shanks. Present each shank with a head of garlic and a few slices of the lemon.

A great pan of tiny, yellow-fleshed, white-skinned, olive-oil-roasted potatoes, chunks of oven-toasted bread, and cold white wine keep luscious company with the Sybarites' fine lamb.

Pesce Spada di Bagnara

SWORDFISH IN THE STYLE OF BAGNARA

Serves 6

Whaling and swordfishing have been the tempestuous business of Bagnara for three thousand years. Wedged as the port is twixt great rocks and the Mar Tirreno at the savage hem of the Aspromonte, it forms a fittingly folkloric tableau for the lumbering black ships trudging out for the hunt. A tower, higher than the masts, is the tight, trembly perch from which one man sights the fish. As did the Greeks from whom they are descended, the harpooners tramp out onto walkways hinged a hundred feet out from the ship over the sea, spears at the ready, to wait for the fish. Once the ships are sighted from the lighthouse, the fishermen's wives gather on the beach with carts and wagons, transport to take the fish to market. Sometimes, fires are laid right there by the water, one fish whacked into trenchers and roasted, a barrel of wine propped against the rocks, the unfolding of an old ceremony. One fishes, one builds a fire, one eats his supper.

> 3 pounds swordfish, cut into $\frac{1}{3}$- to $\frac{1}{2}$-pound steaks
> 2 cups good red wine
> 1 cup extra-virgin olive oil
> 10 bay leaves, crushed

2 small, dried red chile peppers, crushed, or ½ to ⅔ teaspoon
  dried chile flakes
Fine sea salt
Freshly cracked pepper
Whole branches of bay or rosemary

Place the fish in a noncorrosive bowl and pour over the wine, turning the steaks so that each of them is wet. Cover the bowl tightly with plastic wrap and permit the fish to rest in the wine for 1 hour, turning it several times.

In a small saucepan over a medium flame, heat the oil nearly to a simmer and add the crushed bay leaves and the chile peppers. Remove the pan from the flame, cover it, and permit the oil to absorb the seasonings while the fish rests in the wine.

Build a wood fire.

Remove the fish from its bath, drying it on absorbent paper towels. Strain the oil and massage both sides of the fish with ½ cup of it. Sprinkle sea salt and freshly cracked pepper over the steaks. Pound the branches of bay or rosemary with a mallet to release their fragrant oils.

Lay the steaks on a grill over red/white-hot embers and cover them with the pounded branches. Char the steaks for 45 seconds to 1 minute—30 seconds will be suffi- cient if your fire is hot enough—removing the branches, turning the steaks, replacing the branches, and charring their other sides.

Rewarm the remaining ½ cup of oil and pour it over a large, shallow plate. Lay the charred steaks in the oil so their hot flesh can absorb it.

Present the steaks then, still warm, or left to cool a bit if your hunger can abide the wait. You need only honest bread and wine and the warmth of the fire.

Focaccia Dolce Salata Reggina

A SWEET AND SALTY FLATBREAD
IN THE STYLE OF REGGIO CALABRIA

Makes 1 large focaccia

An intriguing bread both sweet with honey and anise and savory with pepper and pancetta, versions of it have been baked for pagan and sacred and secular festivals since the epoch of the Greeks. Giuseppe Fazia sometimes bakes the gorgeous, fragrant bread at his forno in Via Tommasini in Reggio Calabria.

¼ cup extra-virgin olive oil

6 ounces pancetta, minced

2 tablespoons aniseeds

2 teaspoons freshly cracked pepper, plus additional as needed

1 cup warm water

1 package active dry yeast or 1 small cake fresh yeast

6 cups all-purpose flour, plus additional as needed

⅓ cup plus 3 tablespoons dark honey (chestnut,
    buckwheat, etc.)

2 teaspoons fine sea salt

⅔ cup mixed white and dark raisins, plumped in warm red wine

1 large egg, lightly beaten

In a small sauté pan over a lively flame, warm the olive oil and sauté the pancetta, permitting it to render its fat and to crisp. Remove the pancetta with a slotted spoon and reserve it. Add the aniseeds and 2 teaspoons of the cracked pepper, rolling the spices about in the fat for a few seconds to scent it. Set the mixture aside.

In a large bowl, combine the water with the yeast, stirring it a bit before adding 1 cup of the flour, 1 tablespoon of the honey, beating the mixture with a wooden spoon and permitting the yeast to soften and activate for 15 minutes. Add 5 cups of flour, the salt, ⅓ cup of honey, the raisins, the egg, and the spice-infused oil, stirring with a wooden spoon to blend the components.

Turn the mixture out onto a lightly floured work space, kneading it into a velvety, resilient dough—a task that takes at least 8 minutes. Place the dough in a lightly oiled bowl, cover it tightly with plastic wrap, and permit the dough to double its mass, about 1½ hours.

Deflate the dough and, on a parchment-lined baking sheet, roll it or flatten it with your hands into a rather free-form rectangle, about ½ inch in thickness.

In a small pan over a medium flame, heat the remaining 2 tablespoons of honey and drop it in threads over the bread. Strew the top with the reserved, crisped pancetta and grind pepper generously over the bread. Cover the bread with a clean kitchen towel and permit it to rise for ½ hour.

Preheat the oven to 400 degrees.

Bake the focaccia for 25 to 30 minutes, until it is deep gold. Cool the focaccia on a rack for a few minutes before carrying it to table in a flat basket, along with a plate of fresh ricotta or a piece of young, creamy pecorino or a bowlful of mascarpone to eat with the last drops in the bottle—the heel—of a fine red wine for a beautiful *fine pasto*—finish to the meal.

Sammartina

ALMOND WALNUT PASTRY

Serves 6 to 8

Once used only to bake the fanciful soldiers on horseback given to children on the festival of San Martino, the short, buttery dough, in less fantastical shapes and forms, is a daily offering now in every pasticceria, luscious even with the slurring of its namesake.

2 cups all-purpose flour

1 cup brown sugar

¼ teaspoon fine sea salt

8 ounces sweet butter, slightly softened, plus additional for tart
    pan

4 large egg yolks, beaten

2 tablespoons orange-scented liqueur, Cointreau or Grand
    Marnier

Finely grated zest of 1 lemon

Finely grated zest of 1 orange

½ cup white raisins, plumped in warm water

½ cup walnuts, chopped and lightly toasted

½ cup blanched almonds, chopped and lightly toasted

Confectioners' sugar

Preheat the oven to 350 degrees.

In a large bowl, combine the flour, brown sugar, salt, and 8 ounces butter and beat until smooth. Add the egg yolks, one at a time, incorporating each thoroughly. Add the liqueur, the citrus zests, the raisins, walnuts, and almonds, combining them well.

Press the dough evenly into a buttered 10- to 12-inch tart pan with a removable bottom. Bake the pastry for 25 to 30 minutes or until it is deeply golden. Cool the pastry on a rack for 10 minutes before removing the tart pan's ring.

Permit the pastry to cool thoroughly before dusting it generously with confectioners' sugar. Cut the pastry into wedges, serving it with cold, ambered wine.

SICILIA

She could be only an island, this Sicilia. So aloof and pathless is she, less by the caprice of her nature, one thinks, than by her own insolence, as though she might have quit Italy, had she not already been born separate from it.

She is of the lustrous footfalls of the Greeks. She is of splendored epitaphs impressed by Norman kings. She is of temples and castles and cathedrals. And she is of improbably blue-eyed, red-haired babies. All these are her dowry. But in her blood and bones, Sicilia is Alhambra. She is Arabia eternal.

Her temper, her scurillity, resonate Saracen dominion. Sicilia wears her cunning like old Muslim veils. Too, she is of a voluptuous beauty, bounteous lengths of her spilling out over an ancient silence. Storks and wolves abide on the coppered plateaux that look down upon fields fitted in burnished wheat and meadows that swell, then plunge into crevices as though in refuge from an angry sun.

189

The Sicilian farmer does not live on his land. Yet even as he forswears the desolation of rural life by collecting in villages, still he fastens up his solitariness like some breastplate, always reserving, concealing himself beneath it. He works at his patch of earth, small or grand, from sunrise until early afternoon, when he returns to his village. Thus it is not unusual for one to walk or ride a horse or drive an automobile for the latter half of the day through the middling lands, coming upon neither a man nor his dwelling. It shivers up a softly haunting portrait evincing nothing of folkloric embroidery and only stretching at the already swollen quiet.

And so it seems a just thing that the ancient beast of Etna should spew up its blazoned heart onto Sicilia. At the volcano's feet, the land is ecstatic, succulent, raising up three or four or more harvests each year from earth nourished in fat, fecund ashes. But even the stony, parched parts of the island are caressed into some grace, delivering from their spareness forgiving olives and grapes, stands of leafy almonds. A stunningly few hectares of Sicilia languish. Orchards of lemons and oranges are stitched across the haunches of great, liquid green hills and onto valley floors, stopping only at the verges of her seas. And all around her extravagant, thousand-kilometer skirt are couched great succoring coves, curled like Persian scimitars, ports of ingress and flight for pirates and saviors and simple fishermen for a time longer than any of us can know.

It is on the islands of Sicilia, though—outposts of the outpost—that one can best know her, pure and unornamented and as she was.

Most enchanted of all is the Aeolian archipelago in the Mar Tirreno. There, on the island of Vulcano, of a thick, pitch night lit by half a moon, one begins to perceive the cabalistic sap of the Sicilian. Violent crags—sheets of liquid fire gorged up from the rupturing mountains that fell seething into the sea, its coldness freezing, fast and forever, their anguished forms—are the grotesques around which old Aeolus's winds still whine and screech.

But it was, perhaps, the coalescence wrought by Ruggero II d'Altavilla—Roger II of Altavilla, the Norman, the young rogue-king with the auburn curls—that contrived Sicily's finest hours. Though it was his strategies that humbled the two-century Arab reign, Roger the victor was soon to be bedazzled by the conquered. The brutish society of the Normans clashed roaringly with Arab finesse, their ritual aesthetics, the ecstasies of their court, of the harem. Though the Norman hardly crouched at their knees, he dignified the Arab presence in his government and looked to them for counsel in the arts and philosophy. And thus was there a sympathy between the barbarians and the infidels. Roger promenaded in Palermo's elegant avenues and parks, the swashbuckling Norman redressed as a pasha, his white silk caftan flowing, those burnished locks, shocking, exotic against his entourage of raven-headed ministers. And even while Roger restored the feudal systems, built monasteries and cathedrals and brought the island once again under the auspices of Rome, his alliance with the Saracens perplexed, tormented the Church. Roger adored his Sicily, but, too, did he cherish its inviolate Saracen soul. And when I see one of those red-haired, blue-eyed babies, I think of old Roger and his legacies, still ascendant.

Olive Nere e Verdi con Aglio Intero al Forno

ROASTED BLACK AND GREEN OLIVES WITH WHOLE GARLIC

Serves 4 to 6

To tear at a beautiful, newborn bread and eat it with fat, salty olives, a potent red wine sipped between them, is a meal everlasting in its innocence and sensuality. Here follows the simplest of recipes that pairs the soft creaminess of roasted garlic with the olives for a lush result. The dish asks only a little dalliance in the oven. Roasting the olives plumps them, renders them voluptuously fleshy, tender. And when whole, fat garlic—caramelized in a long, slow roasting—confronts the salt-tinged meat of the warm olives, the whole becomes quietly paradisiacal. As beautiful as it is, stray for a moment from the red wine idea and consider a fusion, instead, with an iced Marsala Superiore Riserva or Marsala Vergine or Marsala Soleras Stravecchio—altogether different wine from the often industrially produced sweet varieties that find their way to the States and are used to make zabaglione or to splash sautéed veal. The crackling, almost dry golden chill of them leaves just a point of sweetness on the tongue.

> 4 very large heads of the freshest garlic (late spring and early
>   summer crop with the violet skins are best)
> ¼ cup extra-virgin olive oil, plus additional for oven-toasting
>   bread
> 1 teaspoon fine sea salt
> Freshly cracked pepper
> 24 ounces Sicilian, Greek, or Spanish green, black, or purple
>   olives, or a combination thereof, unstoned
> ½ cup dry Marsala
> 1 round of *pane di semolino di Piana degli Albanesi* (page 213) or
>   another crusty, coarse-textured loaf
> ½ cup fresh mint leaves

Preheat oven to 325 degrees.

Cut through the heads of garlic at their root ends and separate the cloves, leaving their skins intact. Place the cloves in a ceramic or terra-cotta casserole, add the ¼ cup olive oil, tossing the cloves in it, coating them well. Sprinkle on the sea salt and grind pepper generously over the garlic cloves, roasting them for 20 minutes. Add the olives and stir them about, combining them with the softening garlic and the oil. Continue the roast for an additional 20 minutes, checking then to see if the garlic is beginning to collapse and the olives have plumped. Pour over the ½ cup of dry Marsala, raise the oven temperature to 400 degrees, and roast for 5 more minutes.

Having torn the bread into somewhat large and uneven chunks, lay them on an oven sheet, anoint them with oil, and toast the bread along with the olives and garlic for these last 5 minutes. Remove the olives and garlic from the oven, strew them with the mint leaves, and present the dish immediately with the warm, oven-toasted bread and an iced dry Marsala.

Cipolle Arrostite sul Sale Marino con un Pesto di Pistacchi e Olive

ONIONS ROASTED OVER SEA SALT WITH A PESTO
OF PISTACHIOS AND OLIVES

Serves 6

The Onions

Here one heaves great, whole, gorgeous purple-skinned onions into a thick pavement of coarse sea salt and roasts them. Following this primitive exercise, we whack the charred onions in two and then hide inside them a dollop of fragrant pesto before fixing the halves together again. At table, there comes a lovely surprise for those who are prepared to tuck into a roasted onion but find tucked inside it the perfumes of Arabia.

3 cups coarse sea salt
6 firm, unblemished, purple-skinned onions of uniform size

Preheat the oven to 400 degrees.

Spread the sea salt over a shallow ceramic or terra-cotta casserole just large enough to hold the onions without crowding them. Place the onions on top and roast for approximately 40 to 50 minutes, depending upon their size, or until they are very easily penetrated with a thin, sharp knife. It is better to err on the side of underroasting so that the onions maintain their shape. Too long a stay in the oven will lead to their total, graceless collapse.

Remove the onions from the oven and, with tongs, carefully transfer them from their salt bed to a cutting board. Cut them in two, smear one half of each with a generous spoonful of the pesto and place the halves together.

The onions may be served immediately—even reheated for a minute or two in the still-warm oven—or served warm or cool as a starter course or as accompaniment to grilled or roasted meat or fish.

The Pesto

This paste is of the Provençal tapenade brotherhood, as it is kin to the olive pastes of Umbria, Toscana, and Liguria. I have always tried to work with these in a way that seemed not to impinge on their indigenous flavors but that served to quiet their deafening saltiness.

¾ cup shelled pistachios
Zest and juice of 1 large orange
¼ teaspoon ground cloves
¼ teaspoon ground cinnamon
2 teaspoons aniseeds
3 large dried white figs
12 ounces black Sicilian, Greek, or Spanish olives, lightly
   crushed with a mallet, stones removed
1 tablespoon good red wine vinegar
2 tablespoons extra-virgin olive oil

In a small sauté pan over a lively flame, dry-roast the pistachios, tossing them about, until they begin to take on some color; lower the flame a bit and add the orange zest, the cloves, the cinnamon, and the aniseeds, stirring the elements together, permitting the zest and the seeds to roast a bit with the nuts and the ground spices. Keep it moving constantly. After a minute or so, the scents will come up sharp and sweet. Remove the pan from the flame.

Snip the figs into quarters with kitchen shears and place them in a small saucepan with the juice of the orange, heating them gently together. When the liquid approaches a simmer, remove the pan from the flame, cover it, and permit the figs to plump in the warm juice for 10 minutes.

In the bowl of a food processor fitted with a steel blade, process all the ingredients except the oil to a coarse paste. With the machine running, drop in the olive oil in a very thin stream until the sauce is emulsified.

Lo Sfincione di Mondello

THE TRADITIONAL ONION FLATBREADS OF MONDELLO

Makes 2 medium or 12 to 15 small breads

Sitting a few kilometers from the snarls of the city's traffic, Mondello is Palermo's beachfront. Less chic than it is drowsy, the tiny port's center is paved with little trattorie that offer still-writhing sea fish from which one can choose a fine lunch. And at noon, just as bathers and strollers longing for some icy little aperitivo *start off for the bars and* caffès, *a husky, microphoned voice seeming to come from the fat, dark leaves of the old plane trees intrudes on the operetta. With the precision of a corps de ballet, the cast of characters pivots in the direction of a small white truck, chugging slowly, then edging to a stop in their midst. Lo sfincionaro has arrived. In another place, he might be called the pizza man, though his is hardly some prosaic pie. His voice invites: "Just come to see them. They are warm and fragrant. I don't ask that you buy one. I only invite you to admire them."*

We watched as there came a fast gathering of his devoted. Mothers and babies, men in rumply Palm Beach suits, Australian fishermen on holiday, an Englishwoman with a great yellow hat and a silver-headed cane. Children clutching five-lire notes collected, each of them waiting for lo sfincionaro to enfold a great, warm heft of his beautiful onion-scented bread into a sheet of soft gray paper. A traditional confection of Palermo, it is called lo sfincione. It is a crunchy, rich, bread-crusted tart—and close kin to southern France's pissalaidère—*that cradles sautéed onions, dried black olives, sun-dried tomatoes, anchovies, pancetta, and pecorino. Fashioning smaller sfincioni and piling them up, newly born, in an old basket and passing them about with jugs of cold white wine can make for a lovely summer supper.*

The Crust

2 tablespoons active dry yeast or 2 small cakes fresh yeast

1¾ cups plus 1 tablespoon warm water

⅓ cup extra-virgin olive oil

2 tablespoons whole milk or light cream

1 tablespoon plus 2 teaspoons fine sea salt

5 cups plus 2 tablespoons unbleached flour, plus additional to
  knead dough

½ cup finely ground polenta meal

½ cup whole wheat flour

The Filling

2 pounds sweet onions (Vidalia, Texas Sweet, Walla Walla),
    peeled and thinly sliced

¼ cup olive oil

⅓ cup white wine

1 tablespoon red wine vinegar

6 ounces sun-dried tomatoes, drained of their preserving oil
    (reserve the oil)

6 ounces pecorino

8 salt anchovies

8 ounces dried black olives, stones removed

6 ounces pancetta, finely minced

In a large bowl, stir the yeast into the water, letting it soften for 10 minutes. Meanwhile, stir together the olive oil, milk, and salt. Add the flours and the liquids all at once to the yeast/water mixture, blending them well.

Turn the dough out onto a lightly floured work space and knead it to a soft, elastic texture, a task that takes at least 8 minutes. Allow the dough to rise in a lightly oiled bowl, covered with plastic wrap, until it doubles—about 1½ hours.

Meanwhile, prepare the filling. Over a medium flame, slowly soften the onions in the olive oil without browning them. Add the white wine a tablespoon or two at a time, permitting it to evaporate before the next dose. When the onions are very soft and have released and reabsorbed their own liquids as well as the wine—about 25 minutes—remove them from the flame and stir in the tablespoon of vinegar. Set the onions aside. Finely sliver the sun-dried tomatoes. Using a vegetable peeler, shave the cheese thin. Rinse the anchovies of their salt, remove their heads and bones, and lightly dry them on absorbent paper towels before crushing them with a fork.

Preheat the oven to 400 degrees. Deflate the dough, dividing it in two (or cutting it into 12 to 15 pieces for smaller tarts). Roll or pat the dough to a thickness of ⅓ inch, placing each piece on a parchment-lined sheet (or pat the smaller pieces into little rounds, still not more than ⅓ inch in thickness, and place them on parchment-lined sheets).

Spread the cooled onions on the surface of the tarts, leaving a 1-inch border free. Strew the onions with the olives, tomatoes, anchovies, pancetta, and cheese. Allow the *sfincioni* to rise, covered with clean kitchen towels, for 40 minutes. Drizzle 3 tablespoons of the tomato preserving oil over the tarts and bake them—25 minutes for the medium breads and 15 to 18 minutes for the small ones, or until they are golden. Cool them on racks for a very few minutes or not, as appetites and audience dictate.

Pasta con le Sarde

PASTA WITH SARDINES

Serves 6

Harvests from the great, silent fields of sun-bronzed wheat result in more bread than pasta for la tavola siciliana, *yet there is a trio of pasta dishes that is cooked throughout the island. One of them dresses pasta in eggplant and tomatoes perfumed with wild mint and basil, the whole dusted with grated, salted ewe's milk ricotta. Called often* pasta alla Norma *in celebration of Catanian son Vincenzo Bellini it can be a gorgeous dish. Then there is* pasta chi vrocculi arriminati—*dialect for a dish that calls for a paste of cauliflower and salt anchovies studded with raisins and pine nuts. Although it is luscious, it cannot compete with the glories of the island's* pasta con le sarde. *A dish full of extravagant Arab timbres, it employs fresh, sweet sardines, salt anchovies, wild fennel, and a splash of saffroned tomato. One presents the pasta cool, as though heat would be violence against its sensuousness.*

Wild fennel grows abundantly on the lower shanks of Sicily's mountains and, too, along the craggy paths of some of her islands. I used to collect wild fennel along the banks of the Sacramento River and I've heard tell of great clumps of its yellow lace heads bobbing along country roads in America's Northeast. Now I find it a few kilometers from our home in thickets against the pasture fences along the Via Cassia on the road to Rome. Though the scent and the savor of cultivated fennel is sweeter, it behaves well in collaboration with these other elements and yields a still-sumptuous dish.

6 to 8 stalks wild fennel or the fronds and stalks from 1 large
   head of fresh fennel

2 tablespoons coarse sea salt

⅔ cup pine nuts

¼ teaspoon saffron threads

⅓ cup plus 2 tablespoons dry white wine

¼ cup canned tomato puree

4 ounces anchovies, preserved under salt

½ cup extra-virgin olive oil

1 large yellow onion, peeled and minced

16 ounces fresh sardines, filleted, heads and tails removed

½ cup dark raisins, plumped in warm moscato or other ambered,
   sweet wine

16 ounces bucatini or other thick, string pasta

⅓ cup fine, freshly made bread crumbs, browned in 2 tablespoons olive oil

Coarsely chop the stalks of wild fennel with their flowers or the fronds and stalks of culti-vated fennel. Place in a large saucepan, add 5 quarts of cold water, 1 tablespoon of the coarse sea salt, and bring to a simmer, poaching the fennel until the stalks are tender. Drain the fennel, reserving its cooking liquors and press it against the side of the pot to express all its liquid. Finely mince the poached fennel and set it aside.

In a small sauté pan over a medium flame, pan-roast the pine nuts until quite brown and set aside. In a small sauté pan, pan-roast the saffron threads for 1 minute over a low flame. Add the 2 tablespoons of white wine, dissolving the threads in it and then mixing the saffroned wine with the remaining wine and the tomato puree. Rinse the anchovies of their salt, remove their heads and bones, and lightly dry them on absorbent paper towels, finally crushing them gently with a fork.

In a large sauté pan, heat the olive oil and lightly sauté the onion. Add the minced fennel and sauté for 1 minute. Add the crushed anchovies and the sardine fillets, rolling the fish about in the oil with the aromatics for ½ minute before adding the plumped raisins and their juices, ½ cup of the pine nuts, and the saffron/tomato mixture. Stir, amalga-mating the elements and reducing the liquids so that a thick sauce results.

Turn the sauce out into a bowl, permitting it to cool and its perfumes and fla-vors to rest and intensify. Never refrigerate the sauce.

Just before serving, cook the pasta to al dente in the reserved fennel-poaching water, adding 1 additional tablespoon of coarse sea salt. Drain the pasta, leaving it some-what wet, and dress the hot pasta with the sauce, carefully coating each strand.

Serve the pasta in shallow bowls, strewing it with the remaining pine nuts and a dusting of bread crumbs. In high summer, we might sip iced moscato with the pasta, but in cooler weather, a rough, tannic red seems right.

Tranci di Tonno Dolceforte all' Assunta Lo Mastro

TRENCHERS OF TUNA IN A SWEET-SOUR SAUCE
IN THE MANNER OF ASSUNTA LO MASTRO

Serves 6

Perhaps the most elegant version of Sicilian tuna for us was this one that we ate in the kitchen of a tiny, chalk-white house set in the curve of an alley and whose arch-walled garden looked to the sea. The lady who cooked it for us—the owner of the house—was born there in that most ancient parish of Trapani more than ninety years ago. Warm, insistent winds—the breath of Africa, one thinks—billowed up the old blue curtain that was her back door, bidding in the damp, balmy spice of her wisteria as she sat there, beatific, talking and working. It was as though pressing peppercorns into the flesh of a fish was a most magnificent task.

3 pounds tuna, cut into 1- to 1½-inch steaks

2 tablespoons fine sea salt, plus additional to season the tuna

½ cup plus ⅓ cup best-quality red wine vinegar

3 cups dry Marsala

6 tablespoons whole peppercorns, coarsely cracked

6 tablespoons olive oil

2 tablespoons dark honey (buckwheat, chestnut, etc.)

Prepare the tuna in the morning or early afternoon of the evening you wish to eat it. Several hours of *riposo*, rest, help to ripen its rich, luscious savor. Bathe the tuna in cold, sea-salted water (2 tablespoons sea salt dissolved in 2 quarts water) for ½ hour. In a large, noncorrosive bowl, mix ½ cup of the vinegar and 2 cups Marsala. Rinse the tuna under cold water and roll it around in its marinade, covering the bowl with plastic wrap and letting the fish rest for another ½ hour. Remove the tuna from the marinade, patting it dry with absorbent paper towels. Discard the marinade. Press the coarsely cracked pepper onto both sides of the tuna and sprinkle a bit of sea salt over each surface.

Over a medium-high flame, heat the oil in a large sauté pan and cook the fish—2 or 3 pieces at a time or as many as will fit comfortably without touching—for 2 to 2½ minutes to the side. The flesh will be rare at the center, as it should be. As they are cooked, remove the tuna pieces to a deep plate to hold them and their juices.

Pour off the oil from the pan and add the remaining cup of Marsala and ⅓ cup vinegar, along with the accumulated juices from the tuna, stirring and scraping and allowing the liquids to reduce for a minute or two. Stir in the honey and taste the sauce. Neither the sweet nor the sour essence of the sauce should be aggressive. Should the vinegar be too much, soften it with a few drops more of honey.

Pour the very hot sauce over the fish, bathing the pieces as evenly as possible. When the sauce and fish have cooled, cover the dish. Permit the tuna to rest until dinner-time, serving it at room temperature after, perhaps, opening with the *cipolle arrostite sul sale marino* (page 192).

La Tunnina del Rais

TUNA IN THE MANNER OF GIOACHINO CATALDO

Serves 6

A rather sad and barren bit of sand in a Mediterranean archipelago 17 kilometers off the coast of Trapani and 120 kilometers from the brow of North Africa, the island of Favignana is the last of the tonnare—tuna fishing ports—in Sicilia. And it is Gioachino Cataldo who is il rais—"the king," in Arab dialect—of the rite of la mattanza— the ritual slaughtering of migrating tuna practiced first by the Phoenicians and later by the Saracens. La mattanza remains the most powerful spiritual ceremony in the life of the islanders, as it has for a thousand years. And from then until now, its writs are these. Fifteen huge wooden, black-varnished, motorless, sail-less boats are tugged out into the formation of a great quadrangle around the muciara—the boat of il rais that sits at the square's center. Ten kilometers of net are laid in the form of a pouch into which the tuna swim. The great fish migrate from the Atlantic through the Straits of Gibralter to spawn, the Mediterranean being warmer and saltier and, hence, a kinder ambience for reproduction. As the pouch—called the camera della morte, *the death chamber—becomes full,* il rais *gives the command to his fifty-seven soldiers to lift the net. The men bear up the nets by hand, hoisting them and the tuna up to a height at which the fish can be speared and hauled up into the bellies of the boats. The rite remains Arab to its core. Arab are the songs that the tonnaroti—those fishermen who hunt only tuna—sing as they wait for the nets to fill, as are the incantations they chant as they are heaving up the fish and, finally, Arab are the screams the tonnaroti scream as they kill them. We saw them take two hundred tuna in two hours—the fish averaging about seventy kilograms. Those the tonnaroti did not keep for themselves were ferried to Marsala for processing.*

A black-bearded colossus is Gioachino, his face crinkled by the Mediterranean sun, his enormous hands scraggy as an unsharp blade, of a family who, for twelve generations, has birthed men chosen by the Favignanesi to be il rais. The islanders bequeath the post on merit. The credentials, said Favignana's mayor, are: courage, skill, strength, dignity, and honor. And it is the king himself who determines the duration of his reign. Gioachino told us he would remain il rais "finchè le mie forze mi sosterranno"— "while my forces remain uninjured."

In these last ninety-eight years, Gioachino is only the eighth rais of Favignana. This is the simple way he cooked tuna for us, the way he thinks it best. He always uses flesh from the female fish—hence, tunnina—for its more delicate savor, he told us. Il rais harvested the capers for the fish in his garden while we sipped at cold moscato.

> 3 pounds tuna, cut in 4-inch chunks
>
> 2 tablespoons fine sea salt
>
> ½ cup olive oil
>
> 3 fat cloves garlic, peeled, crushed, and minced
>
> 2 large yellow onions, peeled and thinly sliced

2 pounds very ripe tomatoes, peeled, seeded, and coarsely
  chopped
½ cup salted capers, rinsed and dried
8 ounces green Spanish olives, stones removed
4 ounces white raisins
1½ cups red wine
2 tablespoons best-quality red wine vinegar

Bathe the chunks of tuna in cold, sea-salted water (2 tablespoons fine sea salt to 2 quarts water) for ½ hour. Rinse the tuna under cold water and dry the flesh on absorbent paper towels. Over a lively flame, heat the olive oil in a large ceramic or terra-cotta pot and sear the tuna—only those pieces at a time that will fit without touching—browning them well, until crisp on all sides. As the tuna is seared, remove it to a holding plate.

When all the tuna has been seared, lower the flame and add the garlic and onions to the still-hot oil, rolling them about until soft but not colored. After 5 minutes, add the tomatoes, capers, olives, raisins, and the wine. Heighten the flame a bit and permit the sauce to reduce for 3 to 4 minutes. Off the heat, stir in the vinegar.

Add the tuna to the sauce, including any accumulated juices from the holding plate. Over a low flame, braise the tuna in its sauce for 5 minutes, covering the pot with a skewed lid.

Allow the tuna to rest for 1 hour or so and present it, at room temperature, in shallow bowls with a benediction of wine vinegar, chunks of roasted semolina bread, red wine, and tales of the Saracens. The braising sauce is also a wonderfully rich condiment for pasta.

Pesce Spada sulla Brace alla Pantesca

ROASTED SWORDFISH IN THE STYLE OF PANTELLERIA

Serves 6

Daughter-of-the-wind is her name in Arabic—Bent el-Rhia—the gorgeous island of Pantelleria sits seventy kilometers from Tunisia in the Egadian Archipelago. She is full of sea caves and strange, vaporous grottoes. She wears Neolithic ruins among her palms and oleander. And in the contrada, *neighborhood, called Favarotta, we ate swordfish—thin steaks of it cut from the center of the just-caught fish, first rubbed with olive oil and then quickly roasted over a red-sparking grapevine fire. The fisherman/cook laid them over a cool tomato jam and we feasted. Too, we ate yellow-crumbed semolina bread roasted over the then quieter fire, and when its heat was nearly spent, we skewered figs—green ones and the first of the summer—onto grapevine twigs and held them near the fire until their juices were warmed and we ate them with the last sips of Pantelleria's luscious moscato.*

½ cup plus 3 tablespoons extra-virgin olive oil
1½ teaspoons fine sea salt, plus additional as needed
1 teaspoon freshly cracked pepper
Juice of 1 lemon
3 pounds swordfish, cut into ⅓- to ½-inch steaks
2 fat cloves garlic, peeled, crushed, and minced
3 large yellow onions, peeled and thinly sliced
1½ cups moscato di Pantelleria
1 pound green tomatoes, finely diced
1 pound very ripe tomatoes, peeled, seeded, and finely diced
½ cup dark raisins, plumped in warm water
½ cup capers, preserved under salt—*capperi di Pantelleria*—rinsed

Construct a marinade with ½ cup of the olive oil, 1½ teaspoons salt, pepper, lemon juice, and massage it into the fish on both sides. Allow the fish to rest for 1 hour while you prepare a wood fire and an onion/tomato marmalade.

Over a medium flame, heat 3 tablespoons of the olive oil in a large sauté pan and soften the garlic, taking care not to let it color. Add the onions. Soften them for 15 minutes or so, adding 1 tablespoon of the moscato each time the pan seems dry—about ½ cup total. Add the tomatoes, salting them generously, and the remaining cup of moscato. Slowly cook the mixture, stirring it every few minutes until it reduces and thickens almost to a jam—about ½ hour. Drain the plumped raisins and rinse the capers, adding both to the finished marmalade. Stir very well and set the marmalade aside.

When the embers of the fire are red/white-hot, char the swordfish steaks 45 seconds to 1 minute—30 seconds will be sufficient if your fire is hot enough—on each side, removing them to a plate onto which some of the marmalade has been spread. When all the steaks are grilled, spoon a bit more marmalade over them. The warm, charred fish forms a lush fusion with the jam.

Bracioline di Pesce Spada alla Messinese

STUFFED SWORDFISH IN THE STYLE OF MESSINA

Serves 6

One departs Italy—and the European continent—for the journey to Sicilia through the narrow Straits of Messina. The city is an unlovely place, the ravages and wrecks of her face so corrected that she seems benign, with few of her old graces. Snugged inside the tumult of her port sit a few humble houses still dispatching, to the fishermen and the local citizenry, the stews and broths from the old tomes. And it was at one table there where we ate a most luscious rendition of swordfish. A dish typical of Messina, and now of the whole island, it seems, this one was extraordinary for the rich elements of its stuffing, but more for the divine splash of Malvasia in its little sauce.

1½ cups fresh mint leaves

1 cup fresh parsley leaves

2 fat cloves garlic, peeled and crushed

4 ounces pine nuts

6 ounces green Sicilian olives, lightly crushed with a mallet,
stones removed, and coarsely chopped

4 ounces dark raisins, plumped in warm Malvasia delle Lipari or
any sweet, ambered wine

⅓ cup capers preserved under salt, rinsed

4 ounces pecorino

6 ounces freshly made fine bread crumbs, toasted

1 large egg, lightly beaten

Freshly cracked pepper

Fine sea salt, as needed

2 pounds swordfish, sliced into ¼-inch steaks

¼ cup extra-virgin olive oil

⅔ cup Malvasia delle Lipari or any sweet, ambered wine

With a mezzaluna or a very sharp knife, finely mince 1 cup of the mint and parsley together with the garlic to a fine paste and transfer it to a large bowl. Lightly pan-roast the pine nuts. Add the olives, raisins, and any residual liquid and the pine nuts to the bowl along with the capers, pecorino, bread crumbs, and the egg. Generously grind on the pepper. Work the elements to a well-amalgamated paste. The pecorino and capers should be salty enough to flavor the paste, but after tasting it, add a bit more if you wish.

Lay the *bracioline* on a work surface and pound them lightly but firmly with a mallet, thinning the flesh a bit. Spread each steak with a good tablespoon of the paste, roll it into a fat little sausage shape, and secure the *braciolina* with a toothpick. Over a lively flame, heat the oil in a large sauté pan and very quickly cook the *bracioline*, sautéing them well but taking only a minute or so to do it so as not to overcook the fish. Remove the *bracioline* to a holding plate.

When all are cooked, discard any remaining oil and rinse the pan with the ⅔ cup of Malvasia, scraping and stirring and permitting the wine to reduce for 2 to 3 minutes. Pour the sauce over the *bracioline* and present them, strewn with ½ cup mint leaves, warm or at room temperature.

Sacrificing the beauty of the sauce, one could skewer the *bracioline* onto well-soaked grapevine twigs, olive wood twigs, thick branches of rosemary, or metal skewers, alternating them with bay leaves and roasting them over a very hot wood fire for a minute or two on each side, basting them with olive oil. They'll need some accessory—a spoonful of warm tomato vinaigrette would do nicely.

La Vera Caponata

THE TRUE CAPONATA

Serves 8

It is neither a purply, sugared mass nor cold and puckery pap, the true caponata, but a baronial dish first fashioned by the great monzù—*dialect for* monsieur—*the title given to the French chefs imported by the nobility during the reign of the Bourbons. Borrowing from a dish left by the Arabs and tinkered with by the Spanish, the* monzù *exalted the simple braise of eggplant and tomatoes, building a set piece of it, spicing its sauce with oranges and cloves and even a whisper of cacao, then bejeweling it with roasted lobsters and prawns. I thought it, alas, only an historical dish. But with some supplication of a Palermitano friend, ricette antiche—ancient recipes—were unriddled and, after days of bombast and wrangling discourse, one cook was fixed upon who might still build The True Caponata. Two evenings later, I was indulged.*

The dish is a beauty even if one wishes not to garnish it with the roasted seafood. Then, one calls it la caponatina. *Stuffed inside the belly of a whole fish—a sea bass, a salmon, a cod—and wood-roasted, it is splendid.*

4 pounds firm and shiny-skinned eggplant, peeled and cut into
   2-inch cubes
4 tablespoons coarse sea salt for water

½ cup extra-virgin olive oil, plus additional as needed

2 large yellow onions, peeled and thinly sliced

2 pounds very ripe tomatoes, peeled, seeded, and chopped

1 tablespoon freshly ground fine sea salt

1 cup red wine

2 cups finely chopped hearts of celery

Juice of 2 oranges, preferably blood oranges

Zest of 2 oranges

½ teaspoon ground cloves

2 tablespoons unsweetened cocoa powder, preferably Dutch
processed

Freshly cracked pepper

4 ounces blanched almonds, roasted and chopped

1 tablespoon dark brown sugar

5 tablespoons good red wine vinegar

⅔ cup dark raisins, plumped in warm red wine vinegar and
drained

6 ounces green Sicilian olives, stones removed, coarsely
chopped

4 whole lobsters, split

16 prawns, shelled, deveined, heads removed, tails left intact

Soak the eggplant in sea-salted water for 1 hour, then drain, rinse, and dry it on absorbent paper towels.

Over a lively flame, heat the ½ cup olive oil in a large sauté pan and brown the eggplant well, cooking only those pieces at a time that will fit without touching. As the eggplant is sautéed, remove it to paper towels.

Discard all but 2 tablespoons of the remaining oil and, in the same sauté pan, lightly brown the onions, softening them for 2 or 3 minutes before adding the tomatoes, the fine sea salt, and wine. Braise the tomatoes and onions in the wine, stirring, until much of the liquids are absorbed and the mixture has thickened a bit. Set the sauce aside.

Poach the chopped celery in sea-salted water, just enough to cover it, for 2 minutes. Drain and set aside.

Combine the remaining ingredients in a bowl, save the seafood. Add the spiced mixture to the slightly cooled sauce and stir very well. Permit the sauce to cool fully. Finally, stir in the eggplant, the celery, the plumped raisins, and the olives.

Cover the *caponata* and permit it an overnight rest in the refrigerator. Warm to room temperature before serving. Wood-roast the lobster and/or prawns, basting them lightly with olive oil, presenting them, sizzling, atop the room-temperature *caponata*.

Frittelle di Melanzane e Mentuccia Selveggia di Lampedusa

FRITTERS OF EGGPLANT AND WILD MINT IN THE STYLE OF LAMPEDUSA

Serves 6

There is wild tufted mint between the megalithic stones of its befogged and silent fields. And Africa whispers up sultry winds, caressing the place, adding to the sensation of faraway. This is the island of Giovanni di Lampedusa, author of Il Gattopardo, The Leopard. *It is a mystical space etched by the ancients, one after another of them who, having stayed for a while, imprinted it, abandoned it, to its own muffled secrets and to the great lumbering turtles and seals who live there still. Surely not Italy, not, perhaps, Sicilia nor even Africa, it is somewhere else, this Lampedusa.*

Inhabited, finally, without interruption since 1843, when the king Ferdinando II came to claim it, a family descended from this settlement was once our host. The children and their nanny showed us the best, most secret places to collect the wild mint of which we'd grown so fond, we making a salad of its leaves and other wild grasses when enough of it could be foraged. One afternoon, after a particularly good harvest, we emptied our pockets of it onto the kitchen table, thinking we'd all feast on it at dinner, and went upstairs to bathe and rest. Later, the loveliest of perfumes told us that the mint had been seized by the cook and that she'd done something magnificent with it and tomatoes. Here follows a version of her gorgeous frittelle.

The Sauce

3 tablespoons extra-virgin olive oil

2 fat cloves garlic, peeled, crushed, and minced

1 small yellow onion, peeled and minced

3 pounds very ripe tomatoes (which have never been refrigerated), peeled, seeded, and finely chopped, all juices saved

2 cups red wine

Freshly cracked pepper

Fine sea salt

1 cup torn fresh mint leaves

1 cup torn basil leaves

Over a medium flame, heat the oil in a large saucepan and soften the garlic and onion without coloring them. Add the tomatoes, their juices, the red wine, generous grindings of pepper and sea salt. Bring to a quiet simmer, lower the flame, and permit it to cook and reduce for ½ hour or until the tomatoes have reduced to a jam and the wine has all but evaporated.

Off the flame, add the just-torn herbs, stirring them into the thick sauce. Cover the pot and permit the sauce at least 1 hour's rest.

The Frittelle

3 pounds smooth, tight-skinned purple eggplants
3 tablespoons plus 1 cup extra-virgin olive oil
2 cups freshly made coarse bread crumbs
2 cups just-grated pecorino
Freshly cracked pepper
1½ teaspoons fine sea salt
1 scant teaspoon ground cinnamon
½ cup dark raisins, plumped in warm water
1 cup torn fresh mint leaves
1 cup torn fresh basil leaves
3 or 4 large eggs, lightly beaten
Flour

Preheat the oven to 400 degrees.

Slice the eggplants in two lengthwise, brush the cut surfaces with the 3 tablespoons of olive oil and roast them until the flesh is very soft. Remove the eggplants from the oven and cool them slightly.

Scrape the flesh of the eggplants into a bowl. In the work bowl of a food processor fitted with a steel blade, process the eggplant flesh, one-third to one-half at a time, smoothing it into a thick paste. Add ¼ cup of the olive oil through the feed tube in driblets, emulsifying, enriching the paste. Turn out the paste into a large bowl and add to it the bread crumbs, cheese, generous grindings of pepper, salt, cinnamon, raisins, mint, and basil. Add 3 of the beaten eggs and blend the elements well, using your hands or a large wooden spoon. The resultant paste should be light. Lacking that airy texture, add the remaining egg and blend again very thoroughly. Sauté a bit of the paste, tasting for salt and correcting if necessary.

Form the paste into 3-inch ovals of about 1 inch in thickness. Dust them lightly with flour. Over a lively flame, heat the remaining ¾ cup of oil in a large sauté pan and in it cook the little cakes, a few at a time, permitting them to form a bit of a crust before turning them and browning the other side. As they are cooked, remove the *frittelle* to absorbent paper towels. Add a few drops more of oil if the cakes begin to stick. Proceed with the remaining cakes. Alternatively, the fritters can be quickly deep-fried in abundant oil.

Present the fritters immediately on a plate spread with the reheated or room-temperature sauce, offering more sauce at table. You might begin with *olive nere e verdi con aglio intero al forno* (page 191). When gorgeous tomatoes are not to be found, the fritters are also quite wonderful with a only a tiny spoonful of a lemony vinaigrette.

La Minestra di Selinunte

THE WILD CELERY SOUP OF SELINUNTE

Serves 6

Glorious Selinunte was raised up seven centuries before Christ and named by the Greeks after the wild, celerylike plant selinon, *which then blanketed its riparian hills that fell to the sea. For us, the rests at Selinunte, more than any of the other Greek evidences, are the masterworks transcendent on Sicilia. There one can enter the great temples rather than stay, dutifully, achingly, behind a cordon. Hence, the temples there seem more familiar. One can remain, for a while, in the company of the old gods, to see the light change or to watch four chestnut horses, a newly foaled colt, and a fat, fluffy-haired donkey roaming over the fallow of broken marbles as though it were some ordinary meadow. One can eavesdrop on the discourse between two white doves until the silence comes—piano, pianissimo, save only the whisperings of wings.*

Some of the people we met who live in Castelvetrano, near Selinunte, spoke to us of a soup they remembered their grandmothers and aunts having made from a selinon-like plant that grew along the coast. They remembered it being smooth and cold, with a strong, almost bitter sort of celery flavor. Alas, neither selinon *nor other wild grasses of its ilk are to be found. But prompted by our friends' taste memories and our own sweet keepsakes of Selinunte, we fashioned this satiny, soothing soup to be offered on the warmest of days.*

3 tablespoons plus ¼ cup extra-virgin olive oil

4 cups celery and celery leaves, coarsely chopped

1 large yellow onion, peeled and coarsely chopped

⅓ cup barley pearls

2 pounds very ripe tomatoes, peeled, seeded, and coarsely chopped, plus 1 medium, very ripe tomato, peeled, seeded, and coarsely chopped

2 large bay leaves

1½ tablespoons coarse sea salt

1 cup flat parsley leaves

2 fat cloves garlic, peeled and crushed

1 teaspoon fine sea salt

Zest of 1 lemon

In a large soup pot over a lively flame, heat 3 tablespoons of the oil and soften the celery and onion, taking care not to color them. Add the barley and roll it about with the aromatics for 1 minute before adding the 2 pounds tomatoes, bay leaves, coarse sea salt, and 1½ quarts of water. Cook, uncovered, for 1½ hours or until the barley is very soft. Remove the bay leaves.

Cool the soup a bit and, in a food processor fitted with a steel blade, puree it in two or three batches, turning it out into a large bowl. Alternately, one could press the soup through a fine sieve.

Either in a food processor or in a mortar, make a paste of the parsley, garlic, fine sea salt, the remaining tomato, and lemon zest. Slowly drop the remaining ¼ cup of oil through the feed tube or into the mortar, emulsifying and smoothing the paste. Add the paste to the cooled soup, stirring it well.

Cover the soup with plastic wrap and cool it in the refrigerator for at least 3 hours.

Ancient Agrigento—its Greek authors called it Akragas—was a city exquisite in its grace and symmetry. Raised up, half a millennium before Christ, from a hilly plain on a Mediterranean quay, it is now called La Valle dei Templi, The Valley of the Temples. Its ruins offer, perhaps, the island's greatest archaeological wealth, while its fringes are themselves glories. Earth striped in yellow and russet grains and deep-dyed, green silk meadows, all of them are fitted under a cobalt vault of sky and lit by the rages of a meridionial sun.

Some distance from the ancient city sits its medieval incarnation and there, among the thin Arab alleyways and the Norman churches, one can lunch on a warm salad of mussels and prawns and artichokes, sparkled with thick slices of fried lemon, or begin a fine lunch with a small plate of roasted prawns shined in a sauce of honeyed orange. The salad is wonderful presented on a huge platter rather than composed onto small plates. It makes for quite an agreeable little scene with everyone shelling their prawns and sucking at the fine liquors from their mussels and with some one of them saying, always, "I've never eaten a fried lemon before."

Neither of these dishes has a particular history, but they do sidle up to many of the characteristic Sicilian offerings that deal with flavor and texture. Both recipes employ the technique of "flavor reprise"—of repeating the use of certain components in various stages of the cooking. This serves to better define, intensify, the flavors that might otherwise become muddied, diluted, in the process.

Insalata Calda all' Agrigentina

A WARM SALAD IN THE STYLE OF AGRIGENTO

12 to 18 tiny artichokes (the purple-tipped variety about the
  size of a medium plum)

Juice of 1 lemon

1 tablespoon fine sea salt, plus additional as needed

1 cup plus 4 tablespoons extra-virgin olive oil

1 small, dried hot chile

3 fat cloves garlic, peeled, crushed, and minced

6 lemons, unpeeled and sliced into ¼-inch rounds

4 cups dry white wine

3 dozen very large mussels, scrubbed, bearded, and rinsed

½ cup celery leaves

1 fat clove garlic, peeled and wrapped in a bay leaf, fastened
  with 1 whole clove

12 to 18 large prawns, unshelled, heads removed

3 tablespoons best-quality white wine vinegar

Buy only the smallest, tenderest artichokes available, with several inches of their stems intact. Trim only the very ends of the still-soft petals of the young artichokes, leaving them whole if they are very small or slicing them in half if they are a bit larger. If the choke has begun to grow, scoop it out with a small, sharp spoon. Place each of them in a bowl with the lemon juice and toss them about.

Place the artichokes in a large saucepan, covering them with cold water. Add 1 tablespoon of sea salt and bring to a simmer, gently poaching the artichokes for 3 to 4 minutes. They should still be firm and crisp. Drain the artichokes and refresh them under very cold water. Drain them again and set them aside.

Over a lively flame, heat ½ cup of the olive oil in a very large sauté pan and crush the chile between your fingers into it. Lower the flame and stir the oil and the bits of chile for 1 minute, perfuming the oil. Add the garlic and soften it for a few seconds, taking care not to color it. Add the lemon slices, rolling them around in the perfumed oil, sautéing them lightly, and cooking for 4 to 5 minutes. Add the poached artichokes to the pan, rolling them about with the aromatics and the lemons for 2 minutes. Lower the flame, add ½ cup of white wine and cover the sauté pan with a skewed lid, braising the artichokes until the stem end is easily pierced with a sharp knife, about 8 to 10 minutes. Permit the artichokes to cool in the braising liquid, setting them aside.

In a large saucepan, combine the mussels with the celery leaves, the garlic/bay leaf, and 3 cups of wine. Over a lively flame, bring to a simmer, cover the pan, and steam the mussels just until they open. With tongs, remove the mussels to a large bowl, discarding the garlic/bay leaf. Over a lively flame, reduce the mussel liquor to ¾ cup and pour it over the cooked mussels, tossing them about in it. Set them aside.

Last, heat the 4 tablespoons of olive oil in a large sauté pan and add the prawns, rolling them about in the oil. As they begin to rosy a bit, add the remaining ½ cup of white wine and cook the prawns another minute. With tongs, remove the prawns to a large bowl. Over a lively flame, reduce the prawn liquor to 2 or 3 tablespoons and pour it over the cooked prawns, tossing them about in it. Set them aside. The 3 components can be prepared several hours or even half a day in anticipation and held, covered, at cool room temperature.

To assemble the salad: In a very large bowl, combine the 3 components—the artichokes/lemons, the mussels, the prawns—with their respective juices, tossing them together lightly, integrating their juices and liquors. Cover the bowl with plastic wrap and let the salad rest for 10 minutes. Meanwhile, construct a simple vinaigrette with the remaining oil, the vinegar, and a little fine sea salt. Toss the salad once again and turn it out onto a large and beautiful platter, drizzling it with the vinaigrette.

Gamberi Arrostiti all'Arancio e Miele

WOOD-ROASTED PRAWNS WITH A SAUCE OF ORANGE AND HONEY

Serves 6

The Marinade

1 cup freshly squeezed orange juice
¼ cup extra-virgin olive oil
½ cup dry Marsala
24 large prawns, unshelled, heads removed

Combine the orange juice, ¼ cup of the olive oil, and Marsala in a small bowl, whisking together the elements very thoroughly and let them rest while you work at butterflying the prawns.

With a small, sharp scissors, on the outside of the shell, begin cutting through at the larger of the ends, sliding the scissors delicately down to the point where the tail begins to fan out. Stop there and, armed with a small knife, slit the exposed flesh and remove the vein.

Place the prawns into a large bowl and pour over the marinade, tossing the prawns about and coating them well. Cover the bowl with plastic wrap and refrigerate for 2 hours.

The Sauce

2 tablespoons extra-virgin olive oil
1 fat clove garlic, peeled, crushed, and minced
Zest and juice of 2 oranges
1 cup dry Marsala
2 tablespoons dark honey (buckwheat, chestnut, etc.)
1 teaspoon orange flower water
2 tablespoons best-quality white wine vinegar

In a medium saucepan over a lively flame, heat the oil and soften the garlic, taking care not to let it color. Add the zest and roll it about in the oil, permitting its own oils to perfume the olive oil for 1 minute. Add the juice and the Marsala and, over a lively flame, let the liquid reduce for 5 minutes. Lower the flame and add the honey, the orange flower water, and the vinegar. Let the sauce bubble gently for another minute and remove it from the heat. Set the sauce aside.

An hour before you wish to roast the prawns, build a wood fire. Meanwhile, remove the prawns from their bath, draining them very well on absorbent paper towels and reserving the marinade. Roast the prawns, flesh side down, brushing them with the reserved marinade, for 1 minute. Turn the prawns, brushing them again, and roast them for 1½ minutes, fitting in another dose of the marinade.

Remove the sizzling prawns to a platter on which some of the gently reheated sauce has been laid. Drizzle the prawns with a bit more of the sauce and serve them with peeled orange sections and leaves of mint and basil, if you wish. Needless to say, iced dry Marsala is most compatible.

Costoletta di Vitella alla Palermitana

VEAL CHOPS IN THE STYLE OF PALERMO

Serves 2

Cutlets or chops of veal are pressed with oregano, garlic, and bread crumbs, then sautéed or grilled and proffered throughout the island as the fish-phobic's Sicilian supper. One is likely to be presented with a fibrous little cutlet that makes one long to be supping somewhere else. This version, though, inspired by Osteria ai Cascinari in Palermo, begs the rubbing of a good, thick chop with a paste of herbs before giving it a quilt of crumbs mixed with pecorino and sesame seeds and, finally, a brief sauté and a splash of white wine. It makes for a fine dish, especially when accompanied with a bit of pesto di pistacchi e olive *(page 193).*

> 3 tablespoons fresh oregano leaves or 2 teaspoons dried Greek
>   oregano, crumbled
> 2 fat cloves garlic, peeled and crushed
> Zest of 1 lemon
> 2 2-inch-thick veal chops, cut from the loin
> 1 teaspoon fine sea salt
> ½ teaspoon freshly cracked pepper
> ⅔ cup freshly made coarse bread crumbs
> ¼ cup just-grated pecorino
> 2 tablespoons sesame seeds
> 2 tablespoons extra-virgin olive oil
> ⅔ cup dry white wine

Finely mince together the oregano, the garlic, and the zest, making a thick paste. Rub this mixture onto both sides of the chops and leave them to rest for 1 hour at room temperature or as long as overnight, well covered in the refrigerator. Bring the chops back to room temperature before proceeding.

Preheat the oven to 400 degrees. Sprinkle the sea salt and freshly cracked pepper over both sides of the chops. Combine the bread crumbs with the pecorino and sesame seeds and press the mixture thickly onto the sides of the chops.

Over a lively flame, heat the olive oil in a large sauté pan. Brown the chops for at least 2 minutes, building a good firm crust before attempting to turn them. Do the same for the other side. Transfer the sauté pan to the oven and roast the chops, 2 or 3 minutes to the side. Remove the roasted chops to a holding plate and place the sauté pan over a lively flame. Add the wine, stirring and scraping at all those lovely bits of bread and cheese and seeds that will have escaped the chops, and reduce the sauce for several minutes before glazing the veal with it and presenting it straightaway.

Pane di Semolino di Piana degli Albanesi

SEMOLINA BREAD IN THE STYLE OF PIANA DEGLI ALBANESI

Makes 1 very large or 2 medium pagnotte

Piana degli Albanesi is the name of the city settled half a millennium ago when a band of oppressed Albanesi took flight from the Turks and, with the permission of Giovanni II, the then Spanish viceroy in Sicily, took refuge in the countryside near Palermo. A somewhat unmingled populace, cleaving still to its heritage, they perpetuate, in full dress and with great ebullience, the story of their gastronomy. And yet it is a fornaio, a baker, there who makes one of the finest examples of the traditional bread of Sicily. Heavy, cakelike in its wet, golden crumb, its crust is thick, hard, wood-scorched. And to cradle a hunk of it in one's hand is to hold a piece of the ages, it seems. Insofar as things like this can be carried from one part of the world to another, here follows his formula.

3½ teaspoons active dry yeast or 1½ small cakes fresh yeast

⅓ cup warm water

4 tablespoons olive oil

1½ tablespoons fine sea salt

1⅔ cups tepid water

3⅓ cups *farina di grano duro* (hard wheat flour), which is fine
  semolina ("pasta flour"), plus additional as needed

1⅓ cups unbleached all-purpose flour

2 egg whites, beaten to a foam

⅔ cup sesame seeds

In a large bowl, dissolve the yeast in the warm water, permitting it to activate for 15 minutes. In a medium bowl, whisk together 3 tablespoons of the olive oil, sea salt, and tepid water and add it all to the rested yeast. Mix the semolina and all-purpose flours together and add them, in three doses, to the yeast mixture, beating well after each addition. Turn the dough out onto a floured surface and knead it for a minimum of 10 minutes or until the dough develops a satiny finish.

Transfer the dough to a bowl with the remaining 1 tablespoon of olive oil, rolling the dough around in the oil, coating it well. Cover the bowl with plastic wrap and permit the dough to rise for 1½ to 2 hours or until its size doubles. Punch down the risen dough and knead it again for a minute or two, then let it rest for 15 minutes. These last two steps are to give the high-gluten semolina an extra-vigorous workout.

The Sicilians, as you might imagine, exercise their fantasy even unto the shaping of their breads. No form is too intricate. However, the *fornaio* in Piana degli Albanesi is a tranquil sort of fellow who simply pummeled his good yellow dough into great rounds, painted them with a bit of egg white, and pressed sesame seeds generously over the breads' surfaces before heaving them into the his wood-fired ovens.

Divide the dough in two (or even three pieces, if you'd like) or work with it as a whole. In any case, shape the dough into a round form, using cupped hands to stretch the dough, turning the excess under and forming a taut skin over the bread's dome. Line metal baking sheets with baker's parchment and sprinkle the paper lightly with semolina. Position the loaves on the sheets. Paint the foamy egg white over the surface of the breads, coating them well, then gently pressing the seeds overall. Cover the shaped breads with a clean kitchen towel and permit them to rise for 1½ to 2 hours, or until their size has doubled.

Preheat the oven to 450 degrees, with baking stones, if desired.

Just before sliding the loaves onto the stones, sprinkle the stones with semolina or fine cornmeal. Alternatively, place the loaves on the metal baking sheets in the oven. Bake the loaves for 10 minutes, reduce the temperature to 400 degrees, and bake the breads for 20 to 30 minutes more, depending on the size of the loaves. Remove the breads to cooling racks.

To help crisp the crust of these breads, place a dozen or so ice cubes in a baking pan on the floor of the oven just before sliding in the breads. This creates a steamy, humid environment for a few minutes, usually long enough to help form a good crust. Or one can choose to directly spray the breads—using a plant mister filled with ice water. Three or four good mists, three times during the first 8 minutes of baking, is the formula.

La Storia dei Dolci Siciliani
THE HISTORY OF SICILIAN SWEETS

Essentially, it was the Church's holy sisters who created the Sicilian pastry culture early in the fifteenth century. Surely, the Arabs had left behind their own sweet stories, their use of honey and spices and of Etna's snow to fashion ices and the delicate precursors to gelato. Nevertheless, it was the sisters in their convents and monasteries, needing to plump up the Church's coffers, who began to roll out dainties and sweetmeats, biscuits and cakes and tarts of great *raffinatezza*, refinement, dispatching them on feast days—most often through the tiny, wooden-grated doors that were the sisters' only threshold to the world. One first knocked and the door opened. One passed a note of request, accompanied by proper payment. The little door shut. Soon, the door was raised and the sweet parcel appeared.

How beautiful were they, all decorated with exuberant curlicues of orange-flower-scented quince paste, silvered dragées, crystallized fruits and flowers. Molded and carved, flourished and glossed, there was a pastry to celebrate each phenomenon, humble or grand, of Sicilian life. For weddings and funerals and celebrations of the sainted, for births and communions, confirmations, dedications, sowing and reaping festivals, grape and olive harvests and pig stickings, the keen sisters reflected life's passages in sugar and butter, the pastry far more pleasant to swallow, sometimes, than the moment it honored. Each order of nuns composed from its own repertoire, building fame for its own particular set of jewels.

Now the culture of convent sweet-making is all but dissolved, save a few of the orders that produce traditional cakes at Easter and Christmas. It is the *pasticcieri*, the artisan pastry bakers, who feed and soothe Sicily's stunning impulse to devour sweets.

Eaten all day long, all evening long, in the *pasticcerie*, in the bars and *caffès*, in moments of desperation and triumph, alone, in company, in tears, in love, sweets are toted on little paper trays, smartly wrapped and tied, along with newspaper or purse, a briefcase or a sack of peaches. The only and few moments when sweets are denounced might be after lunch and dinner when a fruit or a sliver of cheese, a glass of sweet wine and a handful of roasted almonds are presented as a *fine pasto*—an end to the meal. We know a Sicilian who claims to keep a silver box of exquisitely sculpted marzipan fruits in his bathroom and who nibbles at one each morning while shaving.

Since Sicilians themselves are not concerned with the making of their beloved sweets, it seems an unlikely task to unravel here some pastryman's centuries-old recipe for *cassata siciliana*, the classic cake of ricotta and candied fruits wrapped in sheets of hand-rolled almond paste, scrolled in nougat and beset with crystallized flowers. Better that you taste the glories of cassata in Palermo. Instead, here follow two pastries, never to be found in the pale green satin upholstered windows of the *pasticcerie*. These are the typical pastries of the farmwife, the homey sweets baked with the humble components at hand and the ones that send up perfumes of welcome and comfort.

La Torta Antica Ericina

THE ANTIQUE TART OF ERICE

Serves 6

Bestriding the shoulders of the island's western verges is the perfect borgo medievale *(medieval village) of Erice, called so after he who was the mythical son of Venus, sired by the king of the ancient tribe of the Elimi. There is a fascination about the village, its apocryphal tales and its truths—gifts, one thinks, of the cults that once worshiped the gods of beauty and love there and carved into the village walls scripts still undecipherable.*

Limpid, sweet is its air, and from its sweeping lofts one sees Mt. Etna, her fury diffused in far-off mists. And there on a small piazza sits the pasticceria of Maria Grammatico, who fashions the most gorgeous, most delicious evidences of rustic Sicilian pastry. Many of Signora Grammatico's formulas are borrowed from the epoch of the Ericina convent pastry-making—it, too, having once practiced a temperate rather than a Baroque style. This is a version of the celebrated Ericina ricotta pie.

The Tart Crust

1½ cups all-purpose flour

½ teaspoon fine sea salt

¼ cup confectioners' sugar

½ teaspoon ground cinnamon

9 tablespoons sweet butter, chilled, cut into ½-inch pieces, plus
   additional as needed

4 tablespoons moscato or other sweet wine, chilled

Pulse the flour, salt, confectioners' sugar, and cinnamon two or three times in the work bowl of a food processor fitted with a steel blade. Add the 9 tablespoons very well chilled butter and pulse until it resembles coarse crumbs. With the machine running, pour the cold wine in through the feed tube all at once and process for 4 to 5 seconds, only until the contents just begin to form a dough.

Turn the mixture out onto a large sheet of plastic wrap, gathering up the errant bits and gently pressing it all into a dough. Enclose the dough in the plastic, cover the plastic with a clean kitchen towel and leave it to rest in the refrigerator for 30 minutes.

Roll out the rested dough between two sheets of plastic wrap to ¼ inch. Remove one sheet of wrap and invert the pastry into a buttered 10-inch loose-bottomed tart pan, fitting and trimming the pastry. Cover the pastry with plastic wrap and place it in the freezer for 20 minutes or the refrigerator for 1 hour.

The Filling

1 plump vanilla bean

1½ cups heavy cream

⅔ cup mascarpone

1½ pounds whole-milk ricotta (best if purchased in bulk from an
   Italian grocery or a specialty cheese store)

1 cup confectioners' sugar, plus additional as needed

2 egg whites, beaten to a froth

Split the vanilla bean with a small, sharp knife and scrape out the seeds into a large saucepan. Add the vanilla pod and the cream and, over a medium flame, bring the components to a simmer, permitting the cream to reduce and thicken to 1 cup. Add the mascarpone and heat until the mascarpone is melted and blended with the reduced cream. Cover the pot and permit the vanilla seeds and pod to infuse the cream.

Meanwhile, in the work bowl of a food processor fitted with a steel blade, process the ricotta with 1 cup confectioners' sugar until the cheese is smooth and thick. Add the egg whites and process another 20 seconds to incorporate them well.

Turn the ricotta mixture out into a medium bowl. When the cream/vanilla mixture has cooled, remove the vanilla pod and blend the perfumed cream very well into the ricotta.

Preheat the oven to 425 degrees.

Remove the plastic wrap from the tart shell and bake the shell for 5 minutes, lowering the heat to 400 degrees and baking it for 8 minutes more or until it has begun to firm and is lightly golden. Remove the partially baked pastry from the oven to cool for 10 minutes.

Lower the oven temperature to 350 degrees.

Spread the ricotta mixture over the tart, smoothing it a bit, and bake the tart for 20 minutes or until the ricotta is firm and a very pale golden crust has begun to form on its surface. Do not overbake the tart. Remove it from the oven, setting it on a rack to cool for 5 minutes before removing the pan's sides and permitting the tart to cool thoroughly. Dust the tart with confectioners' sugar.

Crostata di Zucca Invernale e Rhum con Cioccolato Amaro

A TART OF WINTER SQUASH AND RUM WITH BITTER CHOCOLATE

Serves 6

In the late summer and early autumn, in the interior of the island, the great harvests of pumpkin and squash are preserved by the farmwives in varied fashion. Often the flesh is cooked down to a marmalade and sparked with candied oranges, or poached chunks of it are set to rest in a sweet vinegared brine. Too, thick slices of poached flesh are often rolled around in a sugary syrup and left to dry. Of a most luscious flavor, this candied pumpkin is sometimes used with dark rum and a handful of broken, bittersweet chocolate, to make a tart like the one we were served in the village of Milo. I was dazzled by it. But when I heard of the perplexing process by which the tart's author had candied the pumpkin (she began by saying that I should gather fifty to sixty pumpkins), I was slightly shaken. I found, though, that simply roasting the flesh of a pumpkin or squash and then bathing it in caramelized sugar gives a flavor similar and perhaps even richer and requires far less drama.

The Tart Crust

1 recipe tart crust (page 216), substituting dark rum, well
    chilled, for the sweet wine

The Filling

1 3- to 4-pound piece Hubbard squash, butternut squash, or
    pumpkin, seeds removed (these left to dry for later roasting)
1⅓ cups sugar
2 tablespoons sweet butter, plus additional as needed
⅓ cup dark rum
8 ounces extra-bittersweet chocolate, preferably Lindt or
    Valrhona 70% cacao
Confectioners' sugar
Heavy cream or mascarpone (optional)

Preheat the oven to 450 degrees.

On a metal baking sheet, roast the squash until its flesh is tender and collapsing—about ½ hour. Remove the squash from the oven and permit it to cool until you can comfortably scrape the flesh from its shell. Set the flesh aside.

Over a gentle flame, heat the sugar in a large sauté pan, stirring constantly, until it takes on a very dark, golden color. Add the squash and roll it around in the caramel. Because the squash will be colder than the caramel, the caramel will seize and harden, but after a moment or two over the gentle flame, it will melt. Add 2 tablespoons of the butter and the rum, combining the components well. Turn out the squash mixture into a bowl to cool thoroughly.

Meanwhile, butter a 10-inch tart pan with a removable bottom and line it with the pastry, covering the pastry-lined pan with plastic wrap and placing it in the freezer for 20 minutes or in the refrigerator for 1 hour.

Preheat the oven to 400 degrees. Coarsely chop the extra-bittersweet chocolate and combine it with the squash mixture. Spread the squash/chocolate mixture over the well-chilled, unbaked pastry and bake the tart for 15 minutes. Lower the temperature to 350 degrees and bake the tart for an additional 25 minutes or until the pastry is deeply golden.

Permit the tart to cool a bit on a rack, then dust it with confectioners' sugar and present it, very warm, with unsweetened, barely whipped cream or a bowlful of mascarpone, should you wish.

Il Fato di Persephone

PERSEPHONE'S DOOM

Serves 2

Demeter, the goddess of grain, hallowed by i siculi—the warrior tribe that inhabited the island before the Greeks—was all of resplendence, even to the high crown formed from her flaxen braids. It was she who illuminated the magic of sowing seeds beneath the earth and then protecting them, feeding them, and growing them up into ripeness. The tribe's harvests grew ever more abundantly, the goddess conjuring the sun and the rain and the breezes on their behalf, they honoring her with great bonfires under the full moon's light and ritual offerings of bread and wine. The island was Elysium, uninterrupted.

And then, heaving himself up through a rent in the earth's crust, Pluto stole Demeter's daughter, Persephone, as plunder for his abyss. Demeter screeched and mourned and cast Sicilia into darkness. There was nothing to nourish her tribe save the tears Demeter cried down from the heavens.

So clamorously did the goddess petition him that Pluto succumbed, vowing riddance to the child as much as to her shrewish mother. He would liberate Persephone. Only then, though, did Pluto take note that Persephone had cut in two a pomegranate, and that she sat slaking her child's thirst on its juices and its glistening, rosy seeds—a blunder. He howled up at her mother that Persephone had devoured the sacred seeds of fertility, and for this sin he must halve his promise. Just as she had broken the fruit, Persephone would be liber-

ated for only six months of every year. And, as penance, she must, each year and everlastingly, stay six months in the shades of Hades.

And so it was that Demeter heralded the sun and the rain and raised up the wheat, thick and golden, from May through October, when Persephone was at her side, leaving the island barren and under an impotent sun from November until April—her half-mourning an allegory of the seasons, of life and of death.

In the early springtime, one can see still the great roaring fires lit by Sicilian wheat farmers and whole villages in dance and song, invoking the gods' promise to keep safe their newly sown fields. Only now, old, sweet Demeter, pagan that she was, has been supplanted by St. Joseph, her powers having been ferried over into his realm.

Not so long after a woman in Palermo had told us this story of Demeter, we were staying awhile in Enna, an interior agricultural city. One evening, the man who served our supper of rough-cut semolina pasta with a mutton sauce and thick chops of pork, oven-roasted with wild onions, dispatched to our table his mother—a fine country cook—with the sad news that she'd had not a moment to put together some rustic little tart or other that day. There would be no sweet. Unless, of course, she murmured, we'd like a pomegranate with un cucchiaino di zabaglione—*a small spoonful of custard. We agreed.*

What she brought forth to us on an old plate of cranberry-colored glass were two pomegranates that seemed to be broken rather than cut in two, their crimson juices spilling out from the jagged shells with tiny coffee spoons plunged into the hearts of seeds. Two diminutive porcelain pitchers of some winy custard were laid beside the plate. We were urged to pour the custard over, into the pomegranates. Sweet but not quite sweet against the tart, peppery seeds, the sauce was the color of ambered muscadine, its scent that of crushed violets. It was a plate quietly, achingly beautiful to see and to eat.

Later, when we asked her son if we might give our thanks to his mother for the fine supper and, especially, for the pomegranates, he told us that she'd gone upstairs to bed. Thinking to write our thanks in a little note, I asked him, "What is her name?" "Mia madre si chiama Demetra," *said the man. "My mother is called Demeter." Startled, dazed even, for a moment, the story of Demeter came racing to mind. Thinking the note unnecessary, all we said was* "Buona sera. Buona sera e arrivederci." *This is a true story.*

And here follows the recipe for a version of Demetra's pomegranate. It makes for the truly sensual sort of ending one wouldn't think of serving to a great, roaring crowd. Though it might be fine for a foursome of Sybarites, I think it best just for two of you.

2 large, ripe pomegranates
2 tablespoons plus 2 ounces dry Marsala
2 large egg yolks
2 tablespoons sugar

Holding the pomegranate on its side and using a medium-sized, thin-bladed sharp knife, cut through the shell and halfway into the fruit around its diameter. Then, taking the pomegranate in both hands, twist each side of the fruit in opposite directions, breaking it in two. This will fashion pretty, uneven halves that will look less fussed with than had one whacked at them with precision. Pour the 2 tablespoons of cold, dry Marsala into the cavities of the four pomegranate halves, trickling it in slowly, finding little crevices. Set the fruit aside.

In the top of a small double boiler or in a medium bowl that will fit nicely over a saucepan, beat together the yolks with the sugar until the mixture is thickened. Add the remaining 2 ounces dry Marsala and blend it in thoroughly. Over simmering water, whisk the custard until it explodes into a dense, shiny foam.

Pour half the warm custard onto two serving plates, placing two pomegranate halves over the pool of custard on each plate. Present them with a pitcher of more custard to pour into and over the fruit at table.

Gelo d'Anguria

WATERMELON ICE

Makes 1½ quarts

On the curve of Palermo's Via Papireto, just before the entrance to il mercato delle pulci—the flea market—there sits a watermelon stand and a hand-wrought sign: ICED, SWEET WATERMELON, DAY AND NIGHT. *We passed the little place several times each day on our excursions through the great honkings and snarlings of the city traffic. Drawn by its promise, we meant always to stop but never found quite the right convergence of appetite, time, and space in which to park the car. But one Saturday evening, after a long, winy dinner and a dry search for a still-open gelateria, we thought to soothe ourselves with a visit to the watermelon man. Though it was well after midnight, he was there, waiting midst the walls of precisely laid, smooth-skinned fruit, his old Arab eyes illuminated by festoons of pink and green lights. He bid us sit at his one and only tiny, oilcloth-covered table, tucked in the corner farthest from the street. Speaking only in smiles—it was hardly necessary to tell him what we desired—we watched as he chose a melon from those he kept in a basin of iced water and then cleaved it open with a single heft of some ancient tool. Each half he stuck with fork and spoon and, resting the juice-dripping melons on wooden boards, he presented them. He brought a little tin plate in which we might deposit the seeds and two beautifully ironed kitchen-towel napkins.*

The red flesh was crisp under our spoons and each new excavation brought up a yet sweeter, colder mouthful of it. We ate slowly under the pink and green lights, finally resting our spoons against the great, hollowed shells, triumphant, certain we'd spent well that hour of our lives, certain, too, how perfect, how divine was that food.

Lacking a faithful watermelon man, here follows a way to work with a well-ripened, even if not exquisitely fleshed, melon. Perfumed with cinnamon and studded with bitter chocolate and pistachios, it is the traditional ice of ferragosto— the official high summer Italian festival. The gelo is best eaten long after midnight.

6 cups watermelon, seeds removed, cut into coarse chunks

1 to 1½ cups superfine sugar

1 teaspoon just-grated cinnamon dissolved in 2 tablespoons
   warmed Cointreau

3 tablespoons just-squeezed lemon juice

2 ounces pistachios, shelled, roasted, and finely chopped

2 ounces bittersweet chocolate, preferably Lindt or Valrhona
   70% cacao, finely chopped

Iced Cointreau

Puree the watermelon with 1 cup of the sugar, the cinnamon/Cointreau mixture, and the lemon juice in a food processor or a blender. Taste the puree, adding a bit more sugar if you desire.

Pour the puree into a bowl and set it inside another, larger bowl filled with ice and water. Stir the puree, chilling it very well before transferring it to your ice cream maker and freezing it—in two batches, if necessary—according to the manufacturer's instructions. Add the pistachios and chocolate at the point in the process recommended by the manufacturer.

Present the *gelo* with the benediction of a tablespoon or so of iced Cointreau.

I Gelati Artigianali Siciliani
THE HANDMADE ICE CREAMS OF SICILY

The culture of handmade gelato on Sicily is one of lavish proportion. News of who is churning out *fichi d'india*, prickly pear, or fresh fig or *zibibbo*, golden raisin, or some such glory is passed along from one *appassionato* to another—often complete with eye-rolling and the pressing of one's index finger into one's cheek, Sicilian code signifying something that is delicious—with the breathlessness of having just discovered another trajectory around the sun. It might seem that gelato establishes the Sicilian equilibrium along with the other of their life's essentials—espresso, cigarettes, and pastry. Cuddled inside a warm *cornetto* (a croissant-shaped sweet roll) for breakfast, taken in tempered doses throughout the morning between some little *cannolo* (a fried cylinder of pastry filled with candied fruit and chocolate-studded ricotta) or the tiniest pistachio and almond-paste tartlet, the Sicilian sashays, shamelessly, up to the cool glass that separates him from his *dolcezza* again at about four in the afternoon for just *un cucchiaio* (a spoonful) of something, so as not to interfere with the ritual of the five-thirty *aperitivo*. And it is an hour or so after dinner that he takes the last, cold, creamy jot of it, *una coppetta piccola di limone* (a small cup of lemon), just for the digestion and, of course, to pave the way for a little bedtime tray of cookies.

The flavors of the gelato are pure, clean, intense essences of seasonal fruit or some other single and magnificently defined taste. If it is caramel, it is caramel dark and burnished, the sugar just a breath away from burnt. There is no better ice cream than the gelato made in Italy and no better gelato than that from Sicily. As is fancy pastry-making an avenue for only artists, perhaps, too, is this art of coaxing cream and fruit or chocolate or spices into some icy amalgam. We all have memories, I think, of some home-cranked iced peach or strawberry confection of the high summer of our childhoods, but save those and other lush exceptions, the most sumptuous ones are scooped up from the cold metal tubs of the ice cream maker as artist.

Here follow two formulas—neither of which employ eggs and hence are not classic *gelati*—for what might just fall under that category of "lush exception." Both are from a fourth-generation *gelataio* in Trapani.

Un Gelato Barocco

A BAROQUE GELATO

Makes 1 quart

2 plump vanilla beans
3 cups heavy cream
⅔ cup sugar
1½ ounces candied orange peel
1 ounce candied ginger
2 ounces extra-bittersweet chocolate, preferably Lindt or
    Valrhona 70% cacao
2 ounces almonds, blanched, roasted

With a small, sharp knife, slit the beans and scoop out their seeds. Over a lively flame in a large, heavy-bottomed saucepan, combine vanilla seeds and pods, the cream and the sugar, bringing the mixture just to a simmer. Remove from the flame, cover the pot, and permit the vanilla to infuse the cream for an hour.

Meanwhile, finely chop the candied peel, the candied ginger, the bittersweet chocolate, and the almonds. Combine them and set them aside. Strain the infused mixture, cover it with plastic wrap, and chill it for several hours or overnight.

Transfer the mixture to your ice cream maker and freeze it—in two batches, if necessary—according to the instructions of the manufacturer, folding in the fruit and nut mixture at the point in the process recommended by the instructions.

Gelato di Prugne e Semi di Anice

BLACK PLUM AND ANISEED GELATO

Makes 1 quart

This variety of plum, even when ripe, retains a certain tartness that is offset here by the anise and the almond paste, all of which, when lolling about in the cream, seem made for each other.

3 cups heavy cream

1 cup sugar

2 teaspoons aniseeds, lightly crushed

2½ cups fresh black Italian plums

3 ounces almond paste, finely crumbled

Over a lively flame in a heavy-bottomed saucepan, combine the cream, sugar, and aniseeds, bringing the mixture just to a simmer. Remove the pan from the flame and cover, permitting the anise to infuse the cream for 1 hour.

Meanwhile, stone the plums and slip off their skins. Chop the plums and place in a food processor. Process the plums to a coarse puree. Combine the infused cream with the puree, cover it with plastic wrap, and chill for several hours or overnight.

Transfer the mixture to your ice cream maker and freeze it—in two batches, if necessary—according to the instructions of the manufacturer, folding in the crumbles of almond paste at the point in the process recommended by the instructions.

SARDEGNA

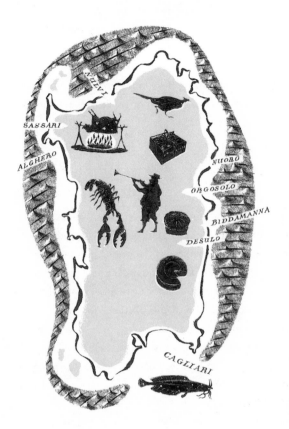

Older than Sicilia, older than Italia, older than the world is Sardegna. Alone in a limpid sea she sits, her stony skirts smoothed by wind and wet caresses, her sand, gold, fine as dust, and tufted with wild lilies. But she is not of the sea, this Sardegna. She is of the ancient and pathless moors of her high plateaux, of a Neolithic tangle of wild olives and figs, juniper and myrtle and thyme entwined with untamed roses, all of it a great and bewitching Stone Age garden. And there, in a silvery dusk, one can see a Sard vested in sheepskins astride a fine Arab horse, the long flap of his white bonnet like a wind sail behind him.

Sardegna is of pastures and forests and stones. Stones piled up thirteen centuries before Christ into humble shelters against the cold, the witches, the giants are her *nuraghi* (archeological remnants). But not these, nothing, no one is older than the Sard himself, the eternal Mesolithic man, he with his penchant to live in small clans, separate from, free from complexities. He is shepherd, swineherd, farmer, hunter, artisan, much as he has been always.

Once he shunned the sea because its edges were malarial infestations. He was safe from its horrors deep inside the moors. Too, there he needn't be troubled by those who came over the seas, those who thought to vanquish him. No one, neither pirate nor soldier, invaded the historical isolation of the Sard, no one. When they came, it was only onto the island's fringes, fetid barriers against the inner spaces of the island. The Sard culture abides, uninjured, inviolate even to his ritual Stone Age cooking. The Sard feasts on the quarry from his hunt, the flesh of his herds, and the thin, crackly bread called *pane carasau*. His is the kingdom of *carraxiu*, the roasting of his supper in ovens carved deep into the earth, smoldering graves for the carcass of a boar, a wild goat, a fat, black pig poached from a barnyard.

Maiale del Bracconiere
A PURLOINED PIG

Tribes of kinsmen still forage and hunt and shelter themselves within *la macchia*—the moors of the *barbagia* (the island's high, central plateau)—resisting the comforts of the villages and towns to live by their wits. And when the old woods yield not enough to feed them, the historical affair of the poacher ensues as one or another of them accepts the mission to go forth from the camp to steal a pig. From a farmer's old barn or a herd bedded on a pasture, *il bracconiere*—the poacher—prevails upon the porcine object of his sustenance and does not return to his fires with an empty sack.

The formula for roasting a pig in the manner of the *bracconiere* is called *porceddu a carraxiu*—in the Sard dialect, "pig roasted under the earth." One sets about the task by digging out a hole, fitting it with fragrant brush and branches and leaves and fashioning a sort of oven with flat stones, heated first over a fire, then positioned on the floor of the hole. The pig, dressed and readied for the ceremony, is laid over the fired stones. Another layer of hot stones is composed atop the pig and, finally, earth is piled and compacted over the subterranean oven, ensuring a slow and smoldering roast. After eight hours or more, the beast is retrieved, his skin nobly burnished, his flesh spiced by the smoke of perfumed woods.

Apart from the province of *i bracconieri*, the pageantry of *carraxiu* is virtually talismanic to the Sard. After three thousand years, he remains certain there is no other prescription to effect the finesse, the savor, that glorifies the flesh—pirated or not—of a pig or a lamb, a goat, a wild boar, roasted under the earth. And whether you shall once be convinced to dig a hole and roast a pig in its musky depths, and taste its sweet, charred goodness, is, perhaps, not a mandate on which you must this moment decide. I offer it to you, though, for I think it a fine thing to collect some gastronomic ritual now and again, if only to feed the sentimental appetite.

La Bottarga Cagliaritana

BOTTARGA IN THE STYLE OF CAGLIARI

Serves 4

The Phoenician port of Karalis is Cagliari and, sitting on the island's southern verges on the Gulf of the Angels, it seems not of Sardegna. The Sards who live away from the port say it is a place doubled-faced and call the Cagliaritani hollow-hearted. They say Cagliari is of the world and not of Sardegna. Sardi falsi—sham Sards—they are called. Surely discordant, as a city, with the Stone Age commonweal of the island's interior, Cagliari's most pleasant quarter seems the one raised up in the serene, medieval tracks of the Pisani. There, embraced by walls, new—as measured in Sard antiquity—one senses, still, some sweet press of sympathy. And it is there on its piazzette, where one can sit under broad, blue-striped umbrellas, to sip at cool Nuragus di Cagliari between melting bites of salty bottarga, the Sards' caviar.

Fashioned from eggs harvested from the cefalo—the gray mullet—the roe sacs are taken whole, compressed under thick hefts of marble, rubbed with unpounded crystals of sea salt, then left to dry on grass mats under the Cagliaritano sun. What emerges after several months of patience is a supple, glossy mass that, when shaved or grated gives up an authoritative yet balmy brininess.

In the humblest of osterie as it is in the ristoranti, this bottarga, the Sards' caviar, is presented with simple adornments. Rather easily hunted up in American specialty stores, look, though, for the bottarga di cefalo rather than the more common, far less delectable, bottarga di tonno, made from eggs of the tuna.

Here follows a recipe for a most uncommon, sensual sort of overture to lunch.

12 ounces of gray mullet *bottarga*
⅓ cup extra-virgin olive oil
Juice and zest of 2 large lemons
Freshly cracked pepper

With a small, very sharp knife, slice the *bottarga* horizontally into thin slivers. Alternatively, shave it with a vegetable peeler. Place the delicate *bottarga* in a single layer on a large, flat plate. Thread it lightly with the olive oil, baptize it with the lemon juice, strew it with the zest, and grind pepper generously over all. Present the *bottarga* as an antipasto with just-toasted bread and cold white wine.

Crostata di Patate di Biddamanna

A POTATO PIE IN THE STYLE OF BIDDAMANNA

Serves 6 to 8

In the Sard dialect, the town of Villagrande is called Biddamanna. There, a vast parcel of Sard earth is su cumonale—owned by everyone of the community. Shepherds can pasture their sheep, townsfolk can collect wood for their fires, a family can cultivate a small orchard, a garden of vegetables. The Biddamannesi can walk kilometer after kilometer through forests, into the mountains, onto the moors, hunting, foraging, gathering, as they have done forever in this town with no walls, no fences. And, too, they cook for each other over great fires laid in the piazza near the village hall on feast days. Cauldrons of thick soups, mutton poached with wild grasses, and beautiful handmade pastas are offered with baskets of pane carasau and barrels of rough, purply cannonau.

Though all Sards seem passionate about making packets of their food, these Biddamannesi seem more devoted, even, to the pursuit. They urge rough doughs into pouches and pillows plumped with all manner of savories and sweets, the bundles tumbled into gurgling oil or baked over wood embers or gently poached. Culingionis are raviolo-like pasta typically stuffed with bitter greens and an acidy, fresh ewe's milk cheese or a paste of potatoes, nutmeg, cloves, wild mint, and pecorino. Though these are luscious, it is a half day's ceremony to make them. Hence, I sometimes wrap the good potato paste in a crisp quilting of cheese pastry, a quickly done deed that gives up all the savor of the culingionis plus the prize of a gorgeous scent as the crostata bakes to crispness.

The Potato Filling

3 tablespoons extra-virgin olive oil

1 large yellow onion, peeled and minced

2 fat cloves garlic, peeled, crushed, and minced

Zest of 1 large orange

1½ pounds new red- or white-skinned potatoes, poached in sea-
   salted water until tender, drained, peeled, and mashed

Generous gratings of nutmeg

½ teaspoon ground cloves

Freshly cracked pepper

1 teaspoon fine sea salt

1 large egg, lightly beaten

⅔ cup just-grated pecorino

⅓ cup minced mint leaves

In a small sauté pan over a medium flame, warm the olive oil and soften the onion, garlic, and orange zest for 5 minutes, permitting the mixture to take on some light color. Transfer the onion, garlic, orange zest combination to a large bowl. Add the mashed potatoes and the remaining ingredients, forming a well-amalgamated paste. Cover the paste and set it aside while you make the crust.

The Pecorino Crust

2⅔ cups all-purpose flour, plus additional as needed to roll out
   dough
⅓ cup coarse polenta
½ teaspoon fine sea salt
⅔ cup just-grated pecorino
7 ounces sweet, cold butter, cut into small pieces
1 large egg, beaten
6 tablespoons very cold dry white wine

In a large bowl, combine the flour, polenta, salt, and pecorino. Using your fingertips or a pastry blender, cut the butter into the dry components until it resembles coarse crumbs. Combine the egg with the cold wine and stir the liquids into the flour mixture, constructing a rough dough.

Turn it out onto a lightly floured work space and gently, swiftly, work it into a smooth dough. Flatten the dough and cover it tightly in plastic wrap, covering the plastic wrap with a clean kitchen towel and leaving the dough to rest in the refrigerator for 1 hour or in the freezer for 20 minutes.

Over a lightly floured work space, roll out the dough into a free-form sort of circle of about 16 inches in diameter. Transfer the pastry to a parchment-lined baking sheet. The pastry will be too large to fit on the sheet but that will soon be remedied.

Place the potato filling in the center of the pastry, working it into a mound and leaving a 2-inch hem of pastry uncovered. Now lift the pastry hem and fold it over, pleating it a bit, covering about 2 inches of the filling. The less symmetric your form, the more homey and beautiful will be your *crostata*. Cover the *crostata* with a sheet of plastic wrap and set it, on its parchment-lined tin, to chill again in the refrigerator for 20 minutes.

Preheat the oven to 400 degrees.

Bake the *crostata* for 25 to 30 minutes or until the crust is deeply golden and the potatoes all golden and crisp.

Permit the *crostata* a 5-minute rest on a cooling rack, transfer it to a cutting board and carry it to table, cutting it into fat wedges. Present it as a first course, to be eaten warm between sips of good red wine.

Burrida Cagliaritana

POACHED FISH WITH WALNUT GARLIC SAUCE
IN THE STYLE OF CAGLIARI

Serves 6

A dish old as the ages, one that pungently depicts the Sards' seminal appetite for the long bathing of fish or game in some puckerish sauce is burrida. *Traditionally prepared with* gattucci di mare—*sea catfish*—*the sauce is enriched with the pounded raw livers of the fish. Here follows a version using* orata—*red snapper*—*or* coda di rospo—*monkfish*—*though river catfish can also be called upon with fine result. Present the* burrida *as an antipasto or a main course to savvy, unshy palates.*

The Sauce

> 4 fat cloves garlic, peeled
> ⅔ cup flat parsley leaves
> ⅔ cup plus 1 tablespoon extra-virgin olive oil
> 1½ teaspoons fine sea salt
> Freshly cracked pepper
> ¼ cup good white wine vinegar
> Livers of the red snapper (optional)
> ½ cup walnuts, toasted and finely chopped
> ⅓ cup pine nuts, toasted and chopped

With a mezzaluna or a very sharp knife, mince the garlic with the parsley to a fine paste. In a small sauté pan over a medium flame, warm ⅔ cup of the olive oil and sauté the paste, taking care not to color it. Add the perfumed oil to a very large bowl, setting the pan aside a moment. Add the sea salt, generous grindings of pepper, and the vinegar, beating the sauce with a fork.

If you are using red snapper and are opting to incorporate their livers into the sauce, take the same small sauté pan and, over a lively flame, warm the 1 tablespoon of olive oil and quickly sauté the livers, tossing them about for 1 minute, mashing them into the oil. Add the livers to the sauce, amalgamating them well.

Add the walnuts and the pine nuts, giving the sauce a final stir. Cover the bowl with plastic wrap while it awaits the fish.

The Fish

6 10- to 12-ounce red snapper, scaled, cleaned, and filleted, the
    livers reserved, or 6 6- to 8-ounce fillets of monkfish
½ cup good white wine vinegar
1 tablespoon coarse sea salt
⅔ cup just-made fine bread crumbs lightly browned in ⅓ cup
    extra-virgin olive oil

Rinse the fish under very cold water. Place cold water in a large pot to the depth of 6 inches and, over a lively flame, bring the water to a simmer, add the vinegar and the sea salt. Lower the flame, add the fish, and permit the liquid to barely simmer around it, poaching it for 8 minutes if you are using snapper, 6 to 8 minutes for the monkfish—depending on the thickness of the fillets—or until the flesh is opaque. Remove the fish with a large, slotted spoon to absorbent paper towels before transferring it immediately to bathe in its sauce.

    With two forks, break up the fish, tossing it about in the sauce, permitting the hot fish to inhale the good flavors. Leave the fish to cool in the sauce. Cover the bowl tightly with plastic wrap.

    The *burrida* can wait several hours in a cool place far from the refrigerator. Just before presenting it, transfer the *burrida* to a large, shallow bowl, strewing it with the warm bread crumbs. Find a white wine that, even cooled to its heart, can fence nicely with each lush layer of the dish's flavors.

La Barbicina di Orgosolo

PASTA WITH BOTTARGA IN THE STYLE OF ORGOSOLO

Serves 4

A tiny place where once lived the paladins of Sardegna is Orgosolo. Only a decade or so ago did they think it prudent, finally, to wander about the steep, tortured alleyways of their mountain village unadorned with a rifle. Orgosolo is the historic lair of Sard banditismo—*banditry. Perhaps the businesses of thieving and bucca-neering seem more gainful in Calabria, for now, the only rapscallions left in Orgosolo are the political artists whose bullying, bitter-sermoned murals irritate walls, housefronts, mountain faces. Too, icons are chafed, gas-tronomically, in Orgosolo, as they are here in this dish, which asks for* bottarga *as well as pecorino, upsetting the proscription, for a moment, against the mingling of fish and cheese.*

> 3 tablespoons extra-virgin olive oil
>
> 6 ounces pancetta, minced
>
> 3 fat cloves garlic, peeled, crushed, and minced
>
> 2 cups canned tomato puree
>
> ¾ teaspoon fine sea salt, plus additional for cooking pasta
>
> ⅔ cup good red wine
>
> 1 tablespoon good red wine vinegar
>
> 1 cup just-grated pecorino
>
> 1 batch *malloreddus di Desulo* (page 234) or 12 ounces of penne,
>   fusilli, ziti, or other short-cut pasta
>
> 8 ounces *bottarga*

In a large terra-cotta or enameled cast-iron casserole over a medium flame, warm the olive oil and sauté the pancetta, tossing it about in the oil for several minutes before softening the garlic in the fat, taking care not to color it. Add the tomato puree, the ¾ teaspoon sea salt, and the wine, bringing the mixture to a gentle simmer and permitting it to reduce for 15 minutes.

Off the flame, add the red wine vinegar and ½ cup of the pecorino, giving the sauce a good stir and letting it to cool, uncovered.

Meanwhile, in abundant, boiling, sea-salted water, cook the *malloreddus* or the other pasta to al dente, draining it and transferring it to a large bowl. Toss the just-cooked pasta with the remaining pecorino, then grate the *bottarga* over it, giving the whole another tossing to distribute the *bottarga*.

Turn the pasta out into the terra-cotta casserole with the still-warm sauce, tossing it about and coating it well. Carry *la barbicina* to the table, serving it in warmed, shallow bowls. Pass around a jug of honorable red wine.

Mazzamurru

A SAVORY SARDINIAN BREAD PUDDING

Serves 4

The poorest, perhaps, of all Sard dishes, some version of mazzamurru *is often a shepherd's supper or humble sus-tenance for a bountyless hunter's family. Made of whatever stuffs might be at hand, the commonalities of* mazza-murru *are rich ewe's milk, some rough bread, and shards of sharp, salty cheese. The ornaments are often a handful of wild grasses or a few sun-dried tomatoes, some olives, a crush of dried herbs. Present the* mazzamurru *with a bowlful of some simple tomato sauce or, better, no sauce at all, its nakedness tasting of such goodness.*

> Trenchers of good country bread, with its crusts intact, 8½
> inches thick by 6 inches long
> 2 cups whole milk
> 2 cups heavy cream
> 2 large eggs, lightly beaten
> 1 teaspoon fine sea salt
> Freshly cracked pepper
> 1½ cups just-grated pecorino
> ¼ cup extra-virgin olive oil
> 2 fat cloves garlic, peeled, crushed, and minced
> 1 small, dried red chile pepper, crushed, or ⅓ to ½ teaspoon
> dried chile flakes

Pave the bottom of a large, shallow terra-cotta or enameled cast-iron casserole with the bread. Warm the milk and the cream to the point just before it simmers. Permit the milk/cream to cool for a minute or two, then beat in the eggs. Pour half the still-hot milk/cream/egg mixture over the bread. Sprinkle on half the sea salt, generous grindings of pepper, and half the pecorino. Repeat the procedure with the remaining bread, hot milk/cream/egg, sea salt, more pepper, and the pecorino. Cover the pudding with a clean kitchen towel and permit the bread to inhale its warm, creamy bath for ½ hour.

Preheat the oven to 400 degrees.

In a small sauté pan over a medium flame, warm the olive oil and soften the garlic, taking care not to let it color. Add the chile pepper and roll it about for 1 minute, scenting the oil. Just before baking the pudding, thread the perfumed oil evenly over it.

Bake the pudding for 35 to 40 minutes or until it is deeply golden.

Malloreddus di Desulo (Vitellini di Desulo)

LITTLE CALVES IN THE STYLE OF DESULO

Serves 4

There is an ancient and savage imperviousness about la barbagia—the high, central plateaux in the Gennargentu Mountains. The Romans named it barbaria—barbarian—they having muddled all campaigns to vanquish the rough Sard clans who lived there, who live there still. And so it was with all who braved ingress onto their wild moors, into their Mesolithic woods.

Of ungenerous earth fit only to pasture sheep and goats, these barbagianesi live simply but somehow not poorly, their uninjured traditions nourishing them as much as the fruits of their hunting and foraging. Too, they are primitive artisans, building, weaving, carving objects of rustic beauty and comfort, enriching their homes and villages, themselves, with a most tender spirit. And riding the thin, tortured roads that thread through the mountains, one is carried back into their unfrayed present. Seeming to seep from the pith of the mountains is the village called Desulo, and there one is greeted by citizens dressed—as they dress always, as they have dressed always—in ancestral costumes of handwoven cloth tinged in the reds and blues and yellows of their allegria, of their perpetual, quiet festival of life.

And, too, one might be invited to sit at a family table to eat mutton boiled with wild bay leaves and wrapped in warm, thin breads baked over embers. But this after a great bowl of malloreddus—vitellini—little calves, for which Desulo is famed. Not calves at all but tiny, plump, hand-rolled, saffroned pasta that, to the Sards, resemble fat little heifers.

The Pasta

16 ounces fine semolina flour, plus additional as needed

2 teaspoons fine sea salt, plus additional for cooking the pasta

¼ teaspoon saffron threads, pan-roasted and dissolved in 2 tablespoons warm white wine

1 cup water, plus additional as needed

On a large wooden board or a pastry marble or in a large bowl, place the 16 ounces of flour with the 2 teaspoons sea salt in a flat mound and form a well in the center. Have the saffroned wine and 1 cup of water at the ready. Pour the water and the saffroned wine into the well, drawing the flour from the inside wall of the mound gently into the liquids. Using your hands, continue to work the elements into a rough paste. Add more water, only drops of it at a time, should the paste seem too dry. Work the paste vigorously, distributing the saffron so that the paste is of a uniform golden color. This is a rustic, dense sort of dough, having nothing in common with the satiny texture of egg-based pasta dough. Building this dough is a bit like building mud pies, in the sense of its compactness. The goal is to end up with a dough that can be molded rather than rolled.

Take an ounce or so of the dough and form it into a rope about ½ inch in diameter. Using your thumb and forefinger, pinch off bits of the rope—each about the size of a dried white bean—and press each bit, rocking it, really, with your thumb, over a rough surface—a tea strainer turned upside down, the tines of a fork turned upside down, or even over a straw place mat. You'll find that the dough, while taking on the imprint of the surface over which it was pressed, also rolls over on itself, forming a fat little dumpling with a hollow. One needs to practice the technique.

Place the finished *malloreddus* on a tray lined with a kitchen towel lightly dusted with semolina. Cover the *malloreddus* with another kitchen towel and let them rest—up to 48 hours—until you are ready to cook them in abundant, boiling, sea-salted water until they are tender. Their cooking time is wholly dependent on how long the pasta has been left to dry.

Drain the pasta, leaving it somewhat wet, tossing it with its good sauce.

The Sauce

¼ cup extra-virgin olive oil

8 ounces fresh, Italian-style sausage, removed from its casing

1 small yellow onion, peeled and minced

2 fat cloves garlic, peeled, crushed, and minced

1 14-ounce can plum tomatoes, with their liquids

2 teaspoons fine sea salt

Freshly cracked pepper

1⅓ cups good red wine

¼ teaspoon saffron threads, pan-roasted and dissolved in 2
   tablespoons warm red wine

1 cup just-grated pecorino

½ cup torn basil leaves

In a large pot over a medium flame, warm the olive oil and sauté the sausage, crushing it into the oil. Soften the onion and the garlic in the oil, taking care not to let them color. Add the tomatoes, the sea salt, generous grindings of pepper, the wine, and the dissolved saffron, bringing the mixture to a gentle simmer. Cook the sauce, uncovered, for 15 minutes.

Off the flame, add the pecorino and the just-torn basil, stirring the sauce well, then permitting it to rest for 1 hour.

Toss the cooked *malloreddus* with half the sauce, passing the remainder at table with more pecorino and sending round a jug of rough red wine.

Quaglie Lessate e Riposate sull' Erbe Selvatiche

WINE-POACHED QUAIL RESTED ON WILD HERBS

Serves 6

The game birds called grive *that are the Sards' quarry in the* macchia *are too small to cook over the open fire, hence they are often poached in white wine, then laid to cool on a palette of myrtle leaves and twigs, with a coverlet of yet more of the leaves, all of them scenting the flesh with soft perfumes, a reprise of the machinations of the old* bracconiere *(page 226).*

Yet another cunning Sard prescription is to tuck the birds inside a paper or cloth sack fitted with the herbs. By fastening the sack securely, one creates a vaporous chamber in which they rest and cool, breathing in the sweet steam. Lacking myrtle bushes, use whole branches of rosemary and thyme, fat leaves of sage, and the fronds of wild or cultivated fennel as lush surrogate bedding for the little birds. A few cloves of barely crushed garlic seem to invigorate the herbs.

Luscious to carry on a picnic, one might prepare the quail—or game hens, a chicken, or a fat capon, adjusting the poaching times accordingly—the evening before, and next day carry along the sack of birds readied for lunch.

1 tablespoon coarse sea salt

1 bottle dry white wine

24 to 27 leaves fresh sage

12 farm-raised quail, cleaned; their livers reserved for another use

12 to 15 large branches of rosemary

8 to 10 branches of thyme

Several wild fennel fronds or the fronds of a bulb of fresh fennel

3 fat cloves garlic, their skins intact, lightly crushed

In a large soup kettle, bring to a simmer 2 quarts of water and the sea salt. Add the bottle of white wine and permit the liquid to return to a simmer.

Place a leaf of sage inside the cavity of each bird. Slide four or more of the quail into the simmering liquids—as many as will fit comfortably. As the liquids once more return to a gentle simmer, lower the flame and poach the birds for 10 to 12 minutes, until their breast flesh feels firm when poked a bit with a finger. The time will vary with the weight of the birds. If you've kept the liquid barely simmering and have resisted leaving the birds too long in their bath, their meat will be succulent, tender.

Have on hand a brown paper bag or a rededicated pillowcase. While the quail poach, ready the sack by laying it on its side and fashioning a cushion of the herbs and garlic. One cannot use too many herbs for this purpose.

Remove the quail from their poaching liquors with a large slotted spoon. Position the birds directly inside the herb-lined sack. Close the sack and continue the poaching process until all the quail are cooked and safely nested inside. If using chicken or capon, relieve the birds of their skins after the poaching process. Fasten the sack with some butcher's twine and leave it to rest at cool room temperature for 8 or 10 hours or as many more as your patience permits. A Sard will tell you to let the birds rest for two days.

When you are ready, serve the quail at room temperature as a starter course, presenting them on cushions of warm, just-toasted bread and glossing them with tears of good, green oil, flattering the savor of the herbed birds. Jugs of cold white wine are welcome.

Cosciotto di Maiale al Coccio del Pastore Sassarese

BRAISED LEG OF PORK IN THE MANNER OF THE SWINEHERD OF SASSARI

Serves 18 to 20

The swineherd, like the shepherd, conducts his life significantly all' aria aperta—*out-of-doors. It is there that he naps and forages, tends to his fires, capriciously bathing himself and one part or another of his clothing in an often swift and single maneuver. He might also cook up some wonderfully scented stew of wild mushrooms or one of dried beans and just-gathered grasses and herbs, as supplement to his staples of cheese, honey, bread, and wine. More than once, though, we took note of purposeful midday couriers visiting a swineherd in the pasture, carrying a basket full of components for him to cook a fine feast of a lunch midst his charges and under the sun. We learned, too, that, once in a while, the swineherd cooks for his family, his friends.*

Here follows a version of a dish as it is prepared by a young Sard herdsman when he slaughters a pig for market. Staging a torchlit supper in his meadow, he braises a haunch of the animal for his neighbors. Its formula was told to us by his wife, she having cooked it for us on the farm where we stayed near Sassari.

1 4-inch stick cinnamon, crushed

10 whole cloves

1 tablespoon whole peppercorns

10 juniper berries

1 12-pound leg fresh pork, its bone intact, its fat well-trimmed

1 bottle plus 1½ cups sturdy red wine

4 to 6 large leaves sage, torn

1 tablespoon minced fresh rosemary leaves

2 tablespoons extra-virgin olive oil

1 tablespoon sweet butter

6 ounces pancetta, finely minced

2 large yellow onions, peeled and finely sliced

6 fat cloves garlic, peeled, crushed, and minced

1½ teaspoons fine sea salt

1 cup late-harvest white wine

In a mortar with a pestle, grind the cinnamon, cloves, peppercorns, and juniper berries to a coarse powder and rub the mixture well onto all the surfaces of the leg of pork, placing it, then, in a large, noncorrosive bowl.

Heat the bottle of red wine to a point just under the simmer, adding the sage leaves and the rosemary. Cover the liquid, allowing it to steep for 30 minutes. Pour the infusion over the spiced pork, covering the bowl tightly with plastic wrap (a conceit not dictated in the original formula) and permitting it to marinate for 6 hours at cool room temperature. If you are a swineherd or a shepherd, a few hours under the shade of an oak tree seems just fine. Strain the marinade from the meat, reserving it and discarding any remains from the spices and herbs. Dry the pork with absorbent paper towels (conceit number two).

Meanwhile, in a very large terra-cotta or enameled cast-iron casserole, warm the olive oil with the butter, adding the pancetta and melting it in the fat. Add the onion and garlic, rolling them about in the fat and softening them to transparency. Remove the onion and garlic to a plate. In the remaining fat, seal the leg of pork, sprinkling on sea salt and permitting the meat to crust and take on deep color. The process takes at least 15 minutes. When the pork is sealed, remove it to a holding plate.

Add the reserved marinade to the casserole, raising the flame, stirring, scraping at the residue for ½ minute before adding 1 cup of the additional red wine and 1 cup of the late-harvest wine along with the pork and the reserved onion and garlic. Over a low flame, bring the liquids just to the point of simmering, cover the casserole with a slightly skewed lid, and braise the pork for 3½ to 4 hours or until the internal temperature at the thickest part of the meat reads 155 degrees. This is the point at which Mariuccia, the swineherd's wife, ended her husband's recipe.

I add the following steps, which detract not a whit from the rusticity of the dish, but serve to intensify its flavors.

Remove the leg of pork to a holding plate and strain the sauce, pressing on and discarding the solids. Return the sauce to the casserole and, over a lively flame, reduce it for 10 minutes. Reacquaint the meat with its sauce, permitting the whole to cool completely, uncovered. Skim any accumulation of fat, gently reheat the pork in its sauce, removing it to large, warmed platter. Add the remaining ½ cup of wine to the sauce, heating it just to the point of simmering, pouring some over the pork.

At table, carve the leg into thin slices, offering it with more of its sauce, chunks of good bread, and a jug of red wine.

averio Gentili is Tuscan by ancient and noble heritage. In the moments imminent to his birth, however, his family was engaged in business on Sardegna. Saverio was born in the town of Nulvi in the north near Sassari. Hence, Saverio was born a Sard. Only a few years passed, though, before his family was restored to the tranquil hills of Arezzo and that sparse, early epoch of his life left him only flitting echoes of the island. Sardegna became some faint prelude.

When he was nearly twenty, there came some talk in the family of a journey back to the island, a sentimental journey to Nulvi to mark Saverio's coming of age in the arms of his Sard paternity. Letters were dispatched, plans were laid, and la famiglia Gentili, once again, traveled to Sardegna. He says now that surely neither he nor his parents nor his older brother could forecast the cordiality of their reception. It seemed that all of Nulvi awaited them, these four souls who had stayed so fleetingly among them and, most especially, the one who had been born among them, to them.

In the fields near the house where Saverio was born, tables were laid for several hundred people. The feasting, the discoursing, the reveling, lasted the day and the night, he says, a mystical invocation of cultish rites and profoundly religious ceremony, all of it to honor the destiny that summoned up Sardegna as his spiritual home. Not of their kith, their blood, even more indissolubly to the Sards, he is of their earth.

From that day until this, when someone asks him of his heritage, Saverio answers simply, "Io sono Sardo." An honorary, cherished citizen of San Casciano dei Bagni, the village where we live, he is our friend, our confidant, our own personal Tuscan-Sard. Here follow two of the dishes he is wont to cook with us.

Impanade di Agnello alla Saverio di Nulvi

PASTRIES OF LAMB WITH OLIVES AND SUN-DRIED TOMATOES
IN THE MANNER OF SAVERIO DI NULVI

Makes 12 to 14 pastries

¼ cup extra-virgin olive oil

3 fat cloves garlic, peeled, crushed, and minced

1 small, dried red chile pepper, crushed, or ⅓ to ½ teaspoon
   dried chile flakes

1½ pounds lamb, cut from the leg, finely minced

1 teaspoon fine sea salt

Freshly cracked pepper

⅓ cup sun-dried tomatoes, finely shredded, 2 tablespoons of its
   preserving oil retained

½ cup dried black olives, stones removed

2 teaspoons fennel seeds, roasted

1 pinch saffron threads, pan-roasted and dissolved in 2 tablespoons warm white wine
1 batch pecorino pastry (page 229)

In a sauté pan over a medium flame, warm the olive oil and soften the garlic for 1 minute, taking care not to let it color. Add the chile pepper and the lamb, sautéing the meat, sprinkling on the sea salt, and generously grinding over pepper.

Turn the mixture out into a bowl and add the sun-dried tomatoes, the olives, the fennel seeds, and the saffroned wine, tossing to combine the components.

Preheat the oven to 400 degrees.

Roll out the chilled and rested pastry to a thinness of ¼ inch. Cut 6-inch circles from the dough and place a generous 2 tablespoons of the lamb over each one, mounding it up in the center.

Reroll the pastry and cut additional circles, placing one atop each of the circles already laid with the lamb. Fold the bottom circle up to cover the edges of the top circle, crimping, sealing, the *impanade*. Brush them with the sun-dried tomato preserving oil and bake them for 18 to 20 minutes or until they are deeply golden.

Remove the *impanade* to cool a very few minutes on racks before presenting them, still warm, with a good red wine.

Fagiano Arrosto alla Saverio di Nulvi

ROAST PHEASANT IN THE MANNER OF SAVERIO DI NULVI

Serves 4

2 fresh Italian sausages
6 tablespoons extra-virgin olive oil
1 small yellow onion, peeled and finely minced
2 pheasants, their livers reserved (each about 2 pounds, preferably "hung" for several days in a cool, dry space, feathers
   removed, cleaned)
1 teaspoon fine sea salt
Freshly cracked pepper
⅔ cup moscato or other sweet, ambered wine
Zest of 2 large oranges
4 large leaves of sage, torn

8 thin slices pancetta

2 cups good red wine

10 to 12 large branches of sage, rosemary, bay, or a combination of them

Pierce the casings of the sausages and poach them for 5 minutes in barely simmering water. Drain and cool the sausages. Remove their casings and mince.

In a sauté pan over a medium flame, warm 3 tablespoons of the olive oil and brown the minced, poached sausages, rolling them about in the fat and crisping them. Add the onion, softening it a bit in the fat, before adding the pheasant livers, breaking them up and amalgamating them with the sausage and the onion. Sprinkle on the sea salt and generously grind pepper over all. Add ⅓ cup of the moscato, letting it evaporate. Add the zest and the sage, combine the components well.

Fill the cavities of the pheasants with the stuffing. Bind their legs with butcher's twine.

Preheat the oven to 400 degrees.

In a shallow terra-cotta or enameled cast-iron casserole over a lively flame, warm 3 tablespoons of the olive oil and, one at a time, seal the birds, browning them well on all sides, then removing them to a holding plate.

After the birds are sealed, lay 4 slices of pancetta over each of their breasts. Rinse the still-hot casserole with the remaining ⅓ cup of moscato and 1 cup of the red wine, stirring, scraping at the residue, and permitting the liquid to reduce for several minutes. Replace the birds in their casserole, cover them with the herb branches, and roast the pheasant for ½ hour or a bit longer, only until the flesh under a leg joint is rosy. Roasting a pheasant to grayness seems a sad thing to do. Remove the birds to a holding plate.

Place the casserole over a lively flame, add the remaining cup of wine, stirring, scraping at the residue, permitting it to reduce for 5 minutes. Whack each bird in two at its breastbone. Lay the halves over a warmed, shallow platter and pour the pan juices over all.

Having, perhaps, begun the feast with the *crostata di patate di Biddamanna* (page 228), one might present the luscious birds with a dish borrowed from Basilicata— *brasato di funghi con aglianico del Vùlture* (page 150) or the spiced chestnuts from Nicola Taurino (page 148). In any case, have at the ready warm bread for the juices and jugs of the same good red wine in which the birds were cooked.

ne of the rare imprints upon Sardegna was trod by the Spaniards. And there, in the northwestern tier of the island at Alghero, still, a thirteenth-century Catalan dialect flatters the air. Lobstermen collect small, sweet, brown specimens, cleave them, still writhing from the sea, roasting the halves on pyres of coal and wood. Soothing the fire-blackened flesh with olive oil, the Algheritani then strew them with crystals of coarse gray salt and offer them, wrapped in glossy white paper, at little kiosks set up on the beach. One might carry them home for supper or ravage them immediately, nearby, sitting cross-legged on the pier, face to a Mediterranean sun, digging into their improbable sweetness with a small wooden fork.

A reproduction more easily staged than the pier lunch is the recipe from another Algheritano on whose little wooden terrace we lingered one evening to eat the lobsters he carried up to us from his fire set down near the sea. Sputtering in a great coppered dish, their fumes sent up the promise of Catalonia. When we returned to him next day for lunch, our Algheritano bestowed on us cold, roasted lobsters, having coated them in a paste of good oil and sweet, salty roe and dusted them with shavings of bottarga.

Aragosta Fredda Algheritana

COLD ROASTED LOBSTER IN THE STYLE OF ALGHERO

Serves 4

4 1½-pound female lobsters, with their roe
1½ cups extra-virgin olive oil
Juice and zest of 2 large lemons
1 teaspoon fine sea salt
8 ounces *bottarga*

Following the directions for *aragosta alla brace algheritana* (page 243), poach, then wood-roast, the lobsters, whacking them in two and rescuing their precious roe (use the tomalley to scent softened butter and use it to enrich a sauce or as a spread for warm bread). After the lobsters have cooled, cover them with plastic wrap and chill them in the refrigerator while you make their sauce.

In a small bowl, beat the olive oil with the juice and zest of the lemons and the sea salt. Beat in the roe, crushing it against the sides of the bowl and into the sauce. Cover the sauce and let it rest at room temperature.

Just before presenting the dish, position the lobsters on one grand plate or on each of four smaller but still ample ones. Beat the sauce and spoon it over the lobsters. Grate the *bottarga* over all and present them, then, with a basket of just-toasted bread, a tiny jug of good, green oil, a dish of fine sea salt, a pepper grinder, and a cooled white wine.

Aragosta alla Brace Algheritana

THE CHARCOALED LOBSTER OF ALGHERO

Serves 4

The Lobsters

4 1- to 1½-pound lobsters
10 quarts seawater or 10 quarts water and 1 cup coarse sea salt

Begin by building a fire of charcoal and fragrant woods—grapevine cuttings, olive wood, oak, or applewood, for example.

Bring the seawater or the water and sea salt to a galloping boil over a lively flame. Give each lobster—one at a time—a 1-minute immersion in the boiling water, lifting each one out to rest while the fire builds. Finally, about 4 inches above white, cindery heat, grill the lobsters whole, turning them almost constantly, for 12 to 15 minutes—not a second more. In a single, sure movement, and with a large and very sharp knife, cut from head to tail, separating each lobster in two. Remove the roe and the tomalley. (Mix the roe, if you've roasted female lobsters, and the tomalley with a bit of softened, sweet butter, smearing the savory salve on hot bread for the cook's *merendina*.)

Position the lobster halves on a warmed tray or plate and spread them with spoonfuls of the sauce.

The Saffroned Almond Sauce

1 large red bell pepper
2 teaspoons plus ¼ to ⅓ cup extra-virgin olive oil
1½ cups blanched almonds
¼ teaspoon saffron threads
2 tablespoons good red wine
4 large, fleshy sun-dried tomatoes, coarsely chopped
2 fat cloves garlic, peeled and crushed
1 small, whole dried red chile pepper, crushed, or ⅓ to ½ teaspoon dried chile flakes
1 tablespoon good red wine vinegar

Dry-roast the red pepper in the oven, or grill it over a wood fire or over a gas flame, turning it until its skin is deeply, completely charred. Place the blackened pepper in a paper bag to steam and cool for 20 minutes.

In a small sauté pan, warm 2 teaspoons of the olive oil and quickly toast the almonds, tossing them about until they are of a dark golden color. Set them aside to cool.

Prepare the saffron by pan-roasting the threads over a medium flame for 30 seconds or so before adding the red wine and allowing it to heat nearly to the boil. Stir the saffron, melting it in the heated wine. Cover the pan and allow the saffron to steep for 20 minutes.

Remove the pepper from the sack, pulling off its charred skin, scraping away its seeds and chopping it roughly.

In the bowl of a food processor fitted with a steel blade, construct the sauce by processing the almonds, the red pepper, the sun-dried tomatoes, the garlic cloves, the chile pepper, and the red wine vinegar for 30 seconds or until the elements are well amalgamated but distinct texture still remains. Scrape the work bowl.

With the machine running, begin adding olive oil in a very thin stream, not much more than droplets at a time, approximately ¼ to ⅓ cup—just enough to bind the sauce into a rather loose paste.

Turn the sauce out into a bowl and begin beating in the saffroned wine, a teaspoon at a time, tasting the sauce after each addition. Stop when the saffron has gently illuminated, integrated the other flavors—when a touch of it on the tongue is all at once sweet, salty, sour, piquant, and with a hushed sort of bitterness at its finish. Dosing the saffron in this manner is good prevention against an acrid-tasting dish.

Allow the sauce to rest an hour or two before presenting it with the just-roasted lobsters. The sauce is lovely tossed with *malloreddus di Desulo* (page 234) or with charred, wood-scented meat or fish.

Sospiri di Limone (Sospirus)

LEMON SIGHS

Makes 30 meringues

Every province on the island claims its own version of this ethereal sweet to be the one-and-only true sospirus. The Oliense hand seems the most gentle with them, though. The very old woman from whom I learned to make them shook her small, kerchiefed head throughout the ceremony, moaning, keening, really, that the confections could only be made from the eggs of Sardinian chickens. Her theory, perhaps valid, was that Sard hens feed on myrtle berries and whey from cheesemaking and that these nourishments render the substance of their eggs less viscous and thus better suited to the construction of delicate pastries. All I know for certain is that I can bake gorgeous sospirus with the eggs of Tuscan hens who eat worms and bugs and corn.

> 2 cups blanched almonds, toasted
> 6 sugar cubes, each moistened with ½ teaspoon grappa or vodka
> Zest of 2 lemons
> Whites of 8 large eggs
> Generous pinch of fine sea salt
> 1⅔ cups sugar

Preheat the oven to 250 degrees.

With a mezzaluna or a very sharp knife, chop the almonds, sugar cubes, and lemon zest together to a fine mince.

In a large bowl, beat—with a whisk or an electric beater—the egg whites with the salt to a foam. Sprinkle on the sugar 2 tablespoons at a time, beating constantly, until the whites hold shiny, stiff peaks.

Gently, swiftly fold into the egg whites the mince of almonds, lemon, and sugar, amalgamating the components well.

On parchment-lined sheets, form the meringues by dropping 3 tablespoons of the mixture into conical, peaked shapes. Leave at least 2 inches of space between them.

Dry the *sospiri* in the oven for 1 hour. Remove them to cool thoroughly before storing them in tins.

Pane di Zibibbo di Sant' Elena in Quartù

THE GOLDEN RAISIN BREAD OF SANT' ELENA IN QUARTÙ

Makes 2 loaves

In the south near Cagliari, in the town of Sant' Elena, is staged a September festival—a tribute to their patroness and a celebration of the vendemmia—the harvesting of the grapes. There are four ascendancies in the week's pageantry. The ancestral dress of the townsfolk, the great, pendulous, ambered muscat grapes, called zibibbo, with which the whole, humble precinct is festooned, the wine pressed from their honeyed juices, and, finally, the luscious breads baked from zibibbi left to dry and crinkle in the sun.

Though the bread is sweetened and ornamented with raisins, it is most compatible with game dishes such as fagiano arrosto alla Saverio di Nulvi, (page 240) or braises such as the cosciotto di maiale al coccio del pastore Sassarese (page 237). We ate pane di zibibbo in Sant' Elena with the sweet, white flesh of a myrtle-roasted pig. The bread, still warm from the oven, or roasted over a wood fire, makes for a gorgeous fine pasto with a piece of young pecorino and a glass of moscato. I reserve the bread's golden-crisped fringes for the baker.

> 1 package active dry yeast or 1 small cake fresh yeast
> 2 cups warm water
> 2 teaspoons dark brown sugar
> 6 cups all-purpose flour
> 1 tablespoon fine sea salt
> ¼ cup dark honey (buckwheat, chestnut, etc.)
> 2 tablespoons extra-virgin olive oil
> ⅔ cup golden raisins, plumped in warm *moscato* or other sweet,
>   ambered wine
> ⅔ cup blanched almonds, toasted and chopped
> Fine semolina flour for turning out dough

In a large bowl, combine the yeast with 1 cup warm water, the dark brown sugar, and 1 cup of the all-purpose flour, stirring, giving the yeast a bit of stimulus from the sugar and flour. Set the bowl aside for 10 minutes.

Add the remaining flour, the sea salt, the honey, the olive oil, and the remaining cup of warm water, incorporating the components well. Turn the mixture out onto a lightly floured work space and knead it for 8 to 10 minutes to a smooth resiliency. Work in the raisins and the almonds and knead another minute or two. Place the dough in a lightly oiled bowl, covering it tightly with plastic wrap, permitting it to double its bulk—about 1½ hours.

Cut the dough in two, covering the waiting piece with a damp kitchen towel while you work with the first. Using a wooden rolling pin or your hands, press the dough into a rough sort of rectangle—about 12 by 8 inches. Roll up the rectangle on its longer edge, forming a tight cylinder. Roll and stretch the cylinder into a rope of 16 to 18 inches in length and curve it into a semicircle. Using a razor blade or a small, very sharp knife, slash the two ends of the semicircle with 10 or 12 closely placed vertical cuts, each about 3 inches long, almost forming fringes.

Line metal baking tins with baker's parchment and sprinkle the paper lightly with semolina. Position the loaves on the tins, covering them with clean kitchen towels and permitting them to rise for 1½ to 2 hours or until their bulk has doubled.

Preheat the oven to 450 degrees, with baking stones, if desired. If you are using baking stones, sprinkle the hot stones lightly with semolina before sliding the loaves onto them. Alternatively, place the loaves into the oven on the metal sheets.

Bake the breads for 35 minutes or until they are deeply golden and have formed a thick hard crust. The process of misting will help accomplish this (page 214). Transfer the loaves to a rack to cool thoroughly. At table, break rather than slice them.

Sebadas Olienese

THE SWEET CHEESE PASTRIES OF OLIENA

Makes 10 to 12 pastries

Sculpted into the shanks of the Sopramonte in the barbagia is Oliena. And drifting toward it from the Nuorese road at sunset, the golden lamplight of the village bedazzles the mountain, splendoring its old, cold grayness as would the gleams of ten thousand torches. Later, inside the village as we sat with our aperitivi, we told a local man how the approach had pleased us. He said that it was ritual for the Olienesi to walk down from the village at crepuscolo (twilight) turning back to face the mountain as the sun softened, sobered down to sleep, before they strolled back up the hill to suppers. And it is from these romantic Olienesi that was begun the tradition of two celebrated Sard dolci—sebadas and sospirus.

Sebadas are typically made with a fresh ewe's milk cheese cushioned inside leaves of pastry, tumbled into bubbling oil, then given a dose of bitter honey. This version asks for ricotta and mascarpone-plumped pastries to be baked, then given a wisp of a honeyed sheen. Present them after some simple supper, such as mazzamurru (page 233), with a tiny glass of icy Malvasia di Cagliari.

The Filling

1 cup whole-milk ricotta
½ cup mascarpone
2 teaspoons orange flower water
Zest of 1 large orange
Zest of 1 lemon

Combine the components in the bowl of a food processor fitted with a steel blade, pulsing the ingredients six or eight times to smooth the ricotta and blend the cheeses to a creamy texture. Turn the prepared cheese out into a bowl, cover and refrigerate it while you make the dough.

The Pastry

2 cups all-purpose flour
½ cup confectioners' sugar
Generous pinch of fine sea salt
Finely grated zest of 1 lemon
5 ounces sweet butter, chilled and cut into small pieces
2 large egg yolks
2 teaspoons orange flower water
2 tablespoons heavy cream
½ cup dark honey (buckwheat, chestnut, etc.), warmed

Preheat the oven to 400 degrees.

In a large bowl, combine the flour, confectioners' sugar, sea salt, and lemon zest. With your fingertips or a pastry blender, quickly work the cold butter into the dry components until it resembles coarse crumbs. Combine the egg yolks, orange flower water, and cream and pour the liquids over the butter and flour mixture, working it very swiftly into a rough dough. Turn the dough out onto a sheet of plastic wrap and press it until smooth.

Enclose the dough in the plastic, wrapping it in a second sheet of plastic, then refrigerate it for 1 hour or place it in the freezer for 20 minutes. Roll the dough between sheets of plastic wrap to a thinness of ¼ inch. Cut 5-inch circles from the dough, stack them between sheets of plastic, wrap them in more plastic, and leave them to rest in the refrigerator while you reroll the scraps and cut additional circles.

When all the dough has been rolled and cut, position half the circles on parchment-lined baking sheets. Place 2 tablespoons of filling on each circle, mounding it in the center. Place another round of pastry over the cheese, folding the bottom circle up to cover the edges of the top circle, crimping, sealing the pastries.

Bake the *sebadas* for 18 to 20 minutes, until they are deeply golden and crisped. Remove the *sebadas* from the oven. Wet a soft pastry brush in the warm honey and paint the just-baked *sebadas*. Permit them to rest a few minutes before giving them another pass with the honey. Remove them to racks to cool a bit, serving them warm or at room temperature.

Aranciata Nuorese

AN ORANGE ALMOND CONFECTION
IN THE STYLE OF NUORO

Makes about 2 pounds

Deep in the interior of the island on the fringes of the barbagia *is Nuoro. It seemed a cultural suicide, wielded by unsentimental politicos over this past half century, that smote Nuoro's picturesque and pastoral life. This, the place on Sardegna where Stone Age man first set his fires, the place least contaminated by the passing of the millennia, was swiftly, gracelessly swept away by those compelled to gentrify her.*

Little has changed about the Nuoresi themselves, though. As best they can midst their fresh new proscenium of concrete, they still dance their simple rhythms, honor legacy and heritage with their reserved sort of gaiety. A sweet—once made only by the Nuorese massaie, *farmwives—is now fabricated in crisp, shiny laboratories and sent then, in its handsome trappings and tassels, to elegant shops on the Continent. Still, the women cook their ancestral* aranciata *at home for feast days, sometimes tucking it into bits of lace, placing little pouches of it at everyone's place at table, then hiding an old silvered tin of it in the back seat of a new friend's automobile.*

24 large, bright-skinned oranges
2½ cups dark honey (buckwheat, chestnut, etc.)
2½ cups blanched almonds, toasted and slivered

Using a swivel-handled peeler, shave the zest from the oranges, avoiding even the barest bits of the bitter pith.

In a saucepan, cover the zest with cold water and blanch it for 1 minute. Drain the zest and refresh it under very cold water, setting it then to rest in a bowl of cold water, covered with plastic wrap, in the refrigerator. Change the water once a day for five days. This long bath sweetens the zest.

Drain and dry the zest on absorbent paper towels.

Place the zest and the honey in a saucepan over a quiet flame, permitting the zest to drink in the honey for 40 minutes. Off the flame, add the almonds, stirring, coating them with the honey and the zest.

Pour the mixture out onto a pastry marble or a double sheet of parchment, leaving it to cool to tepid.

With a sharp, wet knife, cut the confection into tiny squares. Leave the finished *aranciata* to cool completely before storing it in tins. Alas, this artisanal version of *aranciata* has only a short life, giving one the responsibility to see that every last chewy bite of it be dispatched within a few days.

EPILOGUE

As much as I wish I could tell you more, this book is already longer than it was supposed to be. I'm sorry not to have written about the *barista* in Corleone, who harnesses two ten-liter bottles of water to his mule each day and walks with him the few kilometers from a natural spring to his little bar. He uses the water to make fine espresso. The town's own piped water is good enough and I don't think there was even another bar in town with whom he was competing. He just wanted to make *"un caffè più buono possible,"* he told us. Then there was the young and very sunburnt man who worked through *Il Barbiere di Siviglia—The Barber of Seville*—in a handsome *basso profondo* while he sold prickly pears on the roadside between Siracusa and Noto, and the woman who made small, crisp, gold fritters of jasmine blossoms and rose petals and offered them to us after lunch, apologizing for not having had time to make a proper sweet that morning. There isn't even room to tell you about sun-drying figs or tomatoes or how to make the Easter bread of Palermo. There are the foods of whole islands and cities and villages left behind for the sake of space and at least as many stories untold as there are here present. And every time we go to Rome for lunch, or to Naples for a day, or set off on the ferry from Civitavecchia to arrive the next morning on Sardegna, we come home with yet more of them, safe for some other time.

We hear, once in a while, from little Elisabetta and more often from Rosaria who invites us to Gallipoli for every holiday. And Alfonso is going to cook for Erich's birthday next week, a whole menu of seafood dishes. Alfonso is intent on returning north with us for a few days of truffle hunting with another old friend in Norcia.

But we do keep edging southward. We've gone from Venice to Tuscany and now, as soon as the renovations on our home in an eighteenth-century palazzo in the *centro storico di Orvieto* are finished, we'll be a few kilometers more so, this time precisely at Italy's heart. The place is lovely with a very large *salone* with a great carved travertine hearth and a good kitchen in which to host our classes. We'll be a hundred yards from the Duomo. Meanwhile, we're on our way, in a few minutes, for a walk up the road toward Sarteano to watch the sunset. We'll take a quilt and a jug of spiced wine and, afterward, when we're freezing and hungry, we'll tramp back home to our fire and our supper. Life is good but, still, I feel sad to end this book.

19 Gennaio, 1999
San Casciano dei Bagni

GLOSSARY

Al dente: Literally, "to the tooth." A term that describes pasta cooked to a firm texture that still has some bite to it.

Antipasto: Literally, "before the meal." The dish or dishes meant to stimulate the appetite and prepare the palate for the main dishes. The components often include raw vegetables, cured meats, thin slices of grilled bread spread with a savory paste. The term does not mean "before the pasta," as some believe; *pasto* equals "meal."

Aperitivo: A beverage usually, but not always, alcoholic, taken before a lunch or dinner as a stimulant to the appetite; a deep-dyed social ritual in Italy.

Baccalà: Salted, dried cod. The same fish, airdried but unsalted, is called *stoccatisso.* Both must be reconstituted before cooking.

Brasato: A large cut of meat—most often beef—marinated in wine and herbs, then braised for a long time over a low flame.

Bucatini: Literally, "little holes." A thick, hollow spaghetti.

Caciocavallo: "Cheese astride a horse." Christened as such because it resembles two little saddlebags. A semihard or hard cheese made of whole cow's milk, its thin smooth crust varies from golden yellow to light chestnut in color, while its interior is white to pale straw.

Capperi di Pantelleria: These tiny, tight caper buds gathered on the Sicilian island of Pantelleria and preserved under sea salt are the earth's finest and bear slim resemblance to the fat, fleshy ones kept in brine.

Centerbe: Literally, "one-hundred herbs." A potent, often artfully distilled, liqueur made from herbs gatherered on mountain slopes in springtime.

Cèpes: Large, fleshy wild boletus mushrooms that are often available dried; called porcini in Italy.

Chanterelles: Pale coppery-colored wild mushrooms.

Cucina povera: Literally, "cooking of the poor." The term that describes a style of cooking that was based on and limited to a few indigeneous gathered and cultivated components.

Farina di grano duro (semolina): Flour milled from hard wheat; often called "pasta flour."

Fennel: The vegetable is a licorice-scented, crisp-textured, green-and-white bulb with slender stalks and fernlike fronds. In Italy it is served raw, sliced thin, with a simple dressing of olive oil, salt, and freshly cracked pepper known as *pinzimonio;* baked with white wine and Parmigiano; or braised in butter and white wine. Wild fennel is a plant from which the licorice-scented seeds are gathered and whose dried stalks, when added to a grilling fire, give magnificent perfume to meat and fish.

Fine pasto: Literally, "end of the meal." It is the dish, either sweet or savory, that is presented last.

Fusilli: A corkscrew-shaped pasta, the most celebrated version of which has, for centuries, been fashioned, one at a time, by winding thin strands of just-made dough over corkscrew-shaped wires by the women of the village of Felitto in Campania.

Gastronomia: A food shop that offers prepared, table-ready foods among its wares.

Gnocchi: Literally, "bumps." Savory dumplings made from *semolina,* or potato or ricotta sometimes, with a puree of spinach or mushrooms or winter squash; occasionally, even with chestnut flour. (See *Gnocchi di Castagne con Porcini Trifolati,* page 18.)

Grappa: A clear spirit distilled from the pomace or lees—the sediment of skins and pits recovered from the pressing of wine grapes.

Maccheroni: A humble form of flour-and-water pasta fashioned into various shapes— especially short thick tubes bent at the middle, like an elbow—and left to dry.

Marsala: The best known of Italian fortifed wines, roughly comparable to sherry. It takes its name from the city of Marsala in western Sicily. This dessert wine is produced from the Catarratto, Grillo, and Inzolia vines—white grapes—which yield not more than 100 quintals of fruit per hectare. This wine undergoes a complex process of vinification and ageing. Its color varies from amber to tawny, and its alcoholic content is never less than 17 percent. The Marsala tends to greater dryness with greater aging. (For more information, see *Olive Nere e Verdi con Aglio Intero al Forno*, page 191.)

Mascarpone: Originally a product of Lombardy, this thick, naturally sweet cheese is made by curdling cream with citric acids. Used traditionally, sometimes abundantly, in the wintertime sweet and savory cooking of the northern regions, it is not a typical component of southern cooking; sometimes, however, its goodness is borrowed from the northern repertoire and used to enrich a particular dish.

Mezzaluna: A half-moon-shaped blade with handles on each side designed to be "rocked" over the ingredients to be cut or minced.

Mortadelline di Campotosto: A small, plump, rough-textured artfully made pork sausage that is hung to age in the mountain air in the village of Campotosto in the Abruzzo.

Moscato di Pantelleria: The prized, lush, late-harvest, amber sweet wine made from the white Moscato grape on the Sicilian island of Pantelleria.

Mosto: The skins, seeds, and general sediment remaining from the crushing of the grapes.

Mozzarella di búfala: Along the sea between Roma and Napoli, herds of water buffalo graze; their rich milk is collected and fashioned into *mozzarella di búfala*, whose soft, creamy goodness, tasting pristinely fresh and dripping with its own buttermilk, is unforgettable.

Nocino: A thick, syrupy liqueur distilled from crushed walnuts.

Olio santo: Literally, "sainted oil." An affectionate term used to describe good olive oil infused with a generous dose of crushed, dried red chile peppers

Pancetta: Literally, "little belly." It is the salt-cured flesh from the pig's tummy; it can be found either in the flat, thin form of a side of bacon—*panetta stesa*—or rolled into a fat *salame* shape—*pancetta coppata* or *arrotolata*.

Panzarotti: In the Neopolitan dialect, "fat bellies." Pasta or dough that is plumped with a savory filling and then boiled or deep-fried.

Pasta di grano duro: Pasta fashioned with flour milled from hard spring wheat.

Pasticceria: A shop that sells pastries and sweetmeats, most often baked on the premises.

Pecorino: Literally, "a little sheep." A general term for ewe's-milk cheese. As opposed to a geographic name like Gorgonzola, Asiago, or Parmigiano Reggiano, pecorino takes its name from the animal from whose milk it is produced. Many regions of Italy produce pecorino (Lazio, Sicilia, Sardegna, and Piemonte among them), which ranges in taste from fresh and sweet to pungent, sharp, and peppery, depending upon the grazing habits of the ewes, the cheese's maturity, and the way it is aged. The pecorino of Pienza in Tuscany is sometimes rubbed with olive-wood ash or wrapped in tobacco leaves and aged in *tufo* (natural stone) caves, which results in a most assertive flavor. In contrast, *marzolino*, the pecorino fashioned from the spring milk when the ewes have feasted on new grasses and herbs, is softly delicate; the well-aged pecorino most often used in southern cooking is highly piquant.

Pepatelli: Pepper-spiced orange biscuits tradtionally dipped into red wine or iced moscato at the end of dinner; typical of the Abruzzese village of Scanno.

Peperoncino: Small to tiny dried red chile peppers, sometimes called *diavolini* in the south, whose piquancy can vary from warm to hellish.

Pesto: Literally, "paste." Several components are pounded—often in a mortar and pestle—into a paste. The pesto fashioned from basil, pine nuts, garlic, Parmigiano or pecorino, and bound with olive oil is the one Americans know best. But one can also, for example, fashion a pesto from olives, nuts, dried tomatoes, etc.

Polenta: A variously textured meal or flour ground from several strains of dried corn that is cooked in water, milk, and/or wine to form a thick porridge. Polenta can be molded, sliced, grilled, sautéed, or baked and may be served with many sauces and condiments. In its unadorned state, it was and remains the basic dish of *la cucina povera.*

Porcini: Literally, "piglets." Fat, fleshy, wild boletus mushrooms that abound in northern Italy's woods and forests during late August, September, and October.

Portobello: Often-dinner-plate-size, cultivated mushroom that was first developed and grown in Pennsylvania. It is not Italian in origin despite the name—which means "beautiful port"—nor is it or anything like it to be found in Italy.

Prosciutto: Derived from *prosciugare*—to dry—the one and only true air-dried ham cut from the great, mandolin-shaped haunches of Emilian pigs; the salt-cured legs are hung from the rafters of barns and attics in the pre-Apennine hills just south of Parma, in the northern region of Emilia. Though versions of prosciutto are produced in nearly every region of Italy, the ham of Parma remains—by many consumers—the one most coveted.

Puntarelle: A thick-bladed, grasslike herb collected, among other places, in the hills outside Rome. Traditionally, they are lightly poached, dressed in an anchovy-sparked sauce, and served at room temperature.

Ricotta: A fresh cheese by-product left from the process of other cheese-making. It is the re-cooked—in Italian, *ri-cotta*—whey from cow's, goat's, ewe's, or buffalo's milk. *Ricotta Romana* is made with ewe's milk while *ricotta di búfala*, the most rare and delicate of all, is made, near Napoli, from water buffalo's milk.

Ricotta salata: Literally, "salted ricotta." A piquant cheese made by salting fresh ricotta; depending upon how long it is left to age it can be a crumbly, semisoft variety or a hard, grating version.

Robiola: A fresh, soft, creamy cow's milk cheese.

Rosticceria: A food shop whose specialty is roasted, table-ready meats and fowl.

Rucola: Arugola, rocket, and *rughetta* are other names for the often wild (collected near stream and riverbeds), sometimes cultivated, peppery, spicy, green salad leaves.

Salt anchovies: Salted and packed in tins of five to ten kilos and sold by the ounce in every Italian grocery in America, these large russet-skinned anchovies are so superior in taste and texture to the whiffy minuscule ones held in oil that even those who swoon in fear and disgust are swiftly converted. To use salt anchovies, rinse them judiciously under cold running water to remove all traces of salt before relieving them of their heads and bones.

Salumi: The collective name for dried and/or salt-cured, spiced, coarse or fine-textured sausages that are fashioned most often from pork or game.

Scamorza: A supple white cheese made from whole cow's milk, pear-shaped and tied with string around the top. Eaten fresh as a table cheese, it is also often an ingredient in various dishes. It is sometimes smoked (*affumicata*).

Scrippelle: Thin, sweet or savory crepelike pancakes that are traditional in the Abruzzese city of Teramo. (See *Scrippelle 'mbusse alla Teramana,* page 54).

Sea salt: In Italian, "sale marino." Readily available in specialty stores, often collected from Sicilian or French seacoasts. If you are using any other salt—even kosher salt—you are subtly, or not so subtly, altering rather than enhancing the natural flavors of food. Use coarse crystals in the cooking water for pasta and vegetables, or grind the coarse salt directly into the foods being prepared—if your measuring eye is unsure, grind it first onto a plate or a napkin. (Remember that a salt grinder must have hard plastic blades rather than the stainless steel ones appropriate for a pepper grinder to prevent oxidation over long contact with the salt.) Alternatively, use the finer crystals of sea salt that can be measured and employed in much the same manner as regular salt.

Spianatoia: A wooden board or, less often, a slab or marble, over which hot, just-cooked polenta is poured, left to cool and harden slightly, then sauced with any one of numerous savoury sauces. (See *Polenta con Sugo Piccante di Maiale e Peperoni alla Spianatoia di Elisabetta,* page 41.)

Terra-cotta: Literally, "cooked earth." Refers to decorative and utilitarian items fired from native clay. Vessels fired from terra-cotta are best suited to long, slow cooking processes.

Timballo: Literally, "drum." Describes the tall, cylindrical shape of a mold in which a savory pudding or a rich pasta tart is cooked. (See *Timballo di Maccheroni alla Monzù,* page 84.)

Vendemmia: The harvest of the grapes.

Zabaglione: A soft, puddinglike sweet fashioned by whipping egg yolks with wine (usually Marsala), sugar, and spices over a low heat source until the mass thickens and swells.

Zuppa di pesce: A thick, chile-spiced tomato- and garlic-based soup enriched with various fish and other types of seafood.

INDEX